Living Architecture Systems Group White Papers 2016

Library and Archives Canada Cataloguing in Publication

Living Architecture Systems Group. Symposium (2016 : Toronto, Ont.)
[Living Architecture Systems white papers, 2016]

Living Architecture Systems white papers, November 2016 / Philip Beesley &
Ala Roushan, editors. -- Revised edition.

Revision of: Living Architecture Systems white papers, 2016.
ISBN 978-1-988366-10-4 (EPUB)

1. Living Architecture Systems Group--Congresses. 2. Architecture--
Congresses. I. Beesley, Philip, 1956-, author, editor II. Roushan, Ala, editor
III. Title.

NA21.L59 2017   720   C2017-900990-7(c)

Printed and bound in Waterloo, Ontario.
First Edition—November 2016
Final Edition—March 2017

This book is set in Zurich Lt BT and Garamond

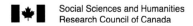 

Social Sciences and Humanities Research Council of Canada

UNIVERSITY OF WATERLOO

LIVING ARCHITECTURE SYSTEMS GROUP

WHITE PAPERS

2016

Contents

Introduction

The Living Architecture Systems Group

Living Architecture Systems White Papers is a dossier produced for the occasion of the Living Architecture Systems Group (LAS) launch event and symposium on November 4 and 5, 2016 at the LAS Sterling Road Studio in Toronto and the University of Waterloo School of Architecture at Cambridge. The White Papers presents research contributions from the LAS partners, forming an overview of the partnership and highlighting opportunities for future collaborations.

Can architecture integrate living functions? Could future buildings think, and care? The Living Architecture Systems Group brings together researchers and industry partners in a multidisciplinary research cluster dedicated to developing built environments with qualities that come close to life— environments that can move, respond, and learn, with metabolisms that can exchange and renew their environments, and which are adaptive and empathic towards their inhabitants. Supported by Social Sciences and Humanities Research Council funding and contributions from numerous partners, LAS is focused on developing innovative technologies, new critical aesthetics, and integrative design working methods, helping equip a new generation of designers with critical next-generation skills and critical perspectives for working with complex environments.

The research of LAS has the potential to change how we build by transforming the physical structures that support buildings and the technical systems that control them. Intelligent controls, machine learning, lightweight scaffolds, kinetic mechanisms, and self-renewing synthetic biology systems are being integrated in prototypes, exploring how these different systems might be fully integrated into new generations of buildings. Core specializations are in advanced structures, mechanisms, control systems, machine learning, human-machine interaction, synthetic biology, and psychological testing. The combined expertise of the group offers integrated design, testing, prototyping and public-scale demonstration facilities.

The LAS partnership is anchored in research centres at universities in North America and Europe, well as collaborations from international design-based research clusters. The LAS partnership is structured by six discipline streams: Scaffold led by Philip Beesley (Architecture, Waterloo and European Graduate School; LAS Director), Synthetic Cognition led by Dana

Kulic (ECE, Waterloo), Metabolism led by Rachel Armstrong (Architecture, Newcastle) Human Experience led by Colin Ellard (Psychology, Waterloo) Interdisciplinary Methods led by Rob Gorbet (Knowledge Integration, Waterloo), and Theory led by Sarah Bonnemaison (Architecture, Dalhousie).

These streams are integrated within a six-year research plan that move in cycles from experimental prototypes to integrated public scales of implementation. Large-scale 'Living Lab' testing spaces offer flexible platforms where specialized researchers and designers can come together to think, experiment, and create. Growing in scale and complexity from prototype interiors to prototype envelopes, researchers are investigating how near-living architecture can integrate machine-based behaviors and how chemical exchanges might be supported. In parallel the group investigates the cognitive, physiological, and emotional responses of occupants.

The production of the LAS group includes dissemination in international gallery and museum installations, runway events, and publications. A number of partners now identified as LAS members have worked together on preceding projects, presented in evolving site-specific installations in some thirty international venues. A number of these projects are illustrated within this current volume, in the section entitled Projects of the Hylozoic Ground Collaboration, 2006-15. LAS is continuing collaborations with international cultural institutions and producers including the The Leonardo Museum for Art, Science and Technology, Salt Lake City, Simons, West Edmonton Mall, Edmonton, and Atelier Iris van Herpen, Amsterdam. These events provide first-hand public interaction with living architecture prototypes and test-beds.

Long-term objectives of the LAS include development of advanced prototype envelopes that have achieved fully integrated self-renewing intelligent, empathetic systems, capable of functioning within existing inhabited buildings. This long-range research has the objective of finding practical strategies for achieving resilience and adaptability within environments that are far from equilibrium.

1 Scaffolds

Stream Leader: Philip Beesley, Architecture, University of Waterloo

Scaffold is focused on advancing resilient architectural test-beds that integrate lightweight and flexible components. These components contain compartments and membranes that incorporate responsive computational and fluid circulation systems. Scaffolds are developed with tensile strength, stability and durability in materials such as acrylics, memory shape alloy and mylar to improve the performative quality of required structures. Permanent integration within occupied buildings is a long-term objective. Projects include: Lightweight Resilient Architectural Scaffolds; Hybrid Building Envelope and Lining; Infrastructures for Fluid, Power, and Data Systems.

2 Synthetic Cognition

Stream Leader: Dana Kulic, Electrical and Computer Engineering, University of Waterloo

Synthetic Cognition integrates computation and controls to develop inter-active systems that visualize and synthesize performance behaviours. The systems integrate multi-modal monitoring and massively distributed sensor arrays employing real-time functions for sensing and learning occupant presence and actions. A learning architecture adapts and responds to continuous feedback and occupant-feedback from test-beds. Permanent integration of empathic technologies into buildings is a long-term objective. Projects include: Sensor, Actuator and Control Systems; Human Interaction Modeling; Scripted Interaction; Autonomous Interaction and Adaptation; Experience Testing of Complex Adaptive Systems.

3 Metabolism

Stream Leader: Rachel Armstrong, Architecture, Newcastle University

Metabolism is focused on developing functional self-renewing systems capable of sustained long-term growth in changing environments. These systems will be integrated in artificial skins and fuels showing qualities of living, composed from fluid-based inorganic chemistries. Synthetic systems of metabolism could act as a regenerative layer for building surfaces, similar to ivy on building structures, and extend beyond the skin to proliferate through the scaffold. Chemical bodies integrated as part of scaffold sustain a kind of the livelihood while being contained. Projects include: Microbial Fuel Cells; Carbon Exchange Systems; Skin Building Systems.

4 Human Experience

Stream Leader: Colin Ellard, Psychology, University of Waterloo

Human Experience explores the emotional and cognitive impact of near-living environments on human occupants. Participant movement, facial expression, and nervous system activity will be used to construct a profile of the relationship between person and the responsive environment. The analysis methods and technical feedbacks gathered from Stream 2 will provide the data required to study human experience in short and long-term time scales. Projects include: Visualizing Emotive Environments; Experience Testing and Analysis Methods.

5 Interdisciplinary Methods

Stream Leader: Rob Gorbet, Knowledge Integration, University of Waterloo

Interdisciplinary Methods studies and develops new working methods for multidisciplinary collaborations within the partnership. Additionally, this stream is interested in teaching methods for interdisciplinary collaboration to impacts curriculum and the future of creative thinking. Projects include: STEAM-based Curriculum Development; Paradigms, Models and Design Methods for Interdisciplinary Working Methods.

6 Theory

Stream Leader: Sarah Bonnemaison, Architecture, Dalhousie University

Theory provides historical and theoretical reflections on the notion of Living in the context of the LAS research partnership. The activities of this stream is working towards developing a collective language and theoretical understanding of living systems through the aesthetic philosophy of Organicism. This stream is also dedicated to developing future trajectories and imagining possibilities offered by living architecture environments in shaping our future Projects will include publications and curated exhibitions.oping a collective language and theoretical understanding of living systems through the aesthetic philosophy of Organicism. This stream is also dedicated to developing future trajectories and imagining possibilities offered by living architecture environments in shaping our future. Projects will include Publications and Curated Exhibitions.

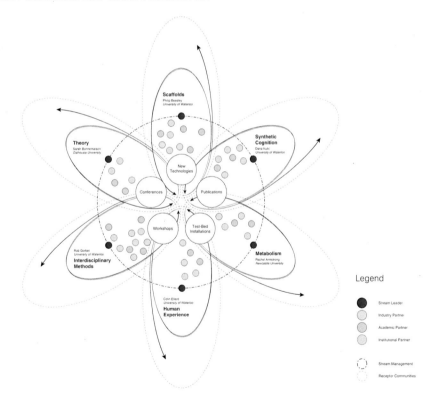

Diagram illustrating the Partnership Structure of the Living Architecture Systems Group.

Dissipative Models:
Notes toward Design Method

PHILIP BEESLEY
University Of Waterloo

In this discussion, I pursue a relationship with the environment embodying the forms of diffusion and dissipation. Seeking essential qualities of emplacement affording subtle phenomena and expanded physiology and measured by mutual relationships of exchange, I will try to articulate a manifesto for architectural design that offers near-living qualities. Rather than polarized working methods that follow only centrally controlled or opposing emergent, incremental models of organization, the fields of the method demonstrated here oscillate. An undulating, quasiperiodic method is evoked by the forms embedded within the projects illustrated here. Deliberate ambivalence is inherent to the approach, yielding qualities where things convulse and stutter in emerging vitality. This personal approach results in shifting boundaries that fluctuate between hard facts and hopeful fictions for exploring the future.

Ilya Prigogine, the great twentieth century physicist, proposed dissipation as a key term for understanding how materials could interact in a constantly evolving and self-organizing world.[1] Prigogine's thought has special value for architectural design, offering a dramatic contrast to embedded traditions. Western architecture has, for the past two millennia, been dominated by paradigms of durability, clarity and stability, enunciated by the first-century Roman Vitruvius in his famous paradigm of 'firmitas'. Vitruvian design education has in turn tended to preserve the ruling philosophy of his Greek predecessor, the philosopher Plato, whose maxims encouraged architecture to harmonize with the natural foundations of the world by following elegant reductions of primary geometry.[2] Applied to architecture, the reductive geometry of Plato's pure circles and simplified crystalline perimeters tends to favour the minimum possible envelope and the maximum possible territory enclosing interior territory. Inspiring such design, pure, reductive geometries can readily be seen within many aspects of natural form finding, exemplified by the space of dew drops and rain drops.[3] Yet the reductive form language that guides such efficiency also makes a mechanism for resisting interaction. The sphere of a raindrop is indeed a reductive machine that rejects interaction. The surface tension of the meniscus encircling a drop of rain pulls inward, and the result is a kind of optimum where the least possible exposing surface encloses the greatest possible mass within. In proportion to its interior volume, there can be no less surface for interaction than that of a sphere. The potency of that equation can hardly be overestimated in its influence on the practice of design.

Similar equations guide the design of a fort that protects, a bullet that pierces, or a bathysphere that can fight the radical forces of the deep. As if guided by a moral compass founded on equations of distillation and purity, western traditions of architecture have tended to value these kinds of pure forms.[4] The resulting architecture tends to seek strength and stability, resisting disruption. Yet why need we assume that the perfectly balanced optimum of a spherical drop of rain is obviously better than the alternate optimum offered by energy-shedding delicate outward-reaching branching spines that radiate from a frozen snowflake? Why, when we think of the myriad of forms that the natural world has offered, should we prefer closed, pure, gloss-faced cubes and spheres to tangled, dissipating masses of fertile soil?

The reductive form-languages of Platonic solids achieve maximum possible territory and maximum possible inertia by minimizing their exposure to their surroundings.[5] Such forms can be effective in a cold climate that requires retention of energy. However, cooling requires the opposite. The opposite of a spherical raindrop appears in the form of frost crystals and snowflakes. Snowflakes epitomize dissipation, optimizing release through an efflorescence of exchange with constantly-unfolding bifurcations determining unique configurations as their thermal reactions expand. Such a form offers a strategy for a diffusive architecture in which surfaces are devoted to the maximum possible intensity and resonance with their surroundings. In turn, following Prigogine, the series of installations and assemblies documented within this paper explore the opposite of reductive spheres and unified crystals. This diffusive architecture pursues qualities similar to those found in veils of smoke billowing at the outer reaches of a fire, the barred, braided fields of clouds; torrents of spiralling liquids; mineral felts efflorescing within an osmotic cell reaction. Such sources are characterized by resonance, flux, and open boundaries lying far from equilibrium.

Gases, Fluids And Membranes

In the natural world, complex systems undergo constant states of per-turbation, which generate disequilibrium. Uniformly organized materials can 'bifurcate' and take alternative potential forms reacting to changes in energy. Simple fluids affected by a change in thermal energy can dissipate to a new state through thermal conduction, moving through states far from equilibrium.[6] Prigogine offers the example of a snowflake as an exemplary dissipative form where "small vibrations around regularly arranged spatial positions… may lie at the vertices of a cube, or the vertices of a regular hexagonal prism and the centers of their hexagonal bases… a case of equilibrium-mediated emergence of order belonging to the class of phase transitions, an important class of natural phenomena that are largely responsible for the polymorphism of matter […]."[7]

Following the need of sheltering enclosures to alternately retain and shed heat, the kind of diffusive form-language embodied within snowflakes offer a paradigm of involvement with their surroundings. Rather than prioritizing enclosed territory and maximum defense, a form like that of a snowflake seems instead to seek a maximum of involvement through its expanded perimeters. Such forms might instruct the design of new batteries, or perhaps can make more efficient bio-generators modeled after the reticulated interior membranes of mitochondria in human cells. By increasing exposure and engagement with the world, such radical exfoliation can also offer a paradigm for building design. At the scale of architecture, such principles might offer alternatives to the conception of enclosing walls and roof surface, reconceiving those surfaces as deeply reticulated heat sinks, and as layered interwoven membrane curtains that modulate the boundaries between inner and outer environments. A new form language of maximization and engagement implies that design may in turn embrace a renewed kind of stewardship.[8] Such a role replaces the sense of a stripped, Platonic horizon with a soil-like generation of fertile material involvement with the world.

Following Prigogine's conceptions, air, gas and fluid can act as design media for architecture. The American mechanical engineer Michelle Addington suggests how energy flows around the body and buildings can be addressed in thermodynamic exchanges, exposing the dynamic of convective plumes around each of us and extending this dynamic into architectural scales.[9] Rather than regarding the air as a void, this approach implies that air is an addressable medium for designers. In contrast to prevailing Modern conceptions of space as a neutralized void, the matrix lying between objects may be seen as populated and structured. This sense of effusive matter also extends to the cell. The US-based cancer research of Dr. Donald Ingber has revealed structural systems occurring within the fluid realm of the cytoplasm, structured in ways that invite manipulation by designers.[10] Ingber's research has demonstrated how the fluid structure of cytoplasm contains interactions between two protein modes: myocin, organized in microtubules offering compression, and actin, working as tensile structures, operating together in a tensegrity grid structuring the viscous medium.

The American zoologist Steven Vogel's seminal research on the structural forms of organisms and their relation to the mechanics of moving fluids illustrates how dynamic forms can lead to highly effective adaptations. The design of organisms responding to drag, flow and lift offers adaptive efficiency. Leaves, exposed to high winds, reconfigure by rolling into conical forms, decreasing their drag.[11] Plants can form themselves into shapes that interact with local air flows to act as pollen traps.[12] The physical adaptations observed in natural forms offer solutions for form-flexible architecture that exists in changing environments. These combined effects could be conceived as a kind of churn that fertilizes relationships between occupants and the environment. The bidirectional exchange between instalment and ecosystem offers a means of constructing new frameworks to build hybrid structures that can mature into more hospitable bionetworks.

Extending the formal structures studied by Vogel and Ingber into the dynamic realm of chemical reactions, artificial life researchers Rachel Armstrong and Martin Hanczyc are part of a movement working with new protocells – prototype cells – exposing the ways designers can work with skin-making mechanisms and carbon-fixing mechanisms.[13] A formation developed by Armstrong and Hanczyc includes a version of a Traube cell, a chemical formulation originally modeled in the nineteenth century as an analysis of the behaviour of living amoebas. Their recapitulation of this study features a delicate copper salt suspended between varying oil densities that permit delicate formations to appear, resulting in the blooming of a mineral felt, powered by osmotic forces pumping solution around a copper sulphate fluid core (figure 1). The dynamic organizations revealed by Prigogine and related researchers invites architectural design to move from the Vitruvian idea of a static world into the dynamic form of a metabolism.

Projects and Methods

Following diffusive form-language, a steadily evolving series of collaborative projects have been developed by the North American and European collaborations of the Living Architecture Systems Group. Recent projects have employed layered systems integrating lightweight scaffolds, simple chemical metabolisms, kinetic mechanisms and distributed computational controls. Structures have tended to be lightweight and ephemeral, organized as resilient textile matrices. The work starts by setting out crystalline forms following diagrids and textile meshworks in order to make lightweight, resonant

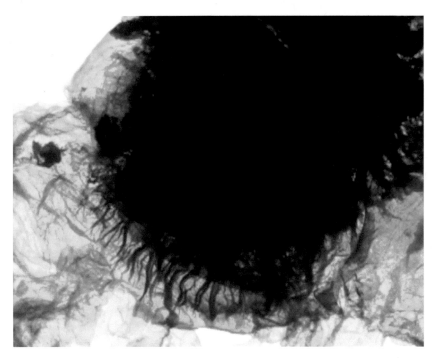

Figure 1   Traube protocells developed for Hylozoic Ground, (Venice Architecture Biennale, Italy, 2010) exhibit osmotic pumping of delicate ferrous membranes, which are formed around copper sulphate vesicles suspended within varying densities of oil.

scaffolds. Flexible lightweight formations are overlaid with microprocessor systems. Kinetic responses are orchestrated by arrayed actuators and sensors, producing turbulent responses that ripple outward (figure 2). Sheet-material derivations expand definitions of space by taking the notion of natural concepts like soil and transforming them into suspended interlinking clouds. In response to human presence, the installation can produce contractile movements, clutching and pulling. Geometries ordering the interlinking structural components used to construct these fields have included quasiperiodic systems where clusters and local arrays can multiply and effloresce, supporting transitions in their interrelationships. A recent stage of development has involved construction of diffusive metabolisms containing protocol liquid reactions creating felt-like chemical skins. This integrated chemistry suggests that buildings could be designed to grow and renew themselves.

Each element within such an environment is gentle, exerting a small response, yet because they are chained together in the hundreds and sometimes the thousands, quite substantial crowd-like responses may occur, suggesting weakly emergent laws of organization. These elements call to mind Prigogine's formulation of systems composed of lattices of identical variables interacting with each other in an environment, where activity from each element is transmitted to its neighbours, in turn affecting the internal state of its "outputting" neighbours leading to emerging properties.[14] In Hylozoic Ground, the individual elements are generated in large arrays where a hyperbolic meshwork stands above the ground making a robust force-shedding structural system with peaks and valleys of doubly curved surfaces. Hovering filters pass convective plumes through them and contain metabolic chemistry that processes and generates new mineral skins by fixing dissolved carbon dioxide from the atmosphere. The bladders, traps and glands seen within these works form soil-like elements. The computation seen here is simple: individual elements chained together produce action akin to a chorus of crickets, or a swarm of insects, or perhaps the opening and closing of polyps in a coral reef. Shift-registers in recent generations of the custom digital control system provide a means of addressing many masses of actuators while using modest micro processing power as the system marches through data sets.

Changing scale in recent work is collaboration in fashion, starting to contribute to the sense of an expanded physiology in literal ways. Iris van Herpen's Amsterdam-based studio has developed clothing that offers a radical intimacy where the skin seems to be rendered as one boundary amongst many. Recent collaboration with Van Herpen[15] includes three dimensional lace made of silicon and impact resistant acrylic. In the recent Voltage series (figures 3), individual components derived from architectural systems were reconceived in miniature form. The layers of this hybrid clothing encourage plumes of air to rise. Fabrics integrate fissured forms configured like leaky heart valves, hovering leaf-like layers that push and pump in gentle waves. A robust silicone meshwork swarms around the body. Individual elements chained together with small silicone tubes make a diagrid of corrugated mesh with diffusive, viscous performance. They make a live performance as they harvest your own energy and ripple around you. Layers lying immediately outside human bodies are organized in octaves of potential exploration, moving into turbulence. Musculature could be considered a mask, and an active fire-like metabolism can be sensed radiating through human skin. A corollary can be seen in a building composed of multiple layers. Traces are pulling at you. You become aware of the impact of your own tread in the world.

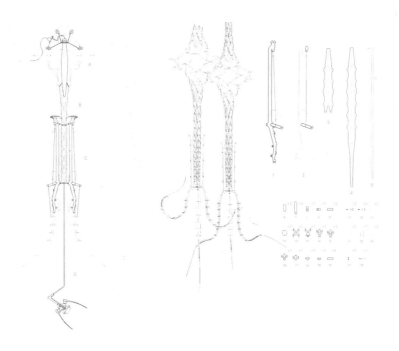

Figure 2   Clusters of flexible meshwork support mounted kinetic tentacles which are activated by optic sensors.

Further Implications: Toward Design of Living Systems

The general principles underlying this work imply mutual relationships and distributed organizations. The hardened boundaries exemplified by Plato's world of spheres and reductive forms might be opened and renewed by form-languages that pursue intense involvement and exchange.[16] This implies a mutual kind of relationship between human occupants and their surrounding environments. In turn, it suggests a craft of designing with materials conceived as filters that can expand human influence while at the same time expanding the influence of the world in an oscillating register: catching, harvesting, pulling and pushing. While personal boundaries can readily be found as functions of central systems – brain, and spine, and hearts define cores that we know well – parallel to those cores lie bundles of ganglia in our elbows or in our sternum and pineal. Neural matter is riddled throughout our bodies, making a series of overlapping networks. Much of our consciousness is bound up in loops and reflexes that happen at the outer edges of cognition. Such a model working internally could be expanded outward. In such a layered space, we could build up a deeply layered, deeply fissure set of relationships in which there are multiple sensitive boundaries. We might be able to build up in a sense of fertility reconstructing a kind of a soil and ground. We could measure values within that constructed ground by measuring resonance. Such a method suggests that the practice of architecture can move closer to the craft of creating living systems.

Figure 3   Finely detailed flexible meshwork structures and translucent fronds form the outer layers of Iris Van Herpen's Voltage collection (Voltage, Haute Couture, Paris, 2013).

For twenty-five hundred years, Western artists and designers have been writing about emulating life. The imagery and forms from this tradition show potent hope for inanimate forms of craft and art coming alive. Yet the speech and evocations of visual art and architecture have often treated 'life' as a kind of boundary defined by separation and distance from human craft. The symbolism that evokes life has been maintained by distinguishing human artifice from the viable organisms of nature. The discipline of architecture seems to have been especially emphatic in maintaining this divide. Architecture seems a counterform to nature, staying deliberately distinct from the living world, preferring instead the role of a stripped stage that supports the living world by means of clear restraint. Perhaps that kind of separation has a moral kind of imperative, avoiding trespass. Yet the distinct progress of science and technology in recent decades invites a change to this strategy of restraint. The achievement of comprehensive information within the human genome project,[17] the accomplishment of potent learning functions in computational control, and the increasing fluency in programming physical materials and projecting complex-system ecological modeling[18] can conspire to demonstrate that living systems no longer need be maintained as a sacrament separate from human intervention. The ability to see our traces and to understand dimensions of the impact with which we thread forms an ethical key to this change. Emerging from the distancing functions of reverence into a new phase of stewardship, living systems can now occupy the space of architectural design.

The qualities of this work offer an alternative to reductive, purifying qualities that have tended to dominate traditions within Western architecture. The morphology described here stands distinctly against prevailing Modern preference for stripped, minimal stages devoted to autonomous freedom. The formal language of this design method instead pursues culpable involvement.[19] Rather than polarized working methods that follow only centrally controlled or opposing emergent, incremental models of organization, the fields of this working method oscillate. Deliberate ambivalence is inherent to the approach, yielding qualities where things convulse and stutter in emerging vitality, characterized by mutual relationships of exchange with surrounding environments. This study opposes Plato's idea of a sphere, the kind of evidently beautiful form embodied by a raindrop. While such a form might claim to be efficient and responsible by reducing consumption, this principle, guiding current minimalism, speaks arguably more of mortality than of fertility. In human culture, spheres can speak of violence and of territorial claims. Instead of such reductive forms I have suggested that snowflakes offer potent form-language that could guide emerging architecture.

In the footsteps of Prigogine, the diffusive, dissipative form-language described here offers a strategy for constructing fertile new architecture. The form-langauge discussion within this approach attempts to open up new spaces bursting with novel potential. The 'mazimizing' interface implied by Ilya Prigogine's conception can guide a fertile generation of architectural design.

Endnotes

This essay previously appeared as Beesley, Philip. "Dissipative Models: Notes toward Design Method." Paradigms in Computing: Making, Machines and Models for Design Agency in Architecture. Ed. David Gerber et al. New York: eVolo, 2014.

1. For Prigogine's conceptions with emphasis on spatial qualities, see Gregoire Nicolis and Ilya Prigogine, Exploring Complexity: An Introduction, New York: W.H. Freeman and Company, 1989.

2. Wallisser, T., "Other geometries in architecture: bubbles, knots and minimal surfaces" in M. Emmer and A. Quarteroni (eds.), Mathknow, Milano: Springer, 2009, pp. 91-111.

3. Chernov, A. A., "Crystal growth science between the centuries" in Journal of Materials Science: Materials in Electronics, vol. 12, no. 8, 2001, pp. 437-449.

4. Skinner, S., Sacred geometry: deciphering the code, New York: Sterling Publishing Company, Inc., 2009.

5. Grimm, V., Revilla, E., Berger, U., Jeltsch, F., Mooij, W. M., Railsback, S. F., ... & DeAngelis, D. L., "Pattern-oriented modeling of agent-based complex systems: lessons from ecology" in Science, vol. 310, no. 5750, 2009, pp. 987-991.

6. Ibid, p. 10.

7. Nicolis and Prigogine, op.cit., p. 41.

8. Hagan, S., Taking shape: a new contract between architecture and nature, London and New York: Routledge, 2001.

9. Addington, D. Michelle, and Daniel L. Schodek. Smart materials and new technologies: for the architecture and design professions, London and New York: Routledge, 2005.

10. Ingber, D. E., "Can cancer be reversed by engineering the tumor microenvironment?" in Seminars in cancer biology, Academic Press, vol. 18, no. 5, Oct. 2008, pp. 356-364.

11. Vogel, Steven, Life in Moving Fluids: The Physical Biology of Flow, Princeton, NJ: Princeton University Press, 1994, p. 123.

12. Ibid, p. 43.

13. Armstrong, R. and M.M. Hanczyc, "Bütschli dynamic droplet system" in Artificial Life Journal, vol. 19, nos. 3-4, 2013, pp. 331-346.

14. Nicolis and Prigogine, op.cit., p. 140.

15. Van Herpen, Iris, "In Conversation with Philip Beesley" in A Magazine, no. 13, pp. 2-7.

16. Youngs, A. M., "The fine art of creating life" in Leonardo, vol. 33, no. 5, 2000, pp. 377-380.

17. Collins, F. S., Morgan, M., & Patrinos, A., "The Human Genome Project: lessons from large-scale biology" in Science, vol. 300, no. 5617, 2003, pp. 286-290.

18. Eliasmith, C., and Anderson, C. H., Neural Engineering: Computation, Representation, and Dynamics in Neurobiological Systems, Cambridge, MA: MIT Press, 2004.

19. Crist, C. P., and Roundtree, K., "Humanity in the web of life" in Environmental Ethics, vol. 28, no. 2, 2006, pp. 185-200.

Philip Beesley, MRAIC OAA RCA, is a practicing visual artist, architect, and Professor in Architecture at the University of Waterloo and Professor of Digital Design and Architecture & Urbanism at the European Graduate School. Beesley's work is widely cited in contemporary art and architecture, focused on the rapidly expanding technology and culture of responsive and interactive systems.

He was educated in visual art at Queen's University, in technology at Humber College, and in architecture at the University of Toronto. He serves as the Director for the Living Architecture Systems Group, and as Director for Riverside Architectural Press. His Toronto-based practice Philip Beesley Architect Inc. operates in partnership with the Europe-based practice Pucher Seifert and the Waterloo-based Adaptive Systems Group, and in numerous other collaborations. The studio's methods incorporate industrial design, digital prototyping, and mechatronics engineering. Beesley frequently collaborates with artists, scientists and engineers. Recent projects include a series of hybrid fabrics developed with Atelier Iris van Herpen, curiosity-based machine learning environments developed with Rob Gorbet and Dana Kulić of the Adaptive Systems Group, and synthetic metabolisms developed with Rachel Armstrong of the University of Newcastle. His most recent collaboration with Iris Van Herpen has translated a shared sensibility for subtle materials, electricity, and chemistry into a collection of highly complex and diverse textile and haute couture collections.

His research focuses on responsive and distributed architectural environments and interactive systems, flexible lightweight structures integrating kinetic functions, microprocessing, sensor and actuator systems, with particular focus on digital fabrication methods and sheet-material derivations. Beesley has authored and edited sixteen books and proceedings, and has appeared on the cover of Artificial Life (MIT), LEONARDO and AD journals. Features include national CBC news, Vogue, WIRED, and a series of TED talks. His work was selected to represent Canada at the 2010 Venice Biennale for Architecture, and has received distinctions including the Prix de Rome, VIDA 11.0, FEIDAD, Azure AZ, and Architizer A+.

Synthetic Cognition: From Reaction to Interaction

DANA KULIĆ
University of Waterloo

The development of cognitive abilities for artificial agents has long been a research interest in robotics (Lungarella 2003, Asada 2009), artificial intelligence (Ikegami 2013) and other interactive systems (Drummond 2009). What does it mean for an agent to possess cognition? A cognitive agent should perceive itself and its environment, by sensing and making sense of its sensory perceptions; plan and act within its environment to achieve its goals; and learn over time through acting and interacting within its environment. The LAS Group has been investigating how cognitive abilities can be imbued into architectural scale environments, to develop near living architecture systems that can engage with visitors during extended interactions and enhance human experience in these immersive environments, learn though the interaction and engage in mutual adaptation with their occupants.

Figure 1   First generation LASG systems prototyped, Hylozoic Ground,
(Venice Architecture Biennale, Italy 2010).

Our Work to Date

Over the last decade, LASG has developed increasingly sophisticated interactive systems and supporting hardware (Gorbet 2015). Early LASG implementations included distributed embedded sensing and actuation, consisting of infrared (IR) proximity sensors and kinetic mechanisms activated by shape memory alloy wire actuators, connected to embedded processors. Within an installation, occupant proximity would be detected by IR sensors, triggering a pre-programmed local response followed by behaviours that feature a "rippling out" effect from the activated node, achieved through communication with, and corresponding response by, neighbouring nodes.

A second series of projects, designed from 2011 through 2014, featured expanded functions including increased density of sensor and actuator arrays, organized within chains, individually controlled by nested sets of microprocessors communicating with a central computer. A fixed set of behaviours was pre-programmed within this series of environments, requiring the designer to specify the sensor and actuator relationship for each behaviour. This model required a programmer to anticipate what gestures the visitors would use to attempt to engage with the sculpture, and what programmed responses would induce a positive reaction. While the distributed structure of the controllers, together with their interconnectivity and variety of human responses created some emergence, the elementary interactions do not change over time, leading to a potential for habituation and predictability during long-term interaction. In addition, designers needed to predict behaviours that could induce positive user reactions, which is very subjective.

To enable long-term, adaptive engagement, a new third series has recently been developed. In these prototypes, the pre-programmed behaviours seen in the preceding series 2 can be replaced or superseded by autonomously generated and evolving behaviours. The aim is to improve the behavioural and perceptual capabilities of the interactive sculpture systems through developing learning algorithms that could acquire novel and engaging behaviours through their interactions with the users. By developing learning algorithms using motivations such as novelty and users' engagement, the behaviours of the sculptures can evolve and improve over time, without requiring detailed programming.

The evolution of the Hylozoic Series hardware platform was motivated by the introduction of the curiosity-based learning algorithm (CBLA) as the control software (Chan 2015), based on Oudeyer et al.'s (Oudeyer 2007) intrinsic motivation approach initially developed for developmental robotics. The CBLA conceptualizes the architectural system as an agent or group of agents that have intrinsic motivations, and generate actions to satisfy them. Specifically, the agents are motivated by curiosity, which induces the system to perform exploratory actions to learn about itself, much like an infant might learn by exercising groups of muscles and observing the response. In its simplest form, the algorithm chooses an action from its action repertoire to perform, and measures the response. At the same time, it generates a prediction of what it thinks should happen. If the prediction matches the measured response, it has learned that part of its sensorimotor space and that space becomes less interesting for future actions. If the prediction fails to match the measured response, it remains curious about that part of its "self", as it obviously still has more to learn. It will create a new prediction and try again. This learning architecture allows the system to learn both about itself, and also about interactions with occupants, whose movements and actions create new and "surprising" responses, activating the system's curiosity.

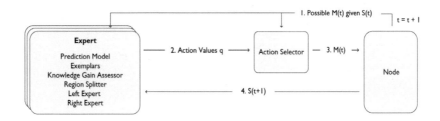

Figure 2   The CBLA Engine: (1) At the start of each time step, the Node outputs the current possible actions M(t)'s given its perceptions S(t). (2) Then, the Expert provides the Action Values q associated with the possible actions M(t) to the Action Selector. (3) After that, the Action Selector selects an action and actuates the Node. (4) After the Node has performed the action, it returns the actual resultant perceptions S(t+1) to the Expert. The Expert can then improve its internal prediction model and update the Action Value associated with SM(t).

To accommodate this algorithm, the system must be able to sense the consequences of its actions, similar to the human capability for proprioception. Similar to human proprioceptors, proprioceptive sensors allow the sculpture to both detect its own actions, and the actions of occupants on its embodiment. For example, an accelerometer on a tentacle senses both when the tentacle actuator is activated, and also when the tentacle is touched by a visitor during interaction. Proprioceptors play an important role in giving the sculpture information about its own state to enable model learning and adaptation.

Using the latest hardware and the developed learning algorithm, we have conducted a pilot user study to investigate how visitors perceive and interact with the learning system in comparison to prescripted behaviours (Chan 2016). Visitors are able to perceive differences between prescripted and learning behaviours, and reported a range of responses to the interaction. While some visitors' interest and engagement increased with the learning system, others became frustrated and disinterested when they could not easily discern the response pattern. The interplay between human and synthetic curiosity is an important direction of our future work.

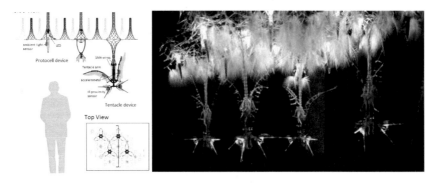

Figure 3   (a) Schematic and (b) Photograph of the multi-cluster prototype installation used for the pilot user study (Chan 2016).

In addition to our work developing algorithms for synthetic learning, we have been investigating more complex perception and action capabilities, particularly exploring the perception and generation of movement. Human movement is known to convey a rich range of information, and is a vital channel of non-verbal communication during human-human interaction. We have been investigating how human affect can be perceived and automatically estimated from human movement (Samadani 2014), and how expertise from dance notation and choreography can be leveraged to generate and modulate affective movement (Burton 2016).

Building on our prior work, the goals of the next stage of system development are to target a step change in the system's cognitive capabilities to enable long term autonomy and architectural scale synthetic cognition, moving towards a system that can engage and co-evolve with its occupants. There are 6 development activities, which together enable the design, development, integration and validation of the interactive systems.

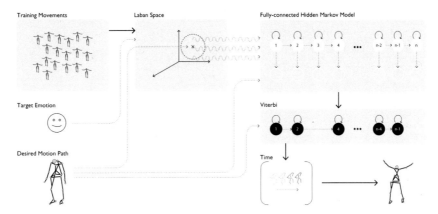

Figure 4   Affective Motion Generation and Modulation based on Laban movement notation. (Burton 2016)

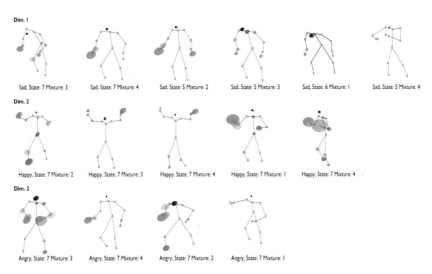

Figure 5   Automatic detection of key movement features which contribute to
affective motion perception (Samadani 2014)

Sensor, Actuator and Control Systems

In this activity, we will develop and integrate actuator, sensor and control systems for large-scale architectural installations. The focus will be on small, low-cost, lightweight distributed sensors and actuators that can be massively replicated to produce large scale installations. The control system design will focus on distributed control which enables complex and emergent behaviour using spatially distributed arrays of simple actuators. The sensing system will enable: (1) proprioceptive sensing of the behaviour of the interactive system, including movement, light and sound, (2) sensing of the visitors in the installation, including location, gaze direction, and body posture, and (3) sensing of the environment, including air flow, temperature and ambient light.

The actuation system will include: (1) articulated movement and vibration, pursuing both expressive machine-human empathetic human communication and environmental modification including air flow and temperature (2) sound generation employing spatial granular synthesis, pursuing expressive empathetic machine-human communication, and (3) light modulation. This work will build on our existing work with Series 2 and 3 Hylozoic Soil actuators, sensors and control systems.

Human Modeling

In this activity, we will use the sensing and actuation technology developed in activity 1 to develop techniques for estimating inhabitant reactions and affect as they interact and respond to the installation. The focus will be on non-verbal communication conveyed through body movement. The goal will be to estimate affective state, level of engagement and level of interest from body movement and gaze direction.

Here, we will build models of the bodily manifestations of affect, engagement and interest; these models will be integrated into the architectural platform and validated through user studies. We will investigate both the measurement of individual visitors, as well as the behaviours that emerge through social interaction of multiple visitors, such as grouping and group dynamics.

Scripted Interaction and Choreography

In this activity, we will develop machine interaction tools to enable choreographers to design joint performances of human and architectural performers. We will develop high level interfaces for the specification and composition of system behaviours, design of scripted local interactions and their distribution over the larger installation. These interfaces will allow choreographers to design and direct installation behaviour without the need for programming or knowledge of the system electro-mechanical implementation. These tools will be used by dancers and choreographers to develop and stage performances incorporating human and architectural "actors". We will start with fully choreographed performances, and, over the course of the project, using the results from the autonomous interaction activity (described below), explore shared autonomy performances which incorporate both choreographed movement and dancer and architectural improvisation.

Autonomous Interaction and Adaptation

In this activity, we will develop models and algorithms for unscripted interaction between inhabitants and the system. We will start with local pre-scripted behaviours, building both on choreographed behaviours and the models of human movement and behaviour generated from the human modeling activity, and develop models of interaction based on user testing within installation test-beds. We will next develop autonomous interaction strategies, building algorithms which autonomously generate interactive behaviours, using inherent system motivation such as curiosity or engagement to drive behaviour adaptation and evolution. These algorithms will use proprioceptive sensing and visitor modeling to generate behaviours which adapt over time, building long term interactions and sustaining inhabitant engagement. This work will build on our work on curiosity based learning algorithms.

Tools for Validation

In this activity, we will develop tools to enable large scale user testing in public environments. The LASG project and its envisioned public installations provide an unprecedented opportunity to validate the developed tools and methodology with a very large and diverse number of users. To enable this validation, we need methods to easily and unobtrusively collect user feedback.

Objective sensing data from proprioreceptive functions and from environment variables (temperature, air quality and movement, illumination) will be integrated with tools for collecting subjective user feedback through the use of experience sampling mobile technologies developed in the Human Experience stream, such as mobile phone based surveys and additional data collection (such as heart rate, accelerometer and location) from mobile wearables.

Outlook

The activities foreseen within the synthetic cognition stream are at the cutting edge of current research in interactive technologies and will provide for an unprecedented application of emerging technologies to architecture. Beyond interactive architecture, the proposed work can be applied to: the design of responsive architecture and environments through the use of adaptive components; for designing interaction strategies for enriched human-robot and human-computer applications; and for the application of distributed computing paradigms. The novel application of existing engineering components to the field of architecture will break new ground as the research is situated at the intersection of human perception, human-robot interaction and embedded technology.

Endnotes

1. J. Drummond, "Understanding Interactive Systems," Organised Sound, vol. 14, no. 02, p. 124, 2009.

2. T. Ikegami, "A design for living technology: Experiments with the mind time machine," Artificial Life, vol. 19, no. 3/4, pp. 387–400, 2013.

3. M. Lungarella, G. Metta, R. Pfeifer, and G. Sandini, "Developmental robotics: a survey," Connection Science, vol. 15, no. 4, pp. 151–190, 2003.

4. M. Asada, K. Hosoda, Y. Kuniyoshi, H. Ishiguro, T. Inui, Y. Yoshikawa, M. Ogino, and C. Yoshida, "Cognitive Developmental Robotics : A Survey," IEEE Transactions on Autonomous Mental Development, vol. 1, no. 1, pp. 12 – 34, 2009.

5. P.-Y. Oudeyer, F. Kaplan, and V. V. Hafner, "Intrinsic Motivation Systems for Autonomous Mental Development," IEEE Transactions on Evolutionary Computation, vol. 11, no. 2, pp. 265–286, 2007.

6. M. T. K. Chan, R. Gorbet, P. Beesley, and D. Kulić, "Curiosity-Based Learning Algorithm for Distributed Interactive Sculptural Systems," in 2015 IEEE/RSJ International Conference on Intelligent Robots and Systems (IROS), Hamburg Germany, 2015, pp. 3435–3441.

7. R. Gorbet, M. Memarian, M. Chan, D. Kulić, and P. Beesley, "Evolving Systems within Immersive Architectural Environments: New Research by the Living Architecture Systems Group," Next Generation Building, 2015.

8. SJ. Burton, A. A. Samadani, R. Gorbet and D. Kulić, Laban Movement Analysis and Affective Movement Generation for Robots and Other Near-Living Creatures, in Dance Notations and Robot Motion, J. P. Laumond and

9. N. Abe (eds), Springer Tracts in Advanced Robotics, pp. 25 – 48, 2016.

10. M. T. K. Chan, R. Gorbet, P. Beesley and D. Kulić, Interacting with Curious Agents: User experience with interactive sculptural systems, IEEE International Symposium on Robot and Human Interactive Communication, pp. 151 - 158, 2016.

11. A. Samadani, R. Gorbet and D. Kulić, Affective Movement Recognition based on Generative and Discriminative Stochastic Dynamic Models, IEEE Transactions on Human-Machine Systems, Vol. 44, No. 4, pp. 454 - 467, 2014.

Dana Kulić received the combined B.A.Sc. and M.Eng. degrees in electro-mechanical engineering and the Ph.D. degree in mechanical engineering from the University of British Columbia, Vancouver, Canada, in 1998 and 2005, respectively. From 1997 to 2002, she worked as a systems engineer designing fuel cell systems with Ballard Power Systems, and developing operational control software for the CanadaArm II at MacDonald Dettwiler.

From 2002 to 2006, Dr. Kulić worked with Dr. Elizabeth Croft as a Ph. D. student and a post-doctoral researcher at the CARIS Lab at the University of British Columbia. The aim of this work was to develop a human–robot interaction strategy to ensure the safety of the human participant. From 2006 to 2009, Dr. Kulić was a JSPS Post-doctoral Fellow and a Project Assistant Professor at the Nakamura-Yamane Laboratory at the University of Tokyo, Japan. The aim of her research was to develop algorithms for incremental learning of human motion patterns for humanoid robots.

Dr. Kulić is currently an Associate Professor at the Electrical and Computer Engineering Department at the University of Waterloo. Her research interests include robot learning, humanoid robots, human-robot interaction and mechatronics.

Metabolic Systems

RACHEL ARMSTRONG
Newcastle University

A characteristic of living systems is their possession of a metabolism but what is a metabolism, and how does one design with it?

Let us surrender for a moment that we inhabit a fully predictable, controllable, rational realm and rather, immerse ourselves in a world that maintains mystery without descending into incomprehensibility. In this domain, substances can spontaneously couple with their neighbors to produce surprising effects and super molecular chemistry gives us the capacity to synthesize matter that has not previously existed in the history of the universe. By spatiality choreographing these strange materialities we may conjure ambiguous landscapes, environments, habitats, and even cities that can surprise and provoke us. Indeed, such an extraordinary matrix may at first seem to exist beyond our capacity to conjure but let me first take a few steps back here in case you mistake my provocations for the poetic hallucinations of a mind that has lost any relationship with its senses. These extraordinary provocations are firmly placed within an experimental world of discovery that can not only be provoked, and designed but also explored.

At the heart of metabolism is the possibility of constructing life, which is a subversive phenomenon that resists the classical laws of physics and therefore has been notoriously difficult to design and engineer with. Consequently its critical operations are not easily described and therefore portrayed through incredibly negative lenses. Even its language is a negation of its radical creativity: non-equilibrium, non-linearity, negentropy, chaos, spookiness, disorder, irreversibility, far from equilibrium, strangeness, co-incidence, messiness, uncertainty and randomness. Feel the darkness within these terms – loaded with revolution, and unpredictability, like a conceptual haunting. Life is defined largely as that which it is not – conceived as multiple destructive acts against the orthodox commandments of matter – a form of material irrationality.

Metabolism ambitiously aims to tackle these difficulties in an ambitious project to conjure life – not through the traditional approach by deducing what liveliness isn't through multiple, strategic dissections that remove parts, which causes its complete collapse – but by attempting to generate life-like phenomena within the material realm in a new kind of synthesis by engaging with the choreography of its difficulties, contradictions and inexactitudes, where boundaries are always blurred, objects semi permeable to each other and its fabrics overwhelmingly hypercomplex.

This is not a fully realized, or easy portfolio of methods, materials, technologies and prototypes, to work with. Indeed, they exist within a hypercomplex and probabilistic realm from which we cannot fully dissociate or observe in its entirety. It could be argued that such fabrics spill beyond the disciplinary domain of architecture and enter into a new multi-disciplinary practice of "worlding"[1] in which the conventional modes of construction that constitute architecture are only a part. Yet, once experienced, it is no longer possible to fully extract ourselves from the charm, magic, or potential of this unchartered domain and even when we begin the explore the details of those operations that form its guts, this territory will always resist our full comprehension remaining, probabilistic, shocking, wonderful and capable of surprise.

Metabolic Systems as Hypercomplex Fabric

Metabolism is a strange fabric, which is in continual flux.[2] It is simultaneously material, technical and phenomenological, arising from the transactions and dynamic couplings within an assemblage of participating chemical bodies that perform "useful" work by resisting energetic decay towards equilibrium and in the process, generate "straightforward environmental images".[3] Another way of approaching metabolism is to understand it as the linking of complex, dissipative bodies, which form loose assemblages with each other and collectively, consume and produces their environment. These dissipative systems, or structures, arise spontaneously in nature across a range of scales such as, crystals, tornadoes and galaxies. While not all meet the technical qualifications of 'life' – all 'life' is a dissipative process. Dissipative structures are paradoxical objects that are confluences of energy/matter flows that spontaneously arise from overlapping fields of activity. Conceptually, they may be imagined as tornadoes that possess a recognisable structure that nucleates around a "nomadic" site – one that is not fixed by spatial coordinates but shaped by its relations, or "hubs" of activity. It maintains stability by dumping energy into its surroundings, and oddly, as it does so, it optimises its organizational capacity to dissipate energy into its surroundings. They exist within a range of limits and are unstable, eventually succumbing to the forces of disorder, or entropy, at which point they lose their lively character. Dissipative structures also interact beyond their boundaries through active fields. Perhaps the best way to imagine a dissipative structure is to think of a tornado. They are unusual to encounter, as they do not behave like classical objects. Imagine a storm chaser encountering a twister, who can feel its presence long before the eye of the storm is reached. Because they are highly complex physical systems that resist collapse they tend to seed the conditions for their next iteration until relative thermodynamic equilibrium is reached. Collectively they produce metabolic fields of activity.

Although metabolic systems are not given the full status of being truly "alive", they are critical to the design process as a set of tactics that may increase the probability of life-promoting events. Metabolism is an unbounded phenomenon that is characterized by constantly unfolding manifolds and landscapes that do not scale linearly, or infinitely. It is therefore a paradoxical fabric, full of contradictions and "invisible" agencies – ones that have not been atomized, named, or formally identified – that shares many characteristics of its constituent dissipative systems operating at far from equilibrium states and whose relationships with its surroundings establish perturbations and channel flows that further perpetuate its existence. We might also think of constructing metabolism as choreographing populations of weakly-linked[4] dissipative systems in time and space.

Metabolism is weather that burns. Not as a dry heat such as combustion but as a wet, ionic field – like storm clouds. Its thunder and lightning carry the seeds of life, ready to charge and re-charge the soaking bodies within its downpour. It is composed from clusters of substances with fluidic tendencies, like clouds, smog, waves, currents, eddies, vortices and hurricanes, whose spatially contextualized exchanges collectively resist the decay towards equilibrium and so result in the materialization and persistence of process. In this way metabolism possesses a character that is consistent with our experience of climate. It has fronts, transitions, quiet days, storms, breezes and even seasonal variations. It is never the same encounter one day to the next and never fully predictable. The theory of "dissipative adaptation" proposes that life-like function directly emerges from the non-equilibrium properties of these chemical substrates and through their persistence their sensate structures change to better perpetuate the flows of matter and energy that forge the weather and enable them to persist through their chemical transformations, so they may begin the transition from nonliving to living matter.[5] "You start with a random clump of atoms, and if you shine light on it for long enough, it should not be so surprising that you get a plant."[6] Metabolic systems embrace many characters, some are fleeting, and a few are constantly evolving, while others – caught in closed loops of exchange – are almost permanent. All metabolisms are in a state of continual flux, oscillating between tipping points before transforming and establishing new configurations. The state of the matrix and the character of the infrastructure in which these relationships are forged facilitate or impede its liveliness. The performance of metabolisms is therefore a question of infrastructure, spatiality, substance and flux. While typically defined within the context of the interior chemical fluctuations that take place within the confines of a cell wall, the semi permeable nature of the membrane extrudes the reach of metabolism beyond the limits of any particular body and leaks its reactive tendrils into the environment – somewhat like an "aura". It draws sustenance from its surroundings and maintains flow of matter and energy through an expanded field of participatory bodies, with their associated matter/energy fluxes. Of course, being a material phenomenon, metabolism possesses limits that are contingent on a host of circumstances – the nature of the participatory substances, the ambient temperature, rate of material flow in the environment, heterogeneity of landscape and the presence of catalysts, to name but a few. Metabolism is an embodied, highly spatial entity. Its potency roams and haunts spaces like hungry ghosts and productive ectoplasms, trembling with uncertainty, generating spooky effects and then vanishing. Being such a diverse assemblage of loosely coupled non-equilibrium objects, "decisions" are not only made from within each dissipative system but also through their external relations. Yet, the notations for indicating these multi-dimensional programs and their operations are largely collapsed into diagrammatic forms that gesture towards web-like structures whose edges are tucked into closed loops and coherent fields of operations. An idea emerges from these modes of representation that metabolisms, life, physiologies and ecologies are "closed loops" of operations – rather than fuzzy, highly spatial fields of uncertainties – more like condensation of breath around a window pane than something that can be channeled through its symbolic representation in straight lines.

Metabolic Systems as Program

The material world computes but not according to the abstractions of numbers that we have become accustomed to with digital computers. We have barely begun to scratch the surface of this realm;[7] a potentiality that was of great interest to Alan Turing.[8] Moreover, matter that computes is by no means

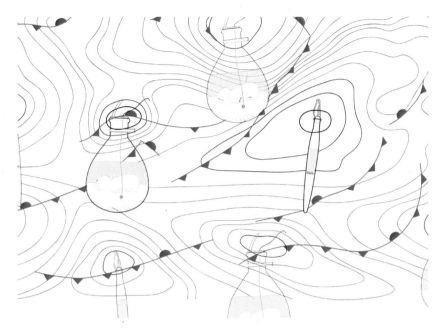

Figure 1   Weather that burns. Diagram of Sentient Chamber clusters – overlaid with notation typically used to illustrate weather fronts indicating thermally active metabolic landscapes.

incompatible with Turing's ephemeral mathematical language. Rather the capacity for lively matter at far from equilibrium states to make decisions, execute commands and produce programmable systems, creates a potent, potentially convergent interface where life, mind, body and symbolic lanugages can mingle to create a Cambrian explosion of new materials, spaces, essences and forms.

Let us consider metabolic systems as analogue computational platforms, whose operative agents are dissipative structures that can complexify space and matter. They function as an iterative system – or 'natural' counting process – that can be ordered to generate a range of program-mable outputs that result in life-like phenomena such as, growth, move-ment and even population-scale interactions. Every iteration – a pulse, a blink, a twitch, or a breath – becomes the material basis for a considered response and action to a context. Imagine, if you will, cellular automata whose pattern generations are produced by their contingencies.[9] Now, think about what that might mean if each "cell" in that operation was a pulsating body, stacks of droplets, or active bodies, capable of materially responding to neighbours in (at least) three material dimensions. We're starting to see a ball of primitive cell-like structures emerge whose potentiality may be likened to that of an early embryo that thickens to form a plate and rolls and folds to produce a more exquisitely complex and performative body.

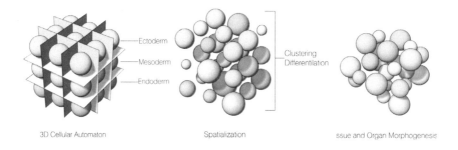

Figure 2   3D chemical cellular automata. Diagram of cuboid grice – overlaid by droplets arranged in 3 layers; ectoderm, mesoderm and endoderm. These then organize through a mechanism that engages cellular automata landscapes to produce highly spacially complex and embryo-like forms.

Dissipative structures are physical bodies that are environmentally sensitive and therefore may be influenced by their context. They are massively parallel computing devices within an excitable gaseous or liquid chemical medium. They act as elementary processors through which different chemistries diffuse, reacting, or transforming in space and time. The actual computation is performed through the meeting of reactive fields at interfaces, and the subsequent propagation of chemical waves, or material depositions caused by these disturbances, which directly feedback into the outputs of the system, so that new spaces and possibilities become accessible. Perhaps surprisingly, dissipative systems are remarkably predictable, although they retain a fundamental capacity for surprise and collapse. They tend to produce a spectrum of outcomes that operate within 'limits' of possibility, which are imposed by the properties of the system, the participating bodies and their contexts. Perhaps think of them like making a cake, whose ingredients and method of cooking may produce a range of outcomes from a dirty black biscuit to a delicious fluffy gateau, depending on how the recipe is executed. Dissipative structures therefore require us to count along with them – not 'for' them by imposing our own expectations on the system's performance. In other words, they require soft control, whose techniques are already known to us as artisan practices and range from cooking, gardening and agriculture – to working with small children, or herding cats. When linked through metabolism, they create the possibility of a technical platform and material that can function as a medium for design. By considering dissipative structures as the iterative process that underpins material computation, the technical operations possess a different set of characteristics than digital computers. Such an apparatus may enable us to work directly with low-level infrastructures, like soils, which produce material programs that directly promote life, or generate structures that provoke lifelike phenomena without reducing or abstracting them. Rather than being purified, homogenized and constrained within bounded spaces, they are open, messy and highly heterogeneous. Lively matter does not need to know the outcome, or the future impact of its interactions, before they respond to changes in their environment. Their capacity of metabolic networks to perform these functions is intrinsic to their materiality, kinetics and context. The incredible parallelism implicit in molecular fields enables them to coherently exist in multiple con-figurations and intermediate states with the potential for phase changes and paradoxical phenomena. Yet, such fabrics are not formless, they produce highly organized structures and even exert a transformative impact on their environ-ment by increasing the liveliness of spaces, or probability of life-like events.

Metabolic Systems as Soil

> Like our bodies, the soil participates in the recirculation and trans-formation of the four major elements, earth, air, fire and water. Like our bodies too it is full of channels and pathways, directing the elements in fertile combinations and transformations at distinct organized levels of the whole structure. And like our bodies, it has a definite genetic form.[10]

The palimpsests and residues of metabolisms are soils. Think of metabo-lism as the outer active layer of a landscape, the foams on a sea crest, the air's dew. Now consider the precipitations, traces, distillates, secretions, crystallizations, dead bodies and countless encounters that finally reach equilibrium, these residues are the soils. They shape the infrastructures upon which metabolisms may fall when the reach equilibrium states and rise again. Yet they are not haphazard and chaotic, they are hypercomplex, highly distributed and burn with the same intense heat that the active foams and smogs that permeate the interfaces between land, sea and air do. Indeed they encourage some metabolisms to migrate further down, seek shelter in their recesses and establish a tangible fabric that enables the transition from inert to lively matter by linking the cycles of life and death through the "compost elevator".

Evolved from the earliest soils – inorganic clays, dusts and sands impregnated by the thinnest scattering of organic matter that draws water into its substance – the compost elevator began as a dance between wind, water and fire, whose footsteps cracked and ground rocks into sands, dusts and clay – that are likely to have had a critical role in biogenesis, catalyzing and spatializing matter into configurations that could persist and transform within their environment as lively assemblages. Yet even clay landscapes act as catalysts for life-like events by providing a mineral coding structure, whose effusive surface offers a land-scape that organic substances may organize around to encounter exactly the kinds of interactions they need to become lively, coherent bodies. Its aperiodic material programs do not in themselves produce life but increase the probability of it happening, Clays stretch and bend energy around chaotic vortices, pro-voke unanticipated unions and offer dynamic containers of information where novelty, creative and synthesis can condense to produce new relationships between molecules. Yet, clay is more than spatially arranged chemistry. It is also a topography of physical forces that attracts oppositely charged particles along its myriad surfaces. Many of these are necessary for organic reactions, including potassium, calcium and nitrates. While the search for biogenesis is focused on the incredible flexibility of the organic molecular realm, the potential contained within the ordering systems of mineral environments is largely overlooked and therefore, the complex events that constitute biosynthesis remain an unbal-anced equation when considering the question of constructing life-like systems. With the formal advent of life, solar energy could be trapped and stored in carbon building blocks to produce biomass bodies and as they perished, they produced organic matter that could be incorporated into early soils so they could draw water and air into their substance to become fertile loams and peats.

Soil has its own material identity that is expressed through a unique tapestry forged from a rich palette of agents including minerals, organic matter, air, water and diverse groups of microbes, which draws together the material residues of the land but also incorporates the possibility of "invisible" or unknown influences in achieving its effects. Indeed, the story of life probably lies beyond full comprehension by any single knowledge canon and therefore invites the overlapping of various knowledge practices from ancient (religious), to corporeal (channeling), to modern science (measurement) and quantum theory (counterintuitive) so that mutual enrichments between these fields may be encouraged. The ultimate aim of the elevator is to prevent the permanent onset of entropy within metabolic networks by continually obfuscating entropic processes using spatial, temporal, material, narrative and phenomenological tactics. It also considers life – not as the result of a single initiating event –but as a succession of highly distributed activation processes with loose controls and multiple authors where – life is transformation as much as transformation is life.

We'll never fully know just how much mineral syntheses have really contributed to primitive ordering systems in biosynthesis, as these apparatuses have been completely replaced by the "Last Universal Common Ancestor", or LUCA, and its biological descendants in nature. Yet, if we are to look for evidence for life's origins, we are most likely to find these processes in geochemistry and its vestiges may yet encountered as strange phenomena.

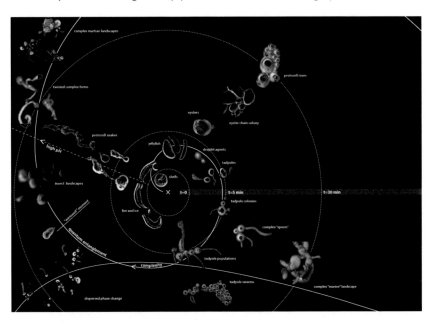

Figure 3   An oceanic ontology of 300 replicate Butschli experiments exploring the creativity of the chemical system as a function time. Drawing courtesy of Simone Ferracina, concept Rachel Armstrong.[11]

This is exactly the right kind of ambiguity in which to reflect upon the kinds of insights and design principles that can be reflected on in considering a practice that operates through metabolic systems and the infrastructures for life. In particular we must consider the invisible agencies that operate within the transition from nonliving to living matter, which have been denied a voice in the modern science laboratory. While vitalisms have been theoretically dismissed for around eighty years or more, they simply have not gone away and remain ghosts in the machine, as the animating forces of nature and life have not been named and atomized. In their stead new terminologies for the invisible lurk within scientific rhetoric as emergence, autopoesis, and self-organization – while these terms indicate a particular phenomenology they do not tell us how or why they work. Both nature and life are unresolved projects. This does not mean that they cannot be designed and interrogated, but that in our explorations we appreciate they harbour the kinds of contradictions that the worlding process of ambient poetics[12] inspires.

Metabolic Systems as Ecology

> "It is interesting to contemplate an entangled bank, clothed with many plants of many kinds, with birds singing on the bushes, with various insects flitting about, and with worms crawling through the damp earth, and to reflect that these elaborately constructed forms, for different from each other, and dependent on each other in so complex a manner, have all been produced by laws acting around us".[13]

The web of living exchanges that foregrounds the participatory processes of active bodies is encapsulated by Charles Darwin's description of an "entangled bank" of organisms where the individual performance and fate of any single organism does not upstage the collective choreography of lively events.[14] Indeed, ecosystems condense where metabolisms and soils begin to converge around the activities of fully alive bodies that occupy discrete habitats and lived spaces. The texturing of these terrains through – "colour, sound, smell, and rhythm, perception and emotion"[15] – produces the characteristic ecology of interactions – whereby landscapes proliferate of their own volition but also respond to and are transformed by the attentiveness of the communities that dwell within them. While Darwin observed the choreography of ecological events as the productive, mutual relationship between organism and niche, he did not identify a specific mechanism to explain the mode of operation of the underlying systems.

The artificial ecologies of the Sentient Chamber are similarly foregrounded ecological fabrics that are paradoxically alien but familiar "entangled banks". Their performativity is not specifically limited by the actions of any particular agent but recognized through the twittering, shivering, sentient fabric that houses the metabolic systems infrastructures and their synthetic soils. The first seeds to arrive within these fertile landscapes are simple chemical structures like ions, droplets, vortices and crystals, with a fundamental appetite for one another, which begin to enliven their host domains. Effervescent turbulence ensues with a first wave of swirling shell-like forms within the city of vessels that harbour the liquid environments. Collectively, they form a river of phantoms that twist like carousels bursting out of each other. Most fall instantly, incarcerated in the crusts of their own product, murdered by the strangeness of their existence. Impossible chemistries appear and fade as phantoms, leaving no traces of their explorations. Interfaces split over invisible trails beckoning swarms of chemical tadpoles, silicon barnacles, soft insect-like bodies, throbbing shellfish residues, inorganic worms, ghosts, accreted oyster chains and kissing corpses, which circle each other for their undetectable nectar. Bodies mirror one another on soft scaffoldings and dance asynchronously – at first with limbs and tails – then together. Others gather in groups knitting crystals and scatter in threads through a gleaming glassy ocean of oil. Matter strings and ribbons decorate this maypole terrain with their turbulence, drawing their names in the snow globe storms that come and go within a city of glass vessels. A few ductile osmotic tubes quietly circle, small, persistent, haunted by their own purpose to join the realms of the unquiet. Now, spent as fossils they settle in spaces that have been drained of their potential and throbbing like upturned flies, reach quiet equilibrium. Living technologies accrete and melt like corals, perpetually building on the residues of their ancestors to create more permanent scaffoldings. Some rupture like fireworks, others activate, a few extrude into forbidden spaces, where it is too hot or dry for life.

At some point, assisted by design tactics, such as the positioning of clusters of hygroscopic materials within the landscape they spill out into new territories expanding the limits of their original realm. Their vagrant active fields and interfaces draw new nutrients towards them which creep through spaces of high flow that invigorates their being and enables them to persist. Panspermic events being organic agency into these landscapes such as, encounters with microbial fuel cells, living batteries that feed on decay and, with augmented proliferative capacities every successive act is an enrichment of what went before. So, where inorganic realm once bloomed now multiple carbon-based bodies, complexify in bursts of punctuated equilibriums, where machines, more sedate than the unruly organic usurpers of the mineral world become gardeners of a new synthetic terrain that possesses coherence, even if its life-forms and relationships are individually unrecognizable. Observing these fabrics through alternative perspectives so that we may work with them ethically and empathetically, so our operations do not devitalize but augment, enliven and provoke these environments to respond empathetically to both human and nonhuman agents. Now, we may begin to observe the kinds of transformations possible within this outlandish environment and discover the potential of artificial evolution to generate new kinds of materials, spaces, landscapes and habitats whose monstrous unorthodoxy nonetheless splendidly dazzles its visitors with extraordinary encounters.

Figure 4   Protocell Phantasmagoria: Portrait of an origins of alternative life. Drawing by Simone Ferracina, movie courtesy Rachel Armstrong, 2016.

"The subject of the experience is not the human but the fielding of the event itself."[16]

Yet, although we see no birds, or plant clusters, no eyes or limbs or faces, the fields of immediacy collide with our memories of the kinds of systems we recognize as nature. Within these novel environments, we begin to perceive the shape of the symphonic score that bonds us to these alien ecologies and understand that we have already encountered them many times before.

Metabolic Systems Within The Sentient Chamber

The Sentient Chamber begins the process of design with complex fabrics that actively explore the possibility of the transition from nonliving to living matter. The exploration is emphatically not a pure form of Enlightenment logic that documents a set of causes and effects but something much stranger that invokes intermodal forms of existence. Nor is it an ancient form of magic that calls upon deities and demons to do the bidding of an architect author that has somehow gained power over their obedience through emerging materials and technological apparatuses. Rather they are a paradoxical material that embodies both the intangible phenomenological realm and its hypercomplex entanglements with matter. The installation is a condensation of ambient poetry, passions, constructed forms, artificial intelligences, human interactions – that together, produce an immersive landscape, an artificial ecosystem, which does not set out to fabricate new anatomical forms but instead, generate immersive experiences that speak to the possibility of provoking fresh encounters with life-like phenomena. These take place within tenuous relationships, distant exchanges, dreams and fears that speak to a greatly extended participatory community than the cause-and-effect narratives that frame Enlightenment discourses. Within the experimental domain of the Sentient Chamber, the processes of composting and renewal begin their rich mixology and start to permeate the environment in ways where the heterogeneous agencies that constitute the installation participate with their audiences through dialogues of unbounded creativity and begin the provocation of becoming "life".

References

1. Singh, R. 2012. Heidegger, World and Death. Plymouth: Lexington Books, p58.

2. Morton, T. 2007. Ecology Without Nature: Rethinking Environmental Aesthetics. Cambridge: Harvard University Press, p84.

3. Morton, T. 2007. Ecology Without Nature: Rethinking Environmental Aesthetics. Cambridge: Harvard University Press, p150.

4. Harman, G. 2012. On the Mesh, the Strange Stranger, and Hyperobjects: Morton's Ecological Ontology. tarp Architecture Manual, Spring 2012. p16-19. [online] Available at: https://issuu.com/tarp/docs/notnature_finaldraft_041012. [Accessed 4 September 2016.].

5. Eck, A. 17 March 2016. How do you say "Life" in physics. Nautilus. [online] Available at: http://nautil.us/issue/34/adaptation/how-do-you-say-life-in-physics. [Accessed 2 September 2016].

6. Wolchover, N. 2014. A New Physics Theory of Life. Quanta Magazine. [online]. Available at: https://www.quantamagazine.org/20140122-a-new-physics-theory-of-life/. Accessed [3 September 2016].

7. Denning P. J. 2007. Computing is a natural science. Communications of the ACM, 50(7), pp.13-18.

8. Turing, A.M. 1952. The Chemical Basis of Morphogenesis. Philo sophical Transactions of the Royal Society of London. Series B, Biological Sciences, 237(641), pp.37-72.

9. Doctorow, C. 11 October 2012. Game of Life with floating point operations: beautiful SmoothLife. Boing Boing. [online] Available at: http://boingboing.net/2012/10/11/game-of-life-with-floating-poi.html [Accessed 20 April 2014].

10. Logan, W.B. 2007. Dirt. The Ecstatic Skin of the Earth. New York: W.W. Norton & Company, p.177.

11. Armstrong, R. 2015. Vibrant architecture: Matter as codesigner of living structures. Warsaw/Berlin: DeGruyter Open, p121.

12. Morton, T. 2002. Why ambient poetics? Outline for a depthless ecology. The Wordsworth Circle, 33(1), P52-56.

13. Darwin, C. 1996. The Origin of Species. Edited by Gillian Beer. Oxford: Oxford University Press, p360.

14. Morton, T. 2011. The Mesh. In (eds.) Stepheniac LeMenager, Terea Shewry and Ken Hiltner, Environmental Criticism for the Twenty-First Century. New York, Routledge, p19-30.

15. Massumi, B. and Manning, E. 2014. Coming alive in a world of texture: For neurodiversity. In (eds.): Brian Massumi and Erin Manning, Thought in the act: Passages in the ecology of experience. Minneapolis: University of Minnesota press, p4.

16. Massumi, B. and Manning, E. 2014. Coming alive in a world of texture: For neurodiversity. In (eds.): Brian Massumi and Erin Manning, Thought in the act: Passages in the ecology of experience. Minneapolis: University of Minnesota press, p14.

Rachel Armstrong is Professor of Experimental Architecture at the School of Architecture, Planning and Landscape, Newcastle University. She is a Rising Waters II Fellow with the Robert Rauschenberg Foundation (April-May 2016), TWOTY futurist 2015, Fellow of the British Interplanetary Society and a 2010 Senior TED Fellow. Rachel is a sustainability innovator who investigates a new approach to building materials called 'living architecture,' which suggests it is possible for our buildings to share some of the properties of living systems. She collaboratively works across disciplines to build and develop prototypes that couple the computational properties of the natural world with the productivity of soils. She calls the synthesis that occurs between these systems and their inhabitants "living" architecture. She is coordinator for the €3.2m Living Architecture project, which is an ongoing collaboration of experts from the universities of Newcastle, UK, the West of England (UWE Bristol), Trento, Italy, the Spanish National Research Council in Madrid, LIQUIFER Systems Group, Vienna, Austria and EXPLORA, Venice, Italy that began in April 2016 and runs to April 2019. It is envisioned as a next-generation, selectively, programmable bioreactor that is capable of extracting valuable resources from sunlight, wastewater and air and in turn, generating oxygen, proteins and biomass. Conceived as a freestanding partition it is composed of bioreactor building blocks (microbial fuel cell, algae bioreactor and a genetically modified processor), which are being developed as standardized building segments, or bricks. Living Architecture uses the standard principles of both photo bioreactor and microbial fuel cell technologies, which are adapted to and combined into a single, sequential hybrid bioreactor system so they will work synergistically together to clean wastewater, generate oxygen, provide electrical power and generate useable biomass (fertilizer). Her work is contextualised in her forthcoming book "Soft Living Architecture: An alternative view of bio-informed design practice" by Bloomsbury Academic, London.

Human Experience

COLIN ELLARD
University of Waterloo

What is the relationship between the built environment and its living occupants? How do the surfaces, the geometry, the movement, and the site of a structure affect the mood, thought processes, and underlying physiology of the human creature enmeshed in such settings?

Sentient Chamber offers a potent environment to explore these questions and assess the impact on human experience. Here the interaction of occupants within a near-living architectural test-bed is observed as a set of relationships that influence our cognitive, psychological and physiological conditions. Sentient Chamber presents a built environment that is moving closer to how humans experience the natural world. In this sense it provides an important context for investigating the triggers that evoke similar reaction to that of experiencing nature.

This interest is grounded in the belief that boundaries between subject and object are permeable and the entirety of human experience relies on grasping the complexities of context. In other words, in order to see inside the mind and understand mental processes, it is necessary to include conditions that matters to a normal functioning brain.

There is a seamless system of interaction between the individual's inner physiology and mental state and their surroundings. Thus the outside is of critical importance to what manifests inside as our human experience. Individuals react to the perceptual qualities of a setting and their reactions influence the organization and meaning of the setting. People respond to architectural elements by the patterns of their gaze, the sounds of their voices, and the movements of their feet. This swirl of biological activity can transform the site itself while simultaneously being transformed by the site.

Studies conducted in both real world settings and simulations in virtual reality, offer some simple predictions about how the formal appearances of complex spaces influence visitor reactions. Using careful spatial analyses based on measurements of complex space, it becomes possible to illustrate the fit between the raw design of a space and the activities, feelings and impressions of those within it. An impressive finding was the degree to which meaning of a space is conditioned less by the location of the walls, ceilings, and windows and more by human activity and interaction. The data stream that is collected from individuals within such settings reflects the operation of complex synergistic relationships between person and place.

Experiments within environments such as Sentient Chamber often include equipping the participants with some simple technology that is designed to probe the state of their minds and bodies while they experience the space. Wanderers carry smart phones that are programmed both to ask them simple questions about their surroundings but also to administer some rapid on-the-spot cognitive tests that tap their cognitive resources—their ability to pay attention and to use their short-term memory. In addition to this, participants wear devices that measure skin conductance (a simple value that gives some insight into the state of their autonomic nervous system). Consumer-grade devices are also used to measure some simple EEG values and the occurrence of eye blinks. This latter measure can be used as a proxy measure of cognitive effort—when we are turning our attention inward to process a scene, our rate of blinking increases.

Experiments conducted thus far reveal some important commonalities in how people respond to variability in the environment. It has been illustrated that complex built spaces produce higher levels of arousal, higher rates of blinking (suggesting increased cognitive processing) and positive affect. In contrast spaces of nature reduce levels of physiological arousal (as measured using skin conductance) but in this case also elicit a strong positive affective response. This interaction between bodily responses and self-reported affective responses suggests that it is important to employ a wide range of different kinds of measures in order to completely fractionate the human response to a setting.

Sentient Chamber offers compelling experiences in forming the relationship between site, structure and human psychological responses. The interactive structures designed as a part of the installation offer a potent context for further exploration of the relationships between the human body and mind and its setting.

On one level, understanding the aesthetic response to the mere appearance of the structures is itself fertile territory. In some ways, the raw appearance of the structures share many properties with the features of natural environments that have been shown by many to be deeply restorative. This effect, though widely documented, is poorly understood. What are the key ingredients of natural settings that produce healthful responses from visitors so dramatic that they can change patterns of brain activity, hormonal states, and even vulnerability to disease? And how much of this effect can be produced by something other than a natural setting?

At a deeper level, it is about understanding the relationship between the response of a visitor to such a structure and the concordant response of the structure itself. There is much to be learned here about the manner in which the dynamic response of a setting to the movements and feelings of an observer feeds back to the feeling state of the observer. In a way, this is not novel. Conventional built settings show the accreted marks of human interaction through their patterns of wear and modification over time, and these marks in turn influence how we respond to an environment. But such marks represent the massed influence of many users over a long period of time and so can rarely reflect individual responses. In a way, such modifications represent a long-term average response rather than an instantaneous one. The opportunity to understand such relationships using a setting that listens and then immediately speaks a reply to an individual observer provides a novel opportunity to dig more deeply into the interactive relationship between a setting and a visitor. It resonates with the conviction that the subject-object divide of most conventional experimental psychology is artificial, oversimplified and deceptive, and it provides us with an opportunity to explore what this means in a tractable, scaled physical system.

More subtly, the interest is in how the interacting system of human and sculpture might be used to explore the way that their linkages emerge over time to reflect memories of the history of their interactions. Is there a shared memory? If so, such memories far transcend the mute, passive relationships between occupant and conventional architecture. For one thing, these relationships might reflect both the mass of experiences accumulated by the sculpture but also the individuated experiences of single identified occupants.

Finally, possibilities for generating therapeutic relationships between occupant and structure can be found within Sentient Chamber as a fundamental opportunity. If a structure can learn the habits, moods, and "pathologies" of a visitor who makes repeated visits, can such visits be considered as a form of therapy? Can a structure heal a person? Or slightly more perversely and with a nod to some more dystopian visions of such relationships in narratives in literature and the other arts, will the structure itself develop pathological systems of responses that mirror those of its occupants?

The vital conditions offered by Sentient Chamber recognizes the profound impact of the environment on human experience. The process of speaking of these conditions calls for the development of proper language to characterize the synergistic relationship between person and the other elements of an interacting system. Avoiding the subject-object divide seems imperative, yet what terminology will capture the life that exists between the two when even the word between itself belies what seems to be wrongful thinking about the problem. New methods of both description and analysis will constitute an important part of the ongoing investigation into vivid spatial environments such as Sentient Chamber. Working towards better understanding human experience within living architecture systems will provide the vocabulary and tools both to look backwards with deeper understanding at the perennial relationship between human and built structure but also to look forward into a future where evolved biological structure, physical invention, and a lived universe teeming with data streams will coalesce into a healthful, sustainable and beautiful new way of thinking about all life—both natural and synthetic.

COLIN ELLARD is interested in how the organization and appearance of natural and built spaces affects movement, wayfinding, emotion and physiology. His approach to these questions is strongly multidisciplinary and is informed by collaborations with architects, artists, planners, and health professionals. His current studies include investigations of the psychology of residential design, wayfinding at the urban scale, restorative effects of exposure to natural settings, and comparative studies of defensive responses. His research methods include both field investigations and studies of human behaviour in immersive virtual environments.

Promoting Creative and Innovative Thinking in the Classroom: The Role of LAS

LUCINDA PRESLEY, ICEE Success
BECKY CARROLL, Redwing Research Inc.
ROB GORBET, University of Waterloo

The Living Architecture Systems Group (LASG) is engaged through its Interdisciplinary Methods stream in developing and testing models and curriculum that address the need for these thinking skills in students of all demographics by integrating formal and informal learning experiences. The classroom approach uses problem-based hands-on learning, integrating Art with traditional STEM domains (STEAM), and is designed in collaboration with classroom teachers to be aligned with mandated curriculum. This paper describes the in-class workshop and reports on the results of pilots in three classrooms from Grade 5 to Grade 8 levels, in the U.S. and Canada.

Introduction

A growing number of researchers, experts, industry representatives, and governmental agencies emphasize that a nation's success in today's global economy will be affected by its ability to innovate and are offering strategies to address these needs.[11,16] As the global need for innovation in many fields increases, so does the importance of creative and innovative thinking. Noted creativity expert R. Keith Sawyer says that we must move beyond associating creativity only with the fine arts, for creativity is important in a wide variety of applications including mathematical theory, experimental laboratory science, and computer software.[13]

One tool in the approach to teaching synthesis and cross-disciplinary creativity is to heed a growing call in education to integrate the Arts and traditional STEM disciplines. In the U.S., an increasing number of schools, school districts, and even state education agencies are using the concept of STEAM, which embraces these intersections of science, technology, engineering, the arts (and humanities) and math. Additionally, the U.S. Congressional STEAM Caucus recently successfully included wording in the new federal Elementary and Secondary Education Act, a major overhaul of the U. S. federal education policy in K-12, that includes art and design as important concepts to integrate with science, technology, engineering, and math. A U.S. coalition of national arts, science, humanities, and higher education institutions, the Innovation Collaborative, found that while the STEAM movement is growing exponentially, there currently exists very little data that demonstrates the impact of the intersections of deep cross-curricular problem-solving on student learning and thinking.

Science scores on the OECD's 2012 Program for International Student Assessment exam, which tests the application, as opposed to memorization, of science facts, show that Canadian students ranked very highly in comparison with other countries.[17] However, it is reported that these scores are declining, that Canada lags in its innovation, and that it must continue to improve students' learning and the outcomes capacity.[17,18] Anecdotal evidence shows that integrated, collaborative, STEAM-based models of teaching can increase students' engagement and understanding of concepts.

The It Lives! classroom program is an effort of the Interdisciplinary Methods stream of the LASG, which capitalizes on the novel physical structures that are the LASG output to inspire students to think more creatively.

The program integrates a growing body of research on learning and cognition that is reflected in the new U.S. Next Generation Science Standards,[19,20] in order to provide a STEAM-based model for teachers and students that improves critical innovation and creative thinking skills in elementary and middle school students, while providing data to support the emerging STEAM education movement. The program promotes content-specific creative and innovative thinking, both individually and as a group, by presenting students with a real-world design problem. The program structure is designed based on strategies recommended by experts in the field of cognitive neuroscience, which promote innovative and creative thinking skills in students.[14,15] The structure asks students to first, select curricular concepts relevant to their problem; second, make connections between these concepts and with the problem; and third, combine concepts to create an innovative solution that reflects the creative thinking.

The It Lives! Project

Taking into account the need for creative and innovation thinking, the strategies that promote these skills, and the realities of the education systems in Canada and the US, It Lives! investigated the integration of these skills with specific science content learning in two schools in the U.S. and one school in Canada. It collaborated with the education department at The Leonardo Museum in Salt Lake City, Utah, and local school districts and educators. It also hired a professional evaluator to assess students' attitudes, their growth in content knowledge, and the effect of their innovation/ inventing experiences on content learning.

It Lives! found the use of brain-based strategies formulated in Chapman's work at the University of Texas at Dallas Center for BrainHealth[14,15] very important in helping students create their inventions and in explaining the growth that we observed. It also discovered the importance of integrating these skills with classroom learning. It Lives! also used research-based education learning and thinking strategies.[21,30]

These education strategies include: hands-on inquiry, knowledge transfer, arts/design thinking, visual thinking, problem-finding/problem-solving based on real-world problems, collaboration, communication, persistence, flexible thinking, inventing, science literacy, and emotional engagement.

The It Lives! project process began during the commissioning of the Philip Beesley exhibit, Hylozoic Veil, in 2011 for The Leonardo Art+Science Museum in Salt Lake City (Figure 1). The It Lives! project team identified an opportunity to bring the multidisciplinary nature and ideas of the sculpture into classrooms, helping to connect students' core art and science curricula and providing a context in which to explore creative and innovative thinking and invention.

Figure 1   The Hylozoic Veil installation in the Leonardo Museum in Salt Lake City, Utah.

They designed the It Lives! workshop – whose name is inspired by the "living" qualities of Beesley's work – as a way to accomplish this. It encouraged student teams to use exhibit-inspired shape memory alloy (SMA), found objects, and craft supplies to create a kinetic device that can demonstrate the interrelationship between synthesized science concepts.

The workshop comprises four sequential sessions: an introduction to the Beesley installation's art, science, and mechanisms that makes explicit connections between these aspects of the sculpture and the core curriculum; a hands-on exploration of mandated science concepts that relate to the sculpture; a creative problem-solving session in which students connect science concepts and use design principles to invent a solution to a real-world problem; and a "making" session in which students fabricate their inventions using shape memory alloy and then present and defend them for the class.

At each site, the classroom material was tailored to the grade- and board-specific core curriculum. The project team worked closely with teachers to identify core concepts from science and art that they wanted to emphasize for their students. These concepts implicitly informed the questions that the project team posed to the students and the hands-on activities that it designed.

In Session 1, *Exploration*, students were briefly introduced to the Hylozoic Veil exhibit (www.hylozoicground.com) by Rob Gorbet, one of the creators of the exhibit. Following this introduction, students rotated in small groups between exploration stations where they used mandated science concepts to observe and interact with components of the sculpture.

In Session 2, *Hands-On*, students connected their experience from Session 1 with hands-on exploration of mandated grade-specific core science concepts. For example, students in Grade 5 studying electricity worked in small groups to explore open and closed circuits, insulators and conductors, using an active exhibit component (Figure 2). Students also were explicitly asked to consider the cross-over of terms such as balance, form, shape and line between science (e.g., in structures) and art, to emphasize the similarity in design thinking and the creative process across these disciplines.

Figure 2   Students using exhibit components to investigate electricity.

In Session 3, *Creative Problem-Solving*, students were assigned to three-person design teams and were given a challenge to create a novel kinetic device using shape memory alloy to demonstrate the intersection of three science concepts. A demonstration lever device was assembled at the front of the classroom, with students following along and constructing their own device (Figure 3).

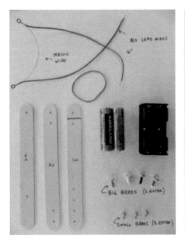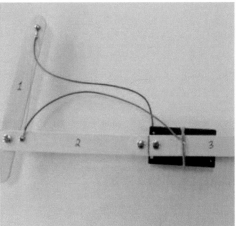

Figure 3   Simple shape memory alloy lever kit for student assembly.

Students then integrated the variety of science information that they had learned in Sessions 1 and 2 with selected key grade-level science concepts. They synthesized that information to come up with a "big idea", and then applied that synthesis to solve a problem. In teams, they drew and labeled their device, integrating their chosen science and art concepts into their work (Figure 4). This phase of the project used the brain-based strategies developed by the UT Dallas researchers.[14,15]

In Session 4, *Making*, students used found objects and craft supplies to bring their 2D solutions demonstrating their science concepts, into 3D, built around their SMA-actuated devices. When complete, each group wrote about their inventions and presented to the class how their invention illustrated their key concepts and why they made the design choices they did. In this session, students solidified and demonstrated their science knowledge as well as their communication skills.

Figure 4   Simple shape memory alloy lever-kit for student assembly.

Results

To study the impact of the It Lives! workshop on students' interests and attitudes toward science and engineering, their knowledge of key content and concepts, and their assessment of how visual thinking and making strategies and experiences affected their learning, we conducted a pilot study in three schools: two classes of 7th grade students at Palestine Junior High, Palestine, Texas; four classes of 5th grade students at Woodrow Wilson Elementary School in Salt Lake City; and one class of 7th grade students and one class of 8th grade students at MacGregor Public School in Waterloo, Ontario, Canada, totaling 213 students. In all three locations, students were given two pre- and two post-assessments: one focusing on attitudes/interests and another on content. In addition, teachers were given a post-assessment to collect data about their perceptions of the program, and the degree to which it promoted science learning, youth engagement in science process skills, and problem-based learning. We also conducted in-person observations of the It Lives! program in Palestine, and interviewed students about their experiences in the program. The studies were approved by the Office of Research Ethics at the University of Waterloo as well as the ethics review committees each local school board.

Data collected from the pilot observations of the program by evaluators, teachers and program implementers, from pre-post attitude and content assessments, and from teacher post-assessments, indicate that It Lives! provided engaging experiences for youth that combined art, rigorous and appropriate science content, and opportunities for students to develop critical thinking, innovation and problem-solving skills.

First and foremost, the It Lives! workshop activities were engaging to students. All of the teachers reported that their students were active participants, and were highly engaged throughout the course of the project. As a teacher reported in post self-assessments:

> Students were engaged, learning and excited. I didn't see one student that was not engaged.

The It Lives! workshop helped students understand important core science concepts, and to make connections between science concepts. For example, two 7th grade students we interviewed in Texas were able to articulate connections they realized between physics and biology concepts, through the building activity with the muscle wire:

> We are making an arm out of popsicle sticks. We wanted to do something with the muscular system and structure. It seemed like force and motion and muscles made sense to combine.

Data in pre-post assessments showed students had made progress in understanding how circuits work, a notoriously difficult concept for students to grasp.[1]

Students appreciated the inquiry-based methods of exploration the project provided, and how that helped further develop their understanding of key concepts. As teachers noted:

> Students were given the opportunity to explore their own questions. It's the way learning should look.

Students also appreciated the ways in which the It Lives! making activity allowed them to better understand the science concepts they had been working with in their classroom throughout the year. As one student we interviewed noted:

> We've been studying muscles in science class. For most people, if you work hands-on, you can understand it better. If you build it, and you see an arm moving up and down, it makes more sense.

The careful design and implementation of activities helped students to engage in productive problem-solving, and to develop critical and innovative thinking skills. As a teacher noted in post assessments:

> I loved how the students were given the responsibility to create their own circuit.

> It was clear that the presentation was designed in such a way that it encouraged investigation and problem-solving, culminating in an activity that required invention and creativity.

Figure 5 highlights pre-post attitude assessment data from one 5th grade class of students. It demonstrates the positive impact of the project activities on student attitudes concerning thinking, problem-solving, inventing, and careers.

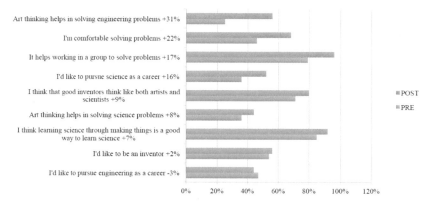

Figure 5   Pre- and post-survey data of student outcomes from grade 5 students in Salt Lake City, Utah (percentage of students agreeing or strongly agreeing with the statement, on a 5-point likert scale; n=25).

Summary and Future Plans

Our experience with the pilot It Lives! sessions show an increase in students' recognition of the importance of making connections, both across disciplines, and between theory and practice. Within the context of the Interdisciplinary Methods stream of the LASG, the next stages of the project will look at refining the workshop, explicitly adopting a Design Thinking framework, scaling the delivery to other grade levels, and developing a train-the-trainer teacher professional development program. This will enable us to further improve the project, multiply the number of students exposed to the workshop, and enable broader delivery. In addition, we will be:

• working within the LASG to develop a series of classroom kits that teachers may use for the hands-on portions of the workshop;

• collaborate with the Innovation Collaborative (IC), a US coalition of National STEM, Arts, and Humanities, and higher education institutions, to develop and validate assessment instruments for creative thinking; and

• work to connect our site classrooms together to enhance their experience of international collaboration and virtual collaboration tools.

Combining these global collaborative skills with creative and innovative thinking and discipline-based knowledge will provide these students a firm foundation for their futures.

Acknowledgement

We would like to acknowledge the support of the Philip Beesley Architect, Inc. group in providing fabrication resources, materials, and time for the in-class demonstrators used to deliver the It Lives! workshop. This work was partially supported through the Social Sciences and Humanities Research Council of Canada's Partnership Development Grant program.

Endnotes

1. Friedman, T. and M. Mandelbaum. 2011. That used to be us: How America fell behind in the world it invented and how we can come back. NY, NY: Farrar, Straus and Giroux.

2. Friedman, T. 2007. The world is flat: A brief history of the 21st century. NY, NY: Picador/Farrar, Straus and Giroux.

3. Robinson, K. 2009. The element. NY, NY: Viking Penguin Group.

4. Florida, Richard. 2003. The rise of the creative class: ... and how it's transforming work, leisure, community, & everyday life. NY, NY: Basic Books.

5. General Electric. 2012. GE global innovation barometer: Global research report. Retrieved from http://files.gecompany.com/gecom/innovationbarometer/GE_Global_Innovation_Barometer_Report_January_2012.pdf

6. National Academies of Science, National Academy Of Engineering, Institute Of Medicine. 2010. Rising above the gathering storm, revisited: Rapidly approaching category 5. Members of the 2005 rising above the gathering storm committee. Washington, DC: National Academies Press.

7. The President's Council of Advisors on Science and Technology. 2010. Prepare and inspire: K-12 science, technology, engineering, and math (STEM) education for America's future. Washington, DC.

8. Lichtenberg, J., C. Woock, and M. Wright. 2008. Ready to innovate: Are educators and executives aligned on the creative readiness of the US workforce. NY, NY: The Conference Board.

9. National Science Board. 2010. Preparing the next generation of stem innovators: Identifying and developing our nation's human capital. Arlington, VA: National Science Foundation.\

10. Association of Universities and Colleges of Canada. 2014. Budget will position Canada as world leaders in research and innovation. Retrieved from www.aucc.ca/media-room/news-and-commentary/budget-2014-will-position-canada-world-leader-research-innovation/.

11. Social Sciences and Research Council of Canada (nd). Strengthening Canada's cultures of innovation: Strategic plan 2013-16. Retrieved from www.sshrc-crsh.gc.ca/about-au_sujet/publications/strategic_plan_2013-16-plan_strategique_2013-2016_e.pdf

12. Science, Technology, and Innovation Council. 2010. Imagination to innovation: Building Canadian paths to prosperity. Retrieved from /www.stic-csti.ca/eic/site/stic-csti.nsf/eng/00043.html

13. Bronson, P. and A. Merryman. 2010, July 10. The creativity crisis. Newsweek. Retrieved from www.thedailybeast.com/newsweek/2010/07/10/the-creativity-crisis.html

14. Sawyer, R. K. 2012. Explaining creativity: The science of human innovation. NY, NY: Oxford University Press.

15. Chapman, S., J. Gamino, and R. Anand. Higher order strategic gist reasoning in adolescence. In The adolescent brain: Learning, reasoning, and decision making. Washington, DC: American Psychological Association, 2012.

16. Chapman, Sandra, and Shelly Kirkland. Make your brain smarter: Increase your brain's creativity, energy, and focus. 2013. NY, NY: Free Press.

17. Council of Ministers of Education, Canada. Measuring Up: Canadian Results of the OECD PISA Study Retrieved from cmec.ca/Publications/Lists/.../PISA2012_CanadianReport_EN_Web.pdf

18. CBC News. Canada's students slipping in math and science, OECD finds Canadian scores above average, but well behind front-running students in Shanghai, China. Retrieved from www.cbc.ca/news/canada/canada-s-students-slipping-in-math-and-science-oecd-finds-1.2448748

19. National Research Council. 2012. A framework for K-12 science education: Practices, crosscutting concepts, and core ideas. Washington, DC: National Academies Press.

20. Next Generation Science Standards 2012. Retrieved from www.nextgenscience.org/next-generation-science-standards

21. Costa, A.L. and B. Kallick. 2008. Learning and leading with habits of mind: 16 essential characteristics for success. Alexandria, VA: Association for Supervision and Curriculum Development.

22. Cropley. A.J.. 2003. Creativity in education and learning: A guide for teachers and educators. NY, NY: Routledge Farmer.

23. Carlson, N. 2012. Physiology of behavior. 11th ed. Upper Saddle River, NJ: Pearson

24. Bransford, J., M. S. Donovan, and J. Pellegrino. 2000. How people learn: Brain, mind, experience, and school: Expanded edition. Washington, DC: National Academy Press.

25. Gardner, H. 2008. 5 minds for the future. Boston, MA: Harvard University Press.

26. Her Majesty's Inspectorate of Education (HMIE). 2006. Emerging good practice in promoting creativity: A report by HMIE. Retrieved from dera.ioe.ac.uk/6273/1/Emerging%20Good%20practice%20in%20Promoting%20Creativity.pdf

27. The Lemelson-MIT Program. School of Engineering, Massachusetts Institute of Technology. (2003). Advancing inventive creativity through education. Boston, MA. Retrieved from web.mit.edu/invent/n-pressreleases/downloads/education.pdf

28. Robinson, K. 2006. Out of our minds: Learning to be creative. Chichester, UK: Capstone Books.

29. Wiggins, G. and J. McTighe. 2006. Understanding by design. 2nd ed. Upper Saddle River, NJ: Pearson

30. Starko, A. 2004. Creativity in the classroom: Schools of curious delight. Mahwah, NY: Erlbaum.

31. Engelhardt, P.V. and R.J. Beichner. 2004. "Students' understanding of direct current resistive electrical circuits." American Journal of Physics, 72(1), pp. 98-115.

Lucinda Presley is Executive Director of ICEE (Institute where Creativity Empowers Education) Success, which develops school programming and curriculum, trains educators, and develop museums in the U.S. and internationally. Ms. Presley also is the founder, Chair, and Executive Director of the Innovation Collaborative, a Washington, DC-based coalition of U.S. arts, science, and humanities institutions that collaborate with higher education to research and promote innovation thinking at STEAM intersections in K-12, and museums. She holds a Master of Arts degree in interdisciplinary studies.

Becky Carroll is an evaluator, whose company, Redwing Research, Inc., has conducted studies of improvements in science, technology, engineering and math education in both formal and informal environments. Areas of interest include studying collaborations and networks, making, and in improvements targeting rural contexts. She holds a B.S. in English and Secondary Education.

Rob Gorbet is an Associate Professor at the University of Waterloo, where he Chairs the Knowledge Integration program, a novel integrative honours degree that emphasizes interdisciplinary collaboration, design thinking, and real-world problem solving. He collaborates with artists and architects to design novel interactive environments that push the boundaries of art and architecture. He holds a PhD in Electrical Engineering and is a registered professional engineer in Ontario.

"Where I Stand"

SARAH BONNEMAISON
Dalhousie University

I "grew up" as an architect, in an intellectual context of analysis and interpretation of natural processes as a valuable source of design inspiration. I took this attitude in my own design of responsive lightweight structures and set up an interdisciplinary research laboratory to develop prototypes to create a healthier built environment. Today, I bring this know-how to the creation of interactive exhibitions to open discussions on ways to build a sustainable future by drawing from the past.

The world of textiles is the fastest growing field in architecture and design today. As Matilda McQuaid says in her catalogue essay for the exhibition titled *Extreme Textiles*, "What can be stronger than steel, faster than a world's record, lighter than air, safer than chain mail, and smarter than a doctor? Hint: it is in every part of our physical environment – lying under roadbeds, reinforcing concrete columns, or implanted into humans." (McQuaid 11) Textiles, of course, is the answer to her riddle, especially technical, high-performance textiles.

Many designers, artists and architects are creating objects and environments that combine these new textiles with software, robotics and sensors. Whether their focus is clothing or immersive environments, their aim is to make textiles that interact with their users not only in visual or tactile terms, or even by being mobile, but which use digital interfaces to respond in all of these ways. According to Lucy Bullivant, the impact of these textiles "is phenomenological, meaning that the body is able to directly experience its environment in a very direct and personal way" (Bullivant 7). As a result, we are seeing a whole new area of avant-garde design – from clothing to large tensile structures that incorporate the event into the artifact – an approach that is valued by museums striving to engage their publics in ever-more interactive attractions and by manufacturers seeking new markets.

These new designs are the products of interdisciplinary collaborations. Clearly, a reactive or interactive garment or environment requires not just software specialists, designers of robotics, and electrical engineers, but often also materials scientists, chemists, specialists in nanotechnology and biomedical engineering. They explore interactive technologies through   creating and adapting clothing, furniture, and the built environment to become communication devices that facilitate personal expression as well as multi-point communication between individuals and groups (Berzowska 32).

The very nature of responsive environments, involving functioning through interfaces that facilitate interaction, is a form of mediation between inner self and the outside world, and it presupposes some kind of event that is not wholly pre-programmed. Input from the real world received via sensors is essential, as are output devices in the form of actuators (mechanisms that transform an electrical input signal into motion), displays and other sensory phenomena to engage with users (Bullivant 9).

As we incorporate technologies into the design of responsive environment, it is important to focus my efforts where it matters and where I can be effective. My efforts are not in a quantitative approach to wellness but rather a qualitative one that attempts to link individuals and social well-being – focusing on developing a sustainable lifestyle and a deeper relationship to nature.

However, designers love to collaborate with specialists and I am no exception. As an architect, I "grew up" in the world of lightweight structures at *The Institute of Lightweight Structures* (IL) in Stuttgart under the leadership of Frei Otto. The philosophy of the IL was entirely based on *Organicism*, well anchored in learning from observing nature, from spider-webs to soap film geometries. While in Stuttgart I was fortunate to work in Bodo Rasch's office with the guidance of Frei Otto on an exceptional design project for 300 umbrellas on the roof of the Great Mosque in Mecca, solar powered and free of cables. A smaller version of the project was realized in 1992 in two courtyards of the Prophet's Holy Mosque in Medina. (Fig.1) A computer chip triggers each umbrella to close under high winds, so the delicate structures are not damaged. This is an early example of tensile architecture in motion, exploring basic responsive capabilities to address environmental conditions (solar exposure, wind load). (Otto and Rasch 9)

I brought this wonderful passion for in-depth research of architectural lightweight structure to my own research laboratory. From 2008-2011, I joined forces with weaver Robin Muller to design and develop electronic textiles for architecture. With funding from ACOA, we formed the *Architextiles Lab*, @ Lab for short. Our goal as leaders of a multidisciplinary team was to design and create architectural prototypes that integrate electronic textiles. (Fig. 2–3) Most research in the field of electronic textiles was for wearable items, like shape-changing and heat-reactive clothing or wearable «soft» computers. The military is a big client for this technology, using for example, communication technology worn next to the body of the soldier. Our designs for electronic textiles focused on a sustainable relationship to our environment, both culturally and technically. They ranged in scale from a curtain, a stage set, and a pavilion. They all explored various combinations of manual and digital craft, from slow tech to high tech. We worked closely with local manufacturers as a way to develop products that could be produced locally in Nova Scotia (Bonnemaison 3).

The prototypes also integrated moving parts. They were as simple as a curtain sliding on a rod, to a complex collapsible pavilion that must telescope,

Figure 1   Umbrellas designed by Bodo Rash in the main courtyard of
the Prophet's Holy Mosque in Medina, 1992. Image Credit: SL - Rash

pivot and fold to shrink to a small fraction of its volume. We learned about collapsible structures from camping tents, folding furniture and retractable objects. Textiles of course, have been valued for millennia for their lightness and portability. To add electronics to these deployable structures, we had to isolate fabric from structure, "skin" from "bones", in order to avoid damaging wires as the structure unfolded. The results were impressive. But as tex-

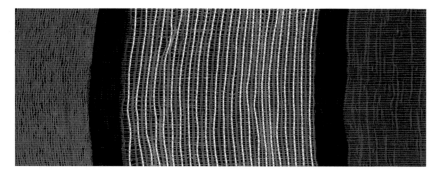

Figure 2   Weaving of EL wires with paper strips and linen for a curtain, @Lab, 2009.
Image Credit: Greg Richardson Photography

Figure 3   Responsive stage set and costume for a Flamenco dance company,
Maria Osende is the dancer. Image Credit: Greg Richardson Photography

tile factories closed one by one all around us the original intent of producing
local products eventually vanished and the research funding drew to a close.

So I returned to the world of ideas and history and decided to bring the
knowledge developed at the @Lab to create exhibitions that draws the past
into the present. Inspired by Ersnt Gadamer's notion that we make sense
of the world through tradition, these exhibitions bring the history of the

modern kitchen for example, into today's concerns for cultural and ecological sustainability. With live performance and interactive "stations', visitors
could participate in the process. This has been satisfying both for me as
as designer and for visitors who understand both in their mind and in their
heart, the ideas that are presented.

One of these exhibitions was called *My Mother's Kitchen* because my
research began in the tiny kitchen of the famous *Unité d'Habitation* designed
by Le Corbusier in 1947-1953 where my mother lived. So true to Gadamer's
philosophy, the exhibition presented major sign posts in the development of
the modern kitchen linking me, standing in the Unité d'Habitation today, all
the way back to the so called *Frankfurt Kitchen* (1920s), *The Frankfurt Kitchen*
was set as the reference point to all the other designs for servantless kitchens
that followed. By weaving the story of this tradition about modernist kitchen
design and uncovering why it was so important in social reproduction it
allowed us to imagine the future.

I will end by describing briefly some elements of the exhibition that shows
where I stand:

A Machine for Living, Frankfurt 1920s

The Frankfurt Kitchen was the focus of an educational film that, according to
its architect, Margarete Schütte-Lihotzky, "explains how to use the kitchen" –
showing a young woman preparing food, cleaning, and ironing with a minimum of effort in this small space that had cleverly-designed features suited
to each task, just as in the galley kitchen of a railway dining car.

The film was projected on a wall of white blocks of different sizes. Using
a computer program called *mad mapper*, the archival footage could be
"mapped" onto the blocks for a perfect fit. Sections of the film thereby isolated
from the narrative emphasized the important comparative points that were
made by Margarete Lihotsky. That way the viewer did not have to sit through
the entire film but could understand the high points through collage (Fig.4).

Participatory Design, Tompkinsville, Cape Breton, 1930s

The 11 houses of Tompkinsville in Cape Breton built in the 1930s are a result of

Figure 4   Archival film of the Frankfurt Kitchen with two dancers, My Mother's Kitchen exhibition, 2014.
Image Credit: Greg Richardson Photography

a heroic collective efforts of miners who no longer wanted to rent a company house own their home. With the support of the *Antigonish Movement*, a blend of adult education, co-operatives, micro-finance and rural community development, a group of men and women found the way to get a mortgage from Nova Scotia's government, buy land and built houses – their descendant still leave in today. In the following years, Tompkinsville became a model for many other working-class people to organize themselves to built new houses, financed cooperatively.

A simple kitchen table had archival images from Tompskinsville projected down onto four "place-mats" that changed according to when and how visitors sit on the chairs surrounding the table. This uses a motion capture camera. (Fig.5)

The Art Of Living, *Chaise Longue* By Charlotte Perriand, 1920s

Charlotte Perriand designed her famous chaise longue that we can still purchase today. Alan Macy adapted the chair with airbags and sensors to picked up the

Figure 5   Table of the Tompkinsville kitchen with projections as "place mats",
                My Mother's Kitchen exhibition, 2014. Image Credit: Greg Richardson Photography

Figure 6   Chandelier linked to breathing apparatus, My Mother's Kitchen exhibition, 2014.
                Image Credit: Greg Richardson Photography

rhythm of the breath of a visitor lying on it. The data was analyzed and sent to a white textile chandelier hanging above the chair and would respond by lighting up in various colours – reds when breathing in and blues when breathing out (Fig.6).

Unité d'Habitation Marseille, France, 1950s

While housing advocates, resident associations and municipal authorities were debating housing policy in social-democratic Germany, intellectuals and artists in Paris had embraced modernity in wholly different ways.

Figure 7   Future kitchen, My Mother's Kitchen exhibition, 2014.
             Image Credit: Greg Richardson Photography

Artists like Marcel Duchamp and Pablo Picasso explored motion studies, mass production, in provocative work that aimed to unsettle and renew cultural assumptions. This is the cultural milieu of Le Corbusier and his professional collaborators – Pierre Jeanneret, Jean Prouvé and, significantly Charlotte Perriand – designed the first apartment building for collective living called Unité d'Habitation in Marseille, France.

In *my mother's kitchen* at the Unité, we re-enacted the preparation of a chocolate cake that was the measuring stick of early Motion Studies to design a more efficient kitchen. We created a nine minutes video of a dancer preparing that particular cake in this particular kitchen designed by Perriand. The video was projected on the rolling furniture pieces that interpret the volumes of the kitchen.

Future Kitchen, the Near Future

Presented as an interactive tool, visitors could design their kitchen of the future by simply moving their body around a white carpet that represented the basic floor plan of the space. Icons would appear and they could place them in space as they wished. This used a tracking software adapted to recognize a human body in motion from above, as opposed to straight on. The icons were meant to generate interest in sustainable kitchen appliances and modes of preparing food such as a solar oven or a terracotta refrigeration units (Fig.7).

References

Berzowska, Joanna. "Memory Rich Clothing: Second Skins that Communicate Physical Memory". Proceedings of the 5th conference on Creativity and Cognition, ACM Press, 2005, pp. 32-40.

Bonnemaison, Sarah. @Lab/ Architextile Laboratory: Electronic textiles in architecture, (with contributions by Berzowska, Macy and Muller), TUNS Press, 2011.

Bullivant, Lucy. "Introduction", Responsive Environments: Architecture, Art And Design, V&A Publications, 2006.

McQuaid, Matilda. Extreme Textiles: Designing for High Performance, Princeton Architectural Press, 2005.

Otto, Frei. Rasch, Bodo. Finding Form: Towards an Architecture of the Minimal, Edition Axel Menges, 1995.

Sarah Bonnemaison has a doctorate in human geography from the University of British Columbia and degrees in architecture from Pratt Institute and the Massachusetts Institute of Technology. She currently teaches architectural history and theory at Dalhousie University. Sarah is also a writer. Her books include *Architecture and Nature*; *Festival Architecture*; and *Installations by Architects*, as well as numerous contributions to edited volumes and journals. Her passion lies in bringing history and theory to life through interactive exhibitions and installations for performance. Her current research project explores the aesthetic and politics of motion studies in the design of everyday spaces.

Field Work in the Thing Site

ROBERT BEAN
Nova Scotia College of Art & Design

Only where things can be seen by many in a variety of aspects without changing their identity, so that those who are gathered around them know they see sameness in utter diversity, can worldly reality truly and reliably appear.[1]

Hannah Arendt

"Field Work in the Thing Site" considers the importance of Things, historic sites used for social and political gatherings. In Nordic and Germanic culture, the Thing was a public assembly where governance, laws, and the resolution of disputes were explained, debated and negotiated. Organized in open-air locations with distinctive characteristics as well as effective acoustic resonance, the practice of "making things public", a description initiated by Bruno Latour, has contemporary implications for how we represent, experience and utilize social and public space for the potential of expressing democratic principles.[2] No longer bound to a subject/object dichotomy, Latour theorizes a "parliament of things", a network of *actants* where the agency and political reality of human existence is inclusive of non-humans and things. This shift problematizes assumptions regarding democracy, citizenship and the common world and instigates a reassessment of the human affiliation to complex environments and knowledge.

This project is based on fieldwork in two notable Thing Sites, the Althing in Iceland and the Thingstätte in Heidelberg, Germany. References to these Germanic traditions of assembly appear as early as the 1st Century in the ethnographic study Germania by the Roman historian Tacitus. The Althing is one of the most celebrated tourist attractions in Iceland while the Thingstätte in Heidelberg recalls the propaganda narratives of the Third Reich prior to the Second World War. The initial purpose of these sites, however, is not reflected in their contemporary use. Tourism, access to the natural landscape, geological landmarks, walking paths, ruins, outdoor concerts, theatrical reenactment, training sites for athletes and festival venues are just some of the events that describe the current use of these Thing Sites.

The Althing (AD 930), located in a rift valley between the North American and European continental plates, is one of the oldest known parliamentary Thing Sites in the Nordic region. The Thingstätte, inaugurated on June 1935 by Joseph Goebbels, Minister of Public Enlightenment and Propaganda for the Third Reich, is located on the Heiligenberg overlooking the Neckar River in Heidelberg. Goebbels called the Thingstätte a "veritable church of the Reich".

Thingstätte 3, 2015

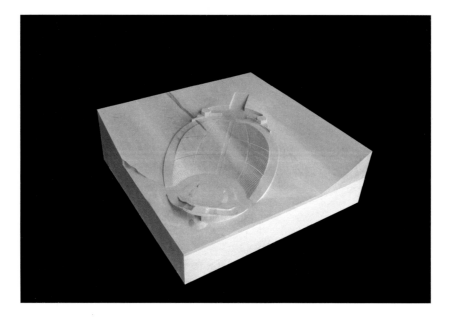

Artifact 1, 2015

Remote Sensing 1, 2015

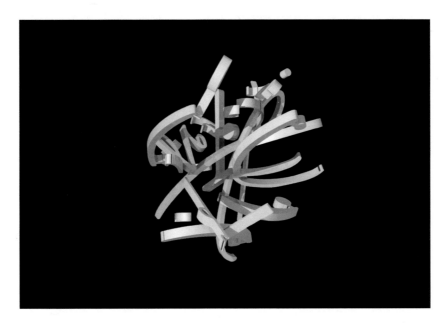

Visible Speech (Hannah Arendt) 2, 2015

Intended to evoke public nostalgia for communal gatherings that recalled the Nordic German traditions, the Thing movement was an early propaganda apparatus. The amphitheaters were sites where quasi-religious Völkisch ceremony and Blut und Boden (Blood and Soil) theatre could be staged. This early form of assembly architecture was ultimately abandoned for the spectacle of Mass Ornament, epitomized by the Nurnberg Zeppelin Field and the 1936 Berlin Olympics. Although the Reich planned for 200 Thing Sites, only 40 were actually completed.

Of significance to this project are the ways in which these historic sites are assemblages influenced by a process of transgenerational memory. The potential for reviewing public visibility and matters of concern that exemplify public space in relation to the transparent or invisible atmosphere that situates the Commons is considered. As Andrea Mubi Brighenti has observed, "… on the one hand, the common is the (invisible) element in which the public comes into existence, and on the other, publicness is what institutes all (visible) commonality."[3]

Following the collective trauma of the Second World War and the moment when Hannah Arendt published her heretic and now commonplace observation about the "banality of evil" in the context of the Israeli trial of Adolf Eichmann, the affective intensities of this observation have not gone unheeded. Continuing to provoke consternation and debate, Arendt's statement is an instance of the political agency that she associates with the public space and the common world. "To live together in the world means essentially that a world of things is between those who have it in common …"[4]

The Thingstätte resides in proximity to the University of Heidelberg, one of the oldest institutions of higher education in Europe. Founded in 1386, the university faculty, alumni and associates include notable figures such as Agricola, Hegel, Herman von Helmholtz, Max Weber, W. Somerset Maugham, Franz Boas, Karl Jaspers, Hans-Georg Gadamer, Erich Fromm, Jürgen Habermas, Hannah Arendt, and Joseph Goebbels. Others associated with the traditions of philosophical inquiry in Heidelberg include Johann Wolfgang Goethe, Friedrich Hölderlin and Martin Heidegger.

The Philosophenweg (philosophers walk) in Heidelberg is a path that links this venerable network of ideas to the Thingstätte.

The fieldwork for this project includes photography, video, architectural artifacts and digital media from the Althing in Iceland and the Thingstätte in Heidelberg. Digital data from this fieldwork will constitute the basis of an acoustic exploration. This process follows on precedents established by Xenakis, Varese and Le Corbusier. The sound work is based directly on a site recordings made at the Thingstätte in Heidelberg as well as the Althing in Iceland. The audio work considers the acoustic space of the Thing Sites as well as Goethe's quotation of Friedrich Schelling that "music is liquid architecture; architecture is frozen music."

Thing Sites is a project dedicated to the memory of Hannah Arendt and her insight regarding the phenomena of "a lesser evil", the bureaucratization of ethical transgression that is endemic to contemporary society.

Endnotes

1. Hannah Arendt, The Human Condition (Chicago: The University if Chicago Press, 1958) 57

2. Bruno Latour, "From Realpolitik to Dingpolitik: Or How to Make Things Public" in Bruno Latour and Peter Weibel (eds.) Making Things Public: Atmosphere's of Democracy (Cambridge: MIT Press, 2005) 14-41

3. Andrea Mubi Brighenti, "The Public and the Common: Some Approximations of Their Contemporary Articulation", Critical Inquiry Vol. 42, No.2 (Winter 2016), 315

4. Hannah Arendt, The Human Condition (Chicago: The University if Chicago Press, 1958) 52

Robert Bean is an artist, writer and curator living in Halifax, Nova Scotia. He is a Professor at NSCAD University. Bean has edited books and published articles on the subject of photography, contemporary art and cultural history. He has been an active contributor to the Cineflux Research Group at NSCAD University and the Narratives in Space and Time art and mobility project. Bean is a recipient of grants from the Social Sciences and Humanities Research Council of Canada (SSHRC) and the Canada Council for the Arts.

Real-time Responsive Spatial Systems:
Design Driven Research Experiments in Interactive Architecture

NIMISH BILORIA
Delft University of Technology

The design-research experiments developed by Hyperbody, TU Delft, Faculty of Architecture, focus on the domain of Interaction design from a spatial perspective. These interactive spaces demonstrate a fusion between the material, electronic and digital domains, which interface with human behavior and associated dynamic activity patterns. Such spaces are visualized as complex adaptive systems, continually engaged in activities of data-exchange resulting in physical and ambient adaptations of their constituting components in response to contextual variations. Equally critical is the underlying interactive process involved in the creation of such dynamic architectural bodies. A collaborative and strategic co-evolution of technical knowledge between the Industry, Praxis, and Academic research gives shape to these interactive constructs, developing an information bridge between three critical knowledge sectors.

Underpinnings

Developing Real-Time Responsive spatial systems is an intricate agenda of Hyperbody's S.M.A.R.T. research agenda led by Dr. Nimish Biloria. S.M.A.R.T. is an acronym for Systems & Materials in Architectural Research and Technology. As a research umbrella, S.M.A.R.T. Environments interrogates the intricate relationship between information systems and associative material formations. This interrogation is deeply rooted in exploring novel interdisciplinary design strategies and nonlinear processes for developing generative meta-design systems. These are used to conceive multi-scalar Performance Driven Architectures and Real-Time Responsive Environments. The resultant spatial outputs are hybrids, which evolve from the creative fusion of Ubiquitous computing, Parametric design and Material computing. Associated experiments spanning from the Micro to the Macro scales, focus on developing context aware spatial eco-systems embedded with sensing, actuation and control protocols enhanced with engineered computing elements and performance driven material aggregations.

The relevance of such real-time responsive spatial systems in the contemporary information rich era and their implications on the shaping of the Architecture Engineering and Construction (AEC) sector is substantial. The rate at which networked data connectivity between objects, machines and humans is omnipresent and is exponentially increasing and has become a key indicator towards exploring such novel spatial paradigms within the AEC sector. This rate of connectivity in the form of the Internet of Things, will fundamentally transform how people will work through new interactions between humans, machines and the spaces which they inhabit. It will combine the global reach of the Internet with a new ability to directly control the physical world, including machines, factories and infrastructure that define the modern landscape. Such data driven synergistic environments bind architectural space and the human counterpart in a behavioral dialogue, promoting real-time interaction. With the advancement in technology, such enhanced spatial environments, are now also increasingly being delegated the task of being more human. This implies acquiring a higher level of intelligence with attributes such as empathy, compassion, pro-activeness etc. becoming intrinsic qualities. It is thus rather crucial to understand how man perceives and experiences his coexistence with advanced machinic intelligence. Besides this, advancements in computational design and analysis tools and techniques have already begun challenging traditional modes of design. An Architectural Engineering flavor, which deals with advanced performance metrics and hyperlinked knowledge banks, is on the rise and is being heavily experimented with by the design fraternity. Performance at the social, structural, environmental and spatial front is thus underpinning contemporary design in praxis as well as academia. Developing fully parametric meta-design systems to enable today's information architect to succeed in this competitive environment is thus gaining paramount importance. The emergence of a new material culture based on novel methodologies in both design thinking and materialization techniques is thus inevitable.

Prototypes

At Hyperbody, we have built a series of prototypes to study the intricacies of research driven design of interactive architectures. The first in the series, called the NSA Muscle, was specifically built for the NSA (Non Standard Architecture) exhibition in Centre Pompidou, Paris, in 2003.

NSA Muscle

The NSA Muscle is a pro-active inflated space, its surface populated with a mesh of 72 pneumatic muscles, which were all addressed individually by means of regulating the amount of air pressure induced within them. The prototype is programmed to respond to human visitors through its sensing, processing and actuating enhancements. To communicate with the observers, the NSA Muscle has to transduce physical quantities into digital signals (sensors) and vice versa (actuators). People connect to the NSA Muscle by 24 sensors attached to reference points on the structure. These input devices convert the behavior of the human players into data that acts as the parameters for changes in the physical shape of the active structure and the ambient soundscape. The input setup comprises eight sensor plates with three sensors each: motion (for sensing the presence of possible players from a distance of 6 meters), proximity (for sensing the distance of the players to the NSA Muscle within a distance of 2 meters) and touch (for sensing the amount of pressure applied upon the surface). The analogue sensor input channels are converted to digital audio signals (MIDI) and transferred to the computer.

The NSA Muscle is programmed to behave within predefined bandwidths of emotional modes and within these modes it is free to act and to develop a personal mood. Emotional modes include jumping (excited), retracting (scared) and shivering (anger) tactile variations attained by volumetric alterations of the external form, by changing the length of the tensile muscles accompanied by the emission of pre-designed sounds of variable pitch. A three-dimensional visualization of the MUSCLE rendered on a flat screen informs the people about the nature of this being. This model is the computational process itself. From this model the state of each muscle is determined. The activity of the muscles is displayed in three colors in the model: red /inflating state, blue /deflating state, and gray /passive state, and in the internally used organizational 72-digit string. Also represented in the model are eight sensor plates changing scale and opacity upon the activity and overall behavioral state of the MUSCLE. They are visualized as a gradually changing color background. Images of architectural applications using muscle technology complement the graphical display. The real-time model is actively viewed from multiple camera positions so as to feel the behavioral patterns at work. Viewed in combination with the physical model the graphical interface contributes to the public's understanding.

Figure 1   The NSA Muscle at the Centre Pompidou, Paris.

Muscle Re-Configured

The Muscle Re-Configured project succeeded the NSA Muscle and focused on materializing a real time, responsive, habitable space, utilizing pneumatic fluidic muscles from Festo. With the objective of experimenting with an interior space, the prototype is conceived as a 3D habitable Strip: a three dimensional section in space, programmed to respond to its occupants through its sensing (proximity and touch sensors), processing (graphical scripting for real-time output) and actuating (fluidic muscles) enhancements. The construct uses a flexible composite panel's (Hylite) property to bend and the fluidic muscle's property of linear compression in interaction with each other, to transform the otherwise hard-edged (visually) spatial strip into soft, luxuriant variations. Each Hylite panel is coupled with two fluidic muscles to form the basic unit of the strip. Panels join together to create a closed 3D loop, in the process creating series of nodes at the panel's junctions. These nodes are linked in space via their actuation members in a highly interdependent manner, constantly exchanging information in terms of air pressure variations, thus behaving as a collective whole to attain varying spatial reconfigurations.

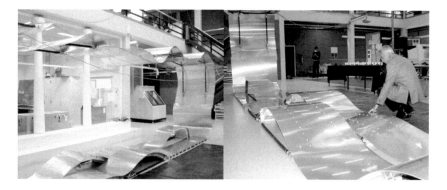

Figure 2   The Muscle Re-Configured being tested for relational curvature variations of all three elements (seating, walls and roof)

This dense network of nodes has two typologies: external and internal. The external (constituting fluidic muscles at the junctions) predominantly deals with sets of sensors and actuators, and the internal (corresponding air valves and their array sequence in the graphical script) deals with computation and data processing elements. A rule-based control algorithm developed in Virtools binds the two node typologies together to produce the desired data exchange and output scenarios (amount of air pressure to be released to the fluidic muscle). The Muscle re-configured project works by means of cumulative coupling of the basic unit mentioned above. This componental interactivity is utilized for developing specific behaviors (in terms of kinetic movements), giving rise to three distinctly behaving elements: responsive floor, ceiling and walls joined together in a closed three-dimensional loop.

These elements are linked in space in a highly interdependent manner, constantly exchanging information (such as occupancy of the seating units, proximity of people, local topology variation of the three elements, etc.). Yet, they behave as a collective whole to attain specific spatial configurations. Seating occupancy triggers a topology modulation in the ceiling and wall units to provide a feeling of being engulfed by the curvature of the ceiling and creates a comfortable viewing angle for projections cast on the wall units.

Emotive Interactive Wall

The Emotive Interactive Wall is composed of 7 separate wall pieces (herein referred to as nodes) that display real time behavior by swinging back and forth, displaying patterns of light on its skin, and projecting localized sound. The primary synchronous behavior of the Interactive Wall is movement. The nodes of the Interactive Wall will bend independently of neighboring nodes in response to the presence of a user. Although responsively independent, each Interactive Wall node synchronizes by constantly readjusting its position in order to align itself with the position of its nearest neighbors.

Augmented modality of the Interactive Wall's behavior is light. The skin of each Interactive- Wall is covered by a unique, irregular distribution of dynamically controlled LEDs that form a highly reactive interface. The LED skins respond directly to user presence by glowing brighter when users are near, and dimmer as they move away. In addition to dimming, the LED skins pulse rapidly and slowly in relation to node position, having a tendency to flash together when the nodes are in sync. The third modality of the Interactive Wall is localized sound. Moments of synchronicity are represented by calmer sounds, while asynchronous behavior results in more intense sound. The propagation of the sound from high to low intensity is varied throughout the Interactive Wall, thus each node is a member of a choir that sings a complex pattern of oscillating chords. Although similar, the physical movements of Interactive Wall, and the light and sound patterns change independently, reacting at varying rates. The synchronous behavior between the Interactive Wall nodes contrasts with the behavior produced by user presence, resulting in a series of complex wave patterns that propagate through the Interactive Wall structure as a whole.

Starting from a clear interactive design concept, we successfully developed a one-to-many interactive system that exhibited emergent behavior and performed like a living system. The result is an independent system built on synchronous behavior that is interrupted by the game-like response of multi-participant interaction. This layered system encourages the intended cycle of observation, exploration, modification, and reciprocal change in the participant, reinforcing believability in the system, and providing a sense of agency to the user.

Figure 3   The Emotive Interactive Wall (commissioned to Hyperbody by Festo).

Ambiguous Topology

Ambiguous topology is an immersive multi-modal installation exploring the tendencies of swarm systems and volumetric projections to generate emergent geometric networks as a response to as well as a trigger for movement of multiple bodies in space and time. The installation operates on the subtle fusion of physical and digital media by means of harvesting and impacting the speed and frequency of movement of the participant's body as a trigger for activating/disturbing a swarm of digital particles in space. The usage of volumetric light projection media (using four HD projectors) in order to visualize this dynamic (simulated) swarm scenario renders abstract three dimensional topological nuances (from projected light) within which the body navigates and experiences new states of ambiguity, dis-alignment and proactive behavior. Technological, human and spatial agency/affordance thus unites into a never-ending looped process of inter-performance through the Ambiguous Topology installation. The installation challenges conventional modes of perceiving space as a dormant object and abolishes the subject-object relationship, which have long been associated with it.

The installation also physiologically and psychologically appeals and instigates our regulated behavioral selves resulting in the generation of novel reactions and interactions. Different geometric instances of the fluid environmental topology are generated via the interplay between the participants and the conceived system, and are materialized via the immersive light projection (volumetric projection) system as a meta-narrative. As a result, an intimate relationship between the overall environment and participants naturally appears during the experiential phase. Meanwhile, an information feedback loop is at play, which binds the physical interactions of the participants, with soft simulation and computation processes to ultimately impact and influence the participants' behavior in real-time. During the interaction process, novel movements, group dynamics and gestural novelty came to the fore.

Figure 4   Ambiguous Topology is a Swarm simulation and Volumetric Projection driven fully immersive
            spatial environment developed at the intersection of art and science
            (Video link: https://vimeo.com/105421757)

Reflectego and Robo-Zoo

Reflectego and Robo-Zoo were interactive installations developed under the EU Culture Grant: METABODY. Reflectego is a real-time interactive architectural installation derived from a kaleidoscopic composition of faceted mirrors, aimed specifically at distorting perception. In the project the user literally becomes the physical object inside a kaleidoscope in which he sees his image scattered and recomposed as a result of his movement in space. The structure consists of a suspended faceted mirror-surface with embedded proximity sensors, which hovers and physically changes the inclination and directions of its facets in real-time based on the people it can sense below it. The user is thus visually displaced, since his perceptual affinity of seeing him/herself in a mirrored surface is suddenly challenged.

Figure 5   Reflectego interacting with its audience at the Media Lab Prado, Madrid, Spain.

Robo-Zoo creates an artificial eco-system from an interactive swarm of robots. The robots, conceived as small-scale bots operate as individual agents, with embedded proximity sensors and servo motors, powered by a battery pack. Each agent thus has a capacity to sense its context (people and obstacles) and propel it in different directions via servo motors attached to structural wheel spokes. The bots and humans, thus inter-activate each other in order to create novel movement patterns of both and in the process constantly redefine space via establishing unspoken ecological dependencies.

Motion and visual expression of each independent robot evokes instanta- neous response in the environment. People perceiving remodeled swarm of artificial creatures are forced to reestablish themselves in the space in real time. Robots and humans thus negotiate interaction boundaries and accep- tance levels mutually.

Conclusion

The real-time responsive spatial prototypes mentioned in this article outline the relationship between information flow, material systems and human behavior. Relational data exchange between multiple parameters becomes embedded in the D.N.A of such real-time interactive environments, convert- ing them into metabolic systemic entities. Such spatial constructs will thus eventually acquire the characteristics of living entities, sending and receiving information, processing this information locally, and producing responsive global output. Such design informatics-based hybrid typologies can be seen as complex adaptive systems, which pave the path for performance based responses to contemporary socio-cultural conditions.

Dr. Nimish Biloria is an Assistant Professor at the, Architectural Engineering and Technology Department (Chair: Hyperbody), TU Delft, The Netherlands. He firmly believes in digitally driven bottom-up methodologies for develop- ing performance driven sustainable and energy efficient design solutions at variable scale. His research and education interests in Performative Design and Interactive Architecture are clubbed under the research umbrella 'S.M.A.R.T. Environments' which investigates the intricate relationships between information flow and associative material formations. Investigations under this research umbrella include the following: Interactive Architectural Systems, Interaction Models and Cognitive Systems, Material Systems and Performative Architecture and Smart Cities. He holds a PhD from the Delft University of Technology in Real-time interactive environments and a Masters in Architecture in Emergent Technologies and Design from the Architectural Association, London, UK. He has lectured at several prestigious institutes globally and has also presented and published his research and design deductions via numerous international journals, design conferences, exhibitions, design books and magazines.

Visualizing Living Architecture: Augmented Reality Visualizations of Sensors, Actuators, and Signal Flows

KATY BÖRNER AND ANDREAS BUECKLE
Indiana University Bloomington

As the built environment becomes increasingly more complex and integrated with new technologies – including the emerging Internet of Things (IoT) – there is an urgent need to understand how embedded technologies affect the experience of individuals that inhabit these spaces and how these technologies can be most appropriately used to improve occupant experience, comfort, and well-being. In addition, the IoT provides an opportunity as well as a challenge when it comes to helping users understand how these intelligent systems gather and process information such as sensor data and internal feedback loops.

The Visualizing Living Architecture project aims to help system architects, designers, and general audiences understand the inner workings of tightly coupled sensor-actuator systems that interlink machine and human intelligence. It aims to empower many to master basic concepts related to the operation and design of complex dynamical systems and the IoT. Specifically, it uses architectural blue prints of living architecture installations together with real-time data streams to visualize the operation of Living Architecture installations (Figure 1). Created by the Living Architecture Systems Group at the University of Waterloo (Canada), these installations can move, respond, and learn; they grow themselves and are adaptive and empathic toward their inhabitants. Börner's team at Indiana University (USA) adds dynamic visualizations to the installations to help visitors, academics, and designers understand the many sensors and actuators used in the design of complex architectural systems, along with artificial intelligence processes rapidly being integrated into next generation architecture.

Figure 1   Details of LASG installation Epiphyte Grove as exhibited Trondheim, Norway (2012).

The visualizations detail how sensory system input (collected via movement, light, and sound sensors but also cameras) is processed by artificial intelligence control circuits and used to control an array of actuators (sound, light, movement) within the living architecture.

In the initial phase of the project, a Cyclops testbed was setup comprising one light sensor (the Cyclops' eye), three actuators, together with hardware and software required to position and drive the sensors/actuators.

The open-code Unity game development software is used to create augmented reality Visualizing Living Architecture applications (VLA app). The VLA app reads the three-dimensional CAD drawing of a Living Architecture installation, e.g., the Cyclops, together with real-time data streams recorded for this installation. The VLA app can be installed and run on laptops, smartphones, and other mobile devices. It geo-registers the Living Architecture by means of a predefined key image or three-dimensional shape then goes into a data visualization mode which visualizes sensor/actuator positions together with signal flows (Figure 2).

Initially, we are interested to answer the following questions: What visual metaphors work best for communicating different sensor and actuator types, positions, and activations? How can signal flows (type and speed) and processing (local and remote) best be communicated? Does speeding up and slowing down time help gaining a more holistic understanding of human-machine intelligence interaction patterns? What visualizations are helpful for experts aiming to optimize Living Architectures? What extensions, if any, are needed to the Visualization Framework (Börner & Polley, 2014, Börner, 2015) to cover these visualizations?

Future work will also aim to answer: What meaningful and qualitative human-machine interactions can be understood from data? How can we design informative and playful augmented-reality environments to engage untrained users with living architectures? How can we enhance data visualization literacy by exposing users to an intelligent system with the comfort and help of our app?

The research will provide a means to analyze and visualize the underlying dynamics within existing interactive architectures, to understand dynamics between space and people, and its larger social impact. The development of novel interfaces will in turn enable individuals, designers, and architects to modify architectural behaviour for greater agency and more meaningful interaction.

Figure 2   Augmented reality visualization of Cyclops sensor and actuator positions.

References

Börner, Katy. Atlas of knowledge: Anyone can map. MIT Press, 2015.

Börner, Katy, and David E. Polley. Visual insights: A practical guide to making sense of data. MIT Press, 2014.

Clark, Andy. "Natural born-cyborg." Minds, Technologies, and the Future of Human 2003

Katy Börner is the Victor H. Yngve Distinguished Professor of Information Science in the Department of Information and Library Science, School of Informatics and Computing. She is a curator of the international Places & Spaces: Mapping Science exhibit and the author of the Atlas of Knowledge and Atlas of Science (MIT Press). She holds a MS in Electrical Engineering from the University of Technology in Leipzig, 1991 and a Ph.D. in Computer Science from the University of Kaiserslautern, 1997.

Andreas Bueckle is a PhD student in Information Science at Indiana University. In his research, he maintains deep interests in developing theoretical frameworks and creating (immersive) data visualization tools that encourage smart decision making.

The Value and Use of Laban Movement Analysis in Observation and Generation of Affective Movement

SARAH JANE BURTON
Sheridan College

This paper discusses Laban Movement Analysis (LMA) and its potential as a comprehensive and precise structure for analyzing and representing expressive movement. This can be of great use for characterizing and generating affective movement for artificial agents, such as robots, animations, kinetic sculptures and environments. In our collaborative work, "Laban Movement Analysis and Affective Movement Generation for Robots and Other Near-Living Creatures,"[1] our goal was to generate compact, informative representations of movement to facilitate affective movement recognition and generation for robots and other artificial embodiments. We hypothesized that LMA, a systematic and comprehensive approach for observing and describing movement, is an excellent candidate for deriving a low-dimensional representation of movement that facilitates affective motion modeling.

In addition to the longstanding research on movement analysis in the dance community, affective movement analysis has more recently received significant attention in other domains. There is a large and active research effort on affective movement perception, recognition and generation in cognitive science, psychology, and affective computing.[2]

Daily we consciously and subconsciously interpret meaning and self-expression by observing body language of others. Our motivation for this research was the question, is it possible to translate emotional expression through an arm movement via algorithms, into a moving sculpture "with feelings"? Our inspiration was one of the immersive, responsive sculptures in a series entitled: Hylozoic Ground, by Philip Beesley and Rob Gorbet. Since people move in response to the sculpture, would it be possible to observe their movements and interact affectively through movement? This capability may be valuable beyond artistic installations, in applications such as human-computer interaction and human-robot interaction. Our goal then was to develop a way to translate between the movement language of humans and the potential movement language of the sculpture.

As a path to reach our goal, our research focused on expressive human gestures of the arm and hand, the parts of the body that would be most similar to the sculpture's moving fronds. Each individual has a unique personal history that influences their movements, as does their physical "architecture" and ability. The challenge of this study, this partnership between the science of robotics and the art of expressive movement, was to attempt to discover and distil the essence of affective movement. The engineers looked to the dance/theatre performance world, where choreographed movements can be specific and repeatable with believable expressive qualities, for a language to analyze and describe movement.

Our approach aimed to quantify and formalize the relationship between perceived movement qualities and measurable features of movements, to enable this relationship to be exploited for automated recognition and generation of affective movement. Another challenge of our research was to develop a common language and shared understanding of movement analysis between interdisciplinary research team members from the dance/choreography and engineering communities.

> "I can't do much for you until you know how to see."
> -José de Creeft, sculptor

The study of Laban Movement Analysis (LMA) trains an observer to see, to become aware of, to attempt to ascertain the different aspects of movement. LMA promotes an understanding of movement from the inside out, as the mover, as well as from the outside in, as the observer. Rudolf von Laban (1879–1958) developed theories and systems of movement and notation. He wrote about the need to find a way to combine movement-thinking and word-thinking in order to understand the mental side of effort and action and re-integrate the two in a new form.

Laban stressed that imitation does not "penetrate to the hidden recesses" of human inner effort. Laban searched for an authentic symbol of the inner vision in order for the performer to make effective affective contact with an audience, and felt that this could be achieved only if we have learned to think in terms of movement.[3] He developed a system of basic principles and movement language that are encompassed in today's Laban Movement Analysis. Bloom argues "that LMA, by providing a vocabulary for articulating the detail of experiential phenomena, provides a valuable framework and a system of categories for bringing the inter-relationships between body and psyche into greater focus."[4] To enable automated movement analysis, a computational understanding of how affect is conveyed through movement was needed. Laban Movement Analysis was used to provide a language useful in the "translation of emotions to algorithms."

Laban Movement Analysis is divided into four overarching themes, both quantitative and qualitative. They comprise a blend of science and artistry. Stability/Mobility describes the natural interplay of components of the body that function to allow the full scope of human movement and balance to occur. Exertion/Recuperation speaks to the rhythms and phrasing of movements, that, similar to the rhythms of breath, may be said to create a "dance" between muscular tension and release. Inner/Outer addresses our connection from our needs and feelings within ourselves to our movement out in the world and the return flow of a response to our environment. Function/Expression differentiates between the aspects of movement that serve a need and the movement qualities that are expressive of affect. The latter two themes were of most interest to this project.

There is some discussion amongst Certified Movement Analysts (CMAs) concerning the dichotomy between quantitative and qualitative analysis, assuming that concepts need to belong in one category or the other.

The implication is that if something cannot be measured then it is qualitative and unprovable. The concepts in LMA are governed by principles, whether or not they are measurable, that Kagan asserts make them "concrete, observable, experientially verifiable, repeatable and predictable."[5] For this reason, we believe LMA is amenable to computational analysis and can be related to measurable features of movement.

Laban Movement Analysis employs a multilayered description of movement, focusing on the components: Body, Space, Effort and Shape. Body indicates the active body parts, and the sequence of their involvement in the movement; Space defines where in space the movement is happening, the directions, spatial patterns and range; Effort describes the inner attitude toward the use of energy; and Shape characterizes the bodily form, and its changes in space. If each of these aspects is understood in terms of its own integrity, one can begin to comprehend how each interacts and illuminates the others.[5] Irmgard Bartenieff (1890–1981), a colleague of Laban, advocates the use of Effort and Shape as a means to study movements from behavioural and expressive perspectives. Application of the concepts of quality, or "inner attitudes towards" movement, are used in the analysis of Effort.[6] Thus among Laban components, Effort and Shape were the most relevant for our specific study.

The members of our research team, in order to communicate, needed to become familiar with each other's language, e.g., the terms "High Level-Low Level" for the engineers referred to qualities of information, but to the choreographer and actor referred to placement in space. Symbols are international in a way that words are not. Laban's terminology and symbols become meaningful with the consciously experienced three-dimensional sculptural movements. For examples of the symbols employed in this research, please refer to our chapter 1.

In designing the movement pathways, inspiration was taken from the types of movements similar to those of the fronds in the sculpture. The goal in designing the choreographed pathways was to choose several simple arm movements that were not already strongly weighted with affect, but were as neutral as possible. It is important to reinforce the fact that different factors such as culture, physique, personal history, and specific environmental circumstances influence a quality of movement. North states that "[i]t is impossible to say either that a particular movement equals a special quality or that a particular quality equals one movement pattern plus a certain shape or space characteristic.

Only generalizations can be made, because a movement assessment is made by the meticulous study of observed movement patterns of each individual."[7]

Based on the study of gestures and accompanying experimentation, three simple pathways were chosen; each was also reversed, making a total of six pathways without strong affective associations. The more limited the prescribed pathway the higher the possibility of measuring subtle significant differences between the emotions. For each of the six paths, a professional actor was asked to act each of Ekman's original Six Basic Emotions: anger, happiness, disgust, sadness, surprise and fear.[8] Prinz acknowledges that they have become the most widely accepted candidates for basic emotions, both psychologically and biologically.[9] In LMA, the word "intent" is used to describe part of the preparation stage of movement and Hackney states "it is at this crucial point that the brain is formulating (even in a split second) the motor plan which will eventually be realized in action."[10] As noted in *Psychology of Dance*, the more vivid, realistic and detailed the image is, the more the senses, thoughts and emotions are involved.[11] The actor relied on her rigorous training in the use of memory and imagination to freshly create and express the emotion aroused internally.

With five tries for each emotion, we captured 180 movement sequences (6 paths, 6 emotions, 5 trials) for each of three data sets. The actor filled out a questionnaire rating her feeling of success at embodying the specific emotion for each try. The training of the actor, the number of tries, and the actor's questionnaire, were attempts at providing high quality motion capture examples of the six emotions.

A coding sheet was devised for the Laban Certified Movement Analyst (CMA) to use while watching the video of each movement. The first LMA factor quantified was Weight Effort, which describes the sense of force of one's movement, with the contrasting elements Strong and Light. The second LMA factor quantified was Time Effort, which describes the sense of urgency, with the contrasting elements Sudden and Sustained. The third LMA factor quantified was Space Effort, which describes the attention to surroundings, with the contrasting elements Direct and Indirect. The fourth LMA factor quantified was Flow Effort, which describes the attitude towards bodily tension and control, with the contrasting elements Bound and Free. The final LMA aspect considered was Shape Directional, which defines the pathway to connect to or from the demonstrator with their goal in space, with the two categories of Arc-like and Spoke-like.

The proposed quantifications were evaluated by comparing the automated quantification values with the annotations provided by the CMA, The results showed a strong correlation between results from the automatic Laban quantification and the CMA-generated Laban quantification of the movements. Based on this, we described in our chapter an approach for the automatic generation of affective movements.

In conclusion, Laban Movement Analysis offers a concise, comprehensive structure for observing, analyzing and representing movement, which can be of great use for generating affective movement for artificial agents, such as robots, kinetic sculptures and environments. Our approach for quantifying LMA components from measurable movement features, and using the proposed quantification within an expressive movement generation framework allows movement paths to be imbued with target affective qualities, a first step towards more expressive human-machine interaction.

In the future, a relatively new academic discipline, Sensory Anthropology, that focuses on how cultures stress different ways of knowing through brain/body maps and the senses[12], might benefit from further investigation of the perception and generation of affective movements. We aim to explore the other datasets collected, where the hand, fingers and arm were not confined to specific pathways. The knowledge gleaned from further research could be used for the development of kinetic affective sculptures and environments.

Endnotes

This paper is an example illustrated from our collaborative work, "Laban Movement Analysis and Affective Movement Generation for Robots and Other Near-Living Creatures."[1]

1. Burton, Sarah Jane and Ali-Akbar Samadani, Rob Gorbet, Dana. Kulić. "Laban Movement Analysis and Affective Movement Generation for Robots and Other Near-Living Creatures." Dance Notations and Robot Motion, edited by Jean-Paul Laumond and Naoko Abe,
Springer International, 2016, pp. 25-48.

2. Karg, Michelle and A. Samadani, R. Gorbet, K. Kuehnlenz, J. Hoey, D. Kulić, "Body Movements for Affective Expression: a Survey of Automatic Recognition and Generation." IEEE Transactions on Affective
Computing 4(4), 2013, pp. 341–359.

3. Laban, Rudolf, revised and
enlarged by Lisa Ullmann. The Mastery of Movement, 3rd ed.,
PLAYS Inc., Boston, 1972.

4. Bloom, Katya. "Interrelationships Between Movement Analysis and Psychoanalysis: a
Qualitative Research Project." Journal of Laban Movement Studies, 1(1), 2009 Spring, pp. 33–43.

5. Kagan, Betsy. "What is spatial tension?" Discussion no. 28, Dance Notation Bureau Theory Bulletin Board, http://dnbtheorybb.blogspot.ca/2010/01/
what-is-spatial-tension.html, 2007.

6. Bartenieff, Irmgard with Dori Lewis. Body movement: coping with the environment, Gordon and Breach
Science Publishers, New York, 1980.

7. North, Marion. Personality Assessment Through Movement, Macdonald and Evans Ltd.,
Estover,
Plymouth, 1972.

8. Ekman, Paul. "Are there basic emotions?" Psychology Review, 99(3), 1992, pp. 550–553.

9. Prinz, Jesse. "Which Emotions Are Basic?" Emotion, Evolution, and Rationality, edited by
D. Evans and P. Cruse, Oxford University Press, 2004, pp.69-88.

10. Hackney, Peggy. Making Connections: Total Body Integration Through Bartenieff Fundamentals, Gordon and Breach, Amsterdam, 1988.

11. Taylor, Jim and Ceci. Taylor. Psychology of Dance, Human Kinetics, Champaign, 1995.

12. Blakeslee, Sandra and Matthew Blakeslee. The Body Has a Mind of Its Own,
Random House, New York,
2007.

Sarah Jane Burton is a Laban Certified Movement Analyst, Ms. Burton has degrees in Movement and Dance from Butler University, IN, and Wesleyan University, CT. As a researcher she has collaborated with computer engineers and has co-written the chapter, "Laban Movement Analysis and Affective Movement Generation for Robots and Other Near-Living Creatures" in Dance Notations and Robot Motion published in 2016 by Springer, as well as given invited talks on the subject in the U.K. and France. Her teaching career includes positions in George Brown's Theatre Dept., the University of Toronto's Faculty of Music, Sheridan College's Music Theatre Dept. and a professorship in Sheridan's co-program in Theatre and Drama Studies with the University of Toronto Mississauga. Ms. Burton received extensive training and performed professionally in dance and theatre in New York, Chicago, Toronto, Ghana, and France. She continues to direct and choreograph professionally, including coaching actors in a television series how to simulate movement in zero gravity. Ms. Burton currently researches the enhancement of expressive movement qualities in people with Parkinson's.

The Intersection of
Art and Technology

ANTONIO CAMURRI & GUALTIERO VOLPE
University of Genova

For a long time, art and science were viewed as distant domains that were only loosely connected, but we're now witnessing more interaction between the two. This has led to an increased awareness of how art and science are indeed two different but strongly coupled aspects of human creativity, both driving innovation as art influences science and technology, and as science and technology in turn inspire art.

Recognizing this mutually beneficial relationship, researchers at the Casa Paganini-Info-Mus Research Centre (www.casapaganini.org) aim to combine scientific research in information and communications technology (ICT) with artistic and humanistic research. We carry out scientific and technological research on human-centered computing, where art and humanistic theories are a fundamental source of inspiration, capable of deep cross-fertilization with "hard" sciences and engineering. Here, we discuss some of our work, showing how our collaboration with artists informed our work on analyzing nonverbal expressive and social behavior and contributed to tools, such as the EyesWeb XMI hardware and software platform (www.infomus.org/eyesweb ita.php), that support both artistic and scientific developments.[1,2] We also sketch out how art informed multimedia and multimodal technologies find application beyond the arts, in areas including education, cultural heritage, social inclusion, therapy, rehabilitation, and wellness.

Research Driven by Art

In keeping with its mission to experiment with and establish synergies between science, technology, and the arts, the premises of Casa Paganini-InfoMus are an ancient monumental building endowed with a 230-seat auditorium and some museum rooms (see www.youtube. com/InfoMusLab for more information). The main lab room enjoys a direct view of the auditorium's stage. This configuration is paradigmatic of the interaction between artistic and scientific and technological research and enables the development of experiments, prototypes, and demonstrations in an almost real world (ecological) scenario (see Figure 1).

Our research into the automated analysis of nonverbal expressive and social behavior, leading to the development of the EyesWeb platform, was heavily influenced by collaborations with composer Luciano Berio and with various artists and researchers, including Nicola Bernardini and Alvise Vidolin. The aim of the collaborations with Berio was to design and develop interactive

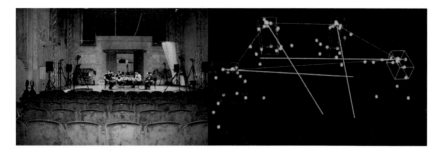

Figure 1   Santa Maria delle Grazie la Nuova, premise of the Casa Paganini- InfoMus research center, is an example of innovative reuse in contemporary information society of a monumental building as a research facility for science, technology, and art. [Left] The main lab room enjoys a direct view of the auditorium is stage. This configuration is paradigmatic of the interaction between artistic and scientific and technological research. [Right] Here, we show an experiment on multimodal recordings (audio, video, motion capture, and physiological signals) of a string quartet.

on-stage technologies for his operas Outis (Teatro alla Scala, Milan, 1996) and Cronaca del Luogo (Salzburg Festival, 1999). EyesWeb aimed to offer synchronized recording and real-time interactive processing and rendering of multimodal data.

For Outis, we answered the following artistic research question: how might an orchestra conductor conduct and synchronize musicians with sounds electronically synthesized in real time, and with the movement of mimes on stage? We developed interactive technologies, detecting the movement of the mimes, to control in real time the electronic sounds, thus simplifying the conductor's task.

In Cronaca del Luogo, the task was more difficult. A major singer of the opera (David Moss) played a schizophrenic character at times appearing wise and calm, while other times appearing crazy, with nervous and jerky movements. We automatically measured some of his movement qualities using sensors embedded in his clothes and a flashing infrared light on his helmet, synchronized with video cameras positioned above the stage (see Figure 2). We used this information to morph the singer's voice from profound (wise) to a harsh, sharp (crazy) timbre. This experience with concrete real-world needs for multimodal analysis and mapping was of paramount importance to shape the requirements for our first publicly available version of EyesWeb.[1]

Figure 2   The sensor systems adopted for the performer David Moss in Luciano Berioi *Cronaca del Luogoi* opera opening at the Salzburg Festival 1999. [Left] Wireless sensors were sewn into his costume and worn in his palms. His helmet included flashing infrared LEDs, synchronized with video cameras in the theater, to track his position [Right] on the whole stage and to measure, in real time, details on his movement qualities, which were used to morph his voice to match characters' schizophrenic behavior.

Furthermore, in our research, art didn't merely inform our requirements. It was also a valuable testbed for assessing computational models, algorithm, interfaces, and techniques. For example, Roberto Doati's musical theater work, Un avatar del Diavolo [A Devil's Avatar] (performed at the Venice Biennale arts organization in Italy in 2005), was our experimental testbed to improve and evaluate multimodal acoustic interfaces exploiting sound propagation in physical objects to localize where a surface is touched and to measure the expressive qualities of such touching gestures. Surfaces of common objects belonging to the scenery on stage (a chair, an old radio, and other furniture) were used in the piece, and we could automatically distinguish, for example, between a caress, a touch with nails or fingertips, and a touch while sitting or while moving around the chair.

Ensemble musical performances and the audience experience were our testbed in the European ICT project SIEMPRE for developing and evaluating models and techniques for measuring creative social interaction between performers, and between performers and the audience, in an ecologically valid framework – that is, in a condition resembling not a laboratory experiment but rather something very near to a real music performance in a concert hall. Experiments with famous artists – such as the Quartetto di Cremona string quartet – led us to novel multimodal techniques, implemented as real-time EyesWeb software libraries, to measure nonverbal social signals, including entrainment (physical alignment between the individuals in a group) and leadership.

Science Explores the Artistic Process

Scientific research digs into our neurophysiological, perceptual, cognitive, affective, and social processes to shed light on the creative mechanisms leading an artist to conceive artwork. Consider the following areas:

- ethnographic observation studies how the original creative idea develops and matures;

- experimental psychology investigates how an artwork engages and conveys emotion to an audience;

- social and organizational sciences address how performers collaborate to reach their common goal; and

- neuroscience focuses on the neural mechanisms enabling all of these activities

Recently, such research has benefited from the availability of advanced physical and mathematical models and from sophisticated technological tools providing accurate measures of the phenomena under investigation, thus helping researchers pair qualitative observation with quantitative analysis. For example, social interaction in music ensembles, ranging from small ones (such as string quartets) to sections of orchestras, was studied by applying techniques, such as sample entropy[2] and Granger causality,[3] originally conceived to analyze time series in physiology and in econometrics, respectively.

Artistic research benefits in many ways from the increasing body of knowledge and tools science offers it. Whereas the growing knowledge of the mechanisms governing the creative processes might help improve such processes 'effectiveness, more importantly, the availability of novel technologies opens formerly unconceivable perspectives and opportunities in terms of extending the artistic language and developing completely new art forms. Consider, for example, dance performances in which the technology extends the choreographic action beyond the dancer's body, coupling it with interactive architectural elements of the environment and with the audience. Or consider novel interfaces for musical expression and collaborative music making, going far beyond the consolidated concept of hyperinstrument, toward novel forms of interaction between instruments, performers, and the audience in distributed environments over the Internet.

New Ways of Creating Art

One way in which our scientific and technological research has affected the arts is through the production of art – that is, in providing content creators (including composers, choreographers, and directors) and performers with tools for extending their artistic language and capabilities. Such an impact mainly emerges when content creators are involved in the participatory design of either an artistic or a scientific project within a multidisciplinary team. Several examples of this process are available in the history of contemporary music. In the 50s and 60s, thanks to available audio and electronic technologies, composers such as Luigi Nono and Karlheinz Stockhausen extended the music language by introducing the 3D spatialization of sound. Then, electroacoustic music and live electronics extended traditional orchestration techniques enabling, for example, complex transformations of sound.[4]

Concerning our research, the techniques we developed to measure movement and its expressive qualities on stage have enabled further degrees of freedom to composers and interactive art artists by allowing real-time control of sound activation and processing through expressive gestures. For example, in Allegoria dell'opinione verbale [Allegory of the Verbal Opinion] (composer R. Doati, 2001), the real-time analysis of the expressive qualities of an actress's lip and facial movements control the sound processing of her voice. In Medea (composer A. Guarnieri, 2002), our EyesWeb platform was used to analyze the movement of trombone players for controlling the 3D spatialization of their sound. In Invisible Line (composer A. Cera, 2007), we sent automatically extracted expressive gesture features over the Internet to make a kind of social and distributed performance in between Genova, Paris, and Hamburg (www.youtube.com/watch? v¼QsPdhO-d4nQ).

Finally, in our ongoing DANCE project (http://dance.dibris.unige.it), the concept of mapping movement onto sound is brought to its extreme consequences – completely inverting the traditional relationship between movement and sound in dance. That is, sound neither inspires body movements in the classical sense nor joins with body movements contingently and accidentally, as in Merce Cunningham's choreographies. Rather, the sound is produced by movement, its qualitative features, and its intrinsic affective and relational meanings. If music is not choreographed, and instead it is the choreography itself that creates music, then dance is conceived as a musical composition (or recomposition and interpretation), changing its traditional dimension into an eminently or exclusively listening experience. Gesture, as an aesthetic object, is experienced as a sounding object. An example of early results from the DANCE project were presented at the SONAR+ Festival in Barcelona in June 2015 (see Figure 3), showing how we developed interactive sonifications of movement qualities such as "fluidity" and "impulsivity."

Figure 3   A snapshot from the booth of the European Horizon 2020 ICT Project DANCE at SONAR©, Barcelona, in June 2015. Short DANCE demos and proof-of-concepts on real-time analysis and interactive sonification of expressive qualities of human movement were developed by the Casa Paganini-InfoMus Research Centre in collaboration with the composer Pablo Palacio and dancers Muriel Romero, Roberta Messa, and Sabrina Ribes. The demo in this picture measures movement qualities using the accelerometers and gyros on two smartphones worn on the danceri￢s right wrist and left ankle. This initiative was organized by the European Commission Project Officer Ralph Dum in the framework of the European Commission Science, Technology and the Arts (Starts) program.

The public availability of our EyesWeb platform since 2001 has enabled several collaborations. For example, New York University established a Music, Dance, and New Technologies summer program in Italy from 2003 to 2006. Students in the program learned EyesWeb, used it in their performance, and continued using it afterward. Also, various international centers for artistic research, including IRCAM [Institut de Recherche et Coordination Acoustique/Musique] in Paris and CIANT [International Centre for Art and New Technologies] in Prague, have used EyesWeb in their productions. Furthermore, artists, including visual artists, commonly exploit EyesWeb for their work after learning about the platform from EyesWeb forums or participating in EyesWeb Week, a one-week tutorial we organize every two years at our research center.

We've also developed techniques to measure, in real time, nonverbal social signals among performers, which might provide novel perspectives of the music language and of dance and interactive arts. For example, in the artistic performance tanGO—Touching Music (www. youtube.com/watch?v¼DckQ5XI B0s), our techniques for analyzing entrainment (that is, temporal and affective synchronization between individuals) and leadership from movement signals captured by mobile devices were exploited to let four dancers and their audience reconstruct a tango. Dancers' quality of movement and nonverbal social signals were used to mold and control the different musical parts of a tango piece.

Artistic Theories Influence Science and Technology

Theories and practices coming from artistic research and developed in the context of humanities offer scientific research an alternative perspective for investigating many facets of human behavior. For example, economists have studied social interaction in string quartets to understand the behavior of typical groups of employees (self-managed teams) that have a total responsibility for a defined project in the industrial world.[5]

Artistic theories provide technology developers with a complementary viewpoint of scientific knowledge to help drive innovation. For example, theories from choreography, such as Rudolf Laban's Theory of Effort,[6] have inspired scientific and technological research on automated analysis of human full-body movement as well as on the expressive emotional content movement conveys. Composer Pierre Shaeffer's[7] concept of a sound object and his typomorphology (a kind of taxonomy of sound and its properties) were influential in developing techniques for automatically analyzing sound quality, synthesizing sounds, and controlling sounding objects.

Artistic theories represent a significant theoretical and methodological background for many either consolidated or emerging scientific and technological research domains, such as affective computing, social signal processing, and sound and music computing. Moreover, many companies, especially those in the high-tech field, agree that major skills at the basis of the artistic process, such as creativity and the ability to involve people, are crucial for innovation. (https://ec.europa.eu/digital-agenda/en/ict-art-startsplatform) Art is thus becoming a valuable catalyst for developing novel value-added products and services for society.

New Ways of Experiencing Art and Cultural Heritage

Technology can also influence how art is experienced – for example, how an audience is exposed to works in art installations. According to Italian philosopher Umberto Eco, narration is like a labyrinthine wood in which the reader must walk, continually losing and finding his or her route. Interactive multimedia and multimodal technologies let us implement this intriguing metaphor and further extend it as a new paradigm for actively experiencing artistic content and cultural heritage – that is, technology lets the audience interactively operate the content, modifying and molding cultural objects in real time, in a novel, concrete, and corporeal way. In the late 90s, we started trying to transform such an idea into interactive multimodal installations with work for Città dei Bambini, a science center for children in Genova,[8] and then with work for science centers such as Città della Scienza (Science City) in Naples, the Museum of Bali in Fano, Italy, and the Museum of La Roche d'Oetre in Normandy, France.

More recently, we further developed the concept for an interactive narrative museum, grounded on nonverbal communication, emotional strategies, and empathic, collaborative forms of social interaction. For example, in permanent museum installations for the Enrico Caruso Museum (Florence, Italy), we developed an interactive environment aimed at recreating an engaging individual or social listening experience of Caruso's voice, starting from the available archives of low-quality audio recordings. The museum's Music Room (see Figure 4) was conceived as an interactive sensitive environment, including a 12-channels 3D interactive audio and loudspeakers system. It lets visitors evoke the artist's voice through queries based on nonverbal full-body movement and behavior. Once a visitor enters the room, each loudspeaker starts simultaneously playing a different fragment of Caruso's voice, subtracted from its harmonic content (so other components of the voice are filtered out). The result is a "whispering" room in which the sound sources surround the visitor. When the visitor moves toward a specific location in the room, a "gush" of a few seconds of the full tenor's voice emerges, related to the content displayed there. Many visitors make several acoustic "gushes" appear, each moving in the room from one visitor to another.

Figure 4   The Music Room at the Enrico Caruso Museum in Florence: [Left] visitors experience music "gushes" of the voice of Caruso while exploring the content in the Music Room, and [Right] detail of one of the infrared video cameras installed on the ceiling to track the behavior of visitors and control the interactive experience with the voice of Caruso. See also www.youtube.com/watch?v=ù6GeTsKlFCbE&list=ùPLEVgkiAQl8zlO9mMU0cUcQdjA8wLHbFAR.

The interactive museum installation, developed as an EyesWeb application, also analyses in real time the individual and social behavior of visitors, such as a visitor "hesitating in the room" or "remaining still near a content object for a significant amount of time," or the "harmonic relation of the trajectories in the room of each single visitor belonging to a group." These expressive and social features are used to build nonverbal queries, which might result in the retrieval, processing, and then interactive experience of audio fragments from the archive of Caruso's music recordings.

Art-Informed Technologies For Society

The impact of art-informed scientific and technological research goes far beyond the artistic domain and extends to many other application areas. Consider, for example, our interactive installations Orchestra Explorer and Mappe per Affetti Erranti [Maps for Wandering Affects] (2) in the framework of our European ICT project SAME. In the Orchestra Explorer installation, a visitor activates and listens to the different instrumental parts of an orches-tral score by simply walking on an empty interactive stage, where a virtual orchestra is located. Moreover, the visitor can modify the sound of the instruments with his or her expressive behavior (for example, an aggres-sive behavior toward a virtual instrument "frightens" it). In Mappe per Affetti Erranti, a group of visitors collaborates in reconstructing a music piece in one out of four different pre-recorded expressive performances (joyful, solemn, shy, aggressive) of the same piece (http://www.w3.org/1999/ xlink"xlink:href="http://www.youtube.com/watch?v=V49hiq6R9eY&list=PLE VgkiAQI8zLU6_ZYEuXW2EOhusFhodcq).

These two installations exemplify how interactive multimedia and mul-timodal technology, joined with the active experience paradigm, could influence education – particularly music education. They provide a unique way to go deep inside a music piece – in its structure and orchestration and its interpretation by letting visitors simultaneously listen to both the whole piece and a single instrument. The inexperienced user can learn, for example, how to distinguish between the timbre of single instruments, and how the single instruments contribute to the piece as a whole. The user can also learn how altering a single music feature affects the performance and expressive intention it conveys.

In this direction, we recently developed two interactive multimedia appli-cations for children.The Potter application helps children experience and learn sound morphology, while BeSound[9] helps them learn the basic ele-ments of music composition (www.youtube.com/InfoMusLab). Both appli-cations, developed in the framework of the European ICT project MIROR, were evaluated by pedagogues at Goteborg and Bologna University, and BeSound was used in an experimental atelier at a local music school in Belgium, where both teachers and students expressed satisfaction. This research direction is going to continue with a specific focus on violin play-ing in the new European ICT project TELMI.

Other relevant application domains include therapy and rehabilitation and social inclusion.

Research has shown that the sonification of movement can increase body awareness and thus improve the performance and effectiveness of rehabili-tation tasks.[10] Art-informed multimedia and multimodal technology enable and enhance movement sonification toward an aesthetic dimension in terms of an active music experience. We adopted this approach to help patients with Parkinson's disease and, more recently, patients suffering from chronic pain.[11] In addition to improving rehabilitation performance, the technology also helped foster social inclusion by, for example, reducing the psychological and social barriers experienced by chronic-pain patients.

Our European ICT DANCE project addresses social inclusion. Sonification of choreutic movement investigates forms of sensory substitution ("to see through listening" – that is, to translate from the visual to the auditory domain the expressive qualities of movement), enabling rapprochement and sharing of spaces and emotions between visually impaired and sighted people. Active experience of artistic content can foster social inclusion in complex situations, such as youth deviance.

Furthermore, we recently created, with the Gaslini Children Hospital in Genova, a new joint laboratory called ARIEL (the Augmented Rehabilitation in Interactive/multimodal Environment Lab), where our paradigms, inspired by performing arts and EyesWeb technology, have been adopted for the therapy and rehabilitation of children. Individual as well as social active experience of multimedia content is the core of our current and future research in these and other application scenarios.

Although current ICT might help shape what anthropologist Marc Aug_e calls the "ideology of the present," entailing the concrete risk of losing our sense of past and history (and therefore our sense of future)[12], art-informed multimedia and multimodal technologies can help us recover our sense of past. Active experience of musical content brings back to music the embodied and social dimension that analog and digital recording technologies suppressed. Music making and listening are clear examples of human activities that are, above all, interactive and social. Yet to date, these activities have been passive, non-interactive, and non-context sensitive. Current technologies, with all their potential for interactivity and communication, have not yet been able to support and promote this essential aspect of music making and listening. This can be considered a significant degradation of the traditional listening and music-making experience, in which the public was (and still is) able to interact in many ways with performers to modify the expressive features of a music piece.

The integration of techniques to automatically measure, in real time, emotions and nonverbal social signals is a promising direction to boost future technology for the active listening of music and, more in general, the active experience of audiovisual content. Active experience of cultural content brings our society back to its identity, roots, and values by letting us reconnect with the shared language and meaning of our artistic heritage. Art-informed scientific and technological research can enable citizens to rediscover cultural heritage contents in an unconventional and charming way by exploiting interactive, multimedia and multisensory paradigms of narration, combining gestures and words, emotions and cognitions, social and personal retrievals.[13]

Acknowledgements

The research projects described in this paper are the work of a whole team of researchers at Casa Paganini InfoMus. We thank our colleagues Paolo Alborno, Corrado Canepa, Paolo Coletta, Nicola Ferrari, Simone Ghisio, Ksenia Kholikalova, Maurizio Mancini, Alberto Massari, Radoslaw Niewiadomski, Stefano Piana, and Roberto Sagoleo. We also thank the European Commission Officers of the projects we coordinated: Loretta Anania (SAME), Teresa De Martino (SIEMPRE), and Ralph Dum (DANCE). We thank the Editor Hayley Hung for her precious suggestions. Note that this research is supported in part by the EU Horizon2020 ICT Project DANCE no.645553.

Endnotes

1. A. Camurri et al., "EyesWeb—Toward Gesture and Affect Recognition in Dance/Music Interactive Systems," Computer Music J., vol. 24, no. 1, 2000, pp. 57–69.

2. D. Glowinski et al., "The Movements Made by Performers in a Skilled Quartet: A Distinctive Pattern, and the Function that it Serves," Front. Psychol., vol. 4, 2013, article no. 841.

3. A. D'Ausilio et al., "Leadership in Orchestra Emerges from the Causal Relationships of Movement Kinematics," PLoS One, vol. 7, no. 5, 2012, article e35757. January–March 2016

4. N. Bernardini and A. Vidolin, "Sustainable Live Electro-Acoustic Music," Proc.
Int'l Sound and Music Computing Conf. (SMC), 2005.

5. A. Gilboa and M. Tal-Shmotkin, "String Quartets as Self-Managed Teams: An Interdisciplinary Perspective," Psychology of Music, vol. 40, no. 1, 2012, pp. 19–41.

6. R. Laban and F.C. Lawrence, Effort, Macdonald & Evans Ltd., 1947.

7. P. Schaeffer, Trait_e des Objets Musicaux, Editions du Seuil, 1966.

8. A. Camurri and A. Coglio, "An Architecture for Emotional Agents," IEEE MultiMedia, vol. 5, no. 4, 1998, pp. 24–33.

9. G. Varni et al., "Interactive Reflexive and Embodied Exploration of Sound Qualities with BeSound," Proc. 12th Int'l Conf. Interaction Design and Children (IDC), 2013, pp. 531–534.

10. A. Singh et al., "Go-with-the-Flow: Tracking, Analysis and Sonification of Movement and Breathing to Build Confidence in Activity Despite Chronic Pain," to appear in Human-Computer Interaction, Taylor & Francis, 2016.

11. Ibid.

12. M. Aug_e, O_u est pass_e l'avenir? [Where is the Future?] Editions du Panama, 2008.

13. G. Volpe and A. Camurri, "A System for Embodied Social Active Listening to Sound and Music Content," ACM J. Computing and Cultural Heritage, vol. 4, no. 1, 2011, pp. 2–23.

Antonio Camurri is a professor at Casa Paganini- InfoMus, which is part of the Department of Informatics, Bioengineering, Robotics, and Systems Engineering (DIBRIS) at the University of Genova. Contact him at antonio.camurri@unige.it.

Gualtiero Volpe is an associate professor at Casa Paganini-InfoMus, which is part of the Department of Informatics, Bioengineering, Robotics, and Systems Engineering (DIBRIS) at the University of Genova. Contact him at gualtiero.volpe@unige.it.

Design & Living Systems
Selected Works

CAROLE COLLET

Central Saint Martins, University of the Arts London

Design & Learning Systems Key Research Questions

Can research at the intersection of design and biology enable us to create compelling sustainable design propositions for future living?

How will the intersection of design and biological fabrication open up to new ways of 'making' and 'crafting' in the future?

Aims and Outputs

The Design & Living Systems Lab explores future sustainable propositions emerging from the intersection of biological tools and design research. By combining a range of projects including practice-based design research, curation and writing, the lab explores new hierarchies for designing with living systems and investigates disruptive methodologies for designing our future materiality.

Sustainability as a Driver

Today, we can witness the effect of climate change, the rapid decline of our biodiversity, and an exponential population growth which is stretching our planet beyond its ability to regenerate. It is estimated that we, as a species, are currently using the equivalent of one and a half planets to sustain our living[i]. Based on known geological reserves, recent studies show that we could run out of some of our critical raw materials within this century.

Yet, new knowledge emerging from life sciences is beginning to offer extraordinary potential for future fabrication and manufacturing. Not only we are beginning to explore the advantage of biological systems in terms of zero waste, minimum use of energy and materials, but with synthetic biology, scientists have developed means to biofabricate like 'Nature' does. We can program and engineer living organisms to grow tailored materials. Such extraordinary tools can trigger a paradigm shift in terms of design and manufacture for the future.

With this emerging biological revolution and a set of extraordinary toolkit that allow us to engineer and program life from scratch, comes a need to re-evaluate the position and potential of design. Designers need to develop a critical and ethical understanding of how best to apply these new biological tools to ensure they can contribute to shaping a truly ecological age post 2050.

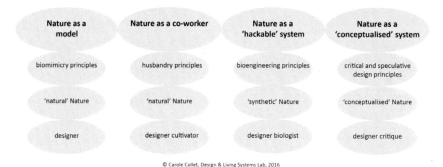

Design & Living Systems Lab: Framework for Biodesign

Nature as a model	Nature as a co-worker	Nature as a 'hackable' system	Nature as a 'conceptualised' system
biomimicry principles	husbandry principles	bioengineering principles	critical and speculative design principles
'natural' Nature	'natural' Nature	'synthetic' Nature	'conceptualised' Nature
designer	designer cultivator	designer biologist	designer critique

© Carole Collet, Design & Living Systems Lab, 2016

Framework for biodesign

Framework

I began mapping the emergence of the biodesign landscape in 2007 and developed a framework to help develop a critical and ethical stance when working with living systems. This framework formed the foundation work for the curation of the exhibition 'Alive, New Design Frontiers' which opened in 2013 in Paris at the Espace Fondation EDF.

The framework proposes a hierarchy in four folds:

- Nature as a model: The most conventional of the three, this is where designers explore biomimicry principles to imitate a behavior, a function or a pattern but may rely on conventional fabrication processes which are not necessarily sustainable.

- Nature as a co-worker: This category combines biomimicry approaches together with husbandry techniques. Here the designer becomes a cultivator that grows and control the morphology of materials by collaborating and cooperating with natural organisms such as bacteria, fungi or algae.

- Nature as a 'hackable' system: This is the most recent approach, only possible since the advances of synthetic biology which allows for the bespoke genetic engineering of simple living organisms, redesigned to produce tailored and tunable substances. Bacteria can be reprogrammed to produce biofuel, yeast to grow vanilla and silk. As designers embrace or rebel against this new biotechnological possibilities, a new array of design propositions can emerge.

- Nature as a 'Conceptualized' system. Developing the imaginary of future technologies belongs to the realm of designers. By exploiting critical and speculative design tools, designers can translate complex scientific research into tangible scenarios and act as 'agents provocateurs' to bring to light new disruptive possibilities, ethical concerns or alternative perspectives on future sustainability.

Design & Living Systems Selected Projects

Alive New Design Frontiers / curation / 2013

Espace EDF Foundation, Paris, April-September 2013. The first international design exhibition dedicated to explore how the interface of biology and design could be leading the path to new sustainable paradigms.

Curator: Carole Collet, Professor in Design For Sustainable Futures, Central Saint Martins, University of the Arts London

Objective: To reveal and question a new design landscape, where fragments of a possible programmable 'synthetic' future are confronted with 'natural' alternative design perspectives.

The seminal exhibition was commissioned and presented at the Espace EDF Foundation to cast light on the quest for different ecological design models in our increasingly bioengineered world. For the first time, it gathered under one roof the work of leading designers, architects and artists driven by nature and biological science, whose thinking ranges from potential sustainable solutions, to poetic interpretations and extreme provocations. The 34 projects, including 6 commissions, featured unraveled a future hybrid world, where our everyday products and manufacturing tools would be 'alive': plants would grow products, and bacteria would be genetically re-programmed to 'biofacture' new materials, artefacts, energy or medicine.

The commissions included: Radiant Soil by Philip Beesley, The Rise by

Radiant Soil, Philip Beesley and The Rise, CITA at 'Alive, New Design Frontiers', Espace Fondation EDF Paris 2013. Photography Laurent Lecat/EDF Foundationwww.thisisalive.com

CITA, The Biocouture Shoe by Suzanne Lee with Liz Ciokajlo-Squire, Seasons of the Void by Alexandra Daisy Ginsberg, Sascha Pohflepp, Andrew Stellitano, Hortus:Paris by EcoLogic Studio, and Botanical Fabrication by ENSCI Les Ateliers & Central Saint Martins) See: www.thisisalive.com

Biolace / Speculative design / 2012

Biolace is a speculative design project which explores the potential of synthetic biology for future textile fabrication. In a future located in 2050, when natural resources have become scarce, and global population has reached 9 Billion, food grows in urban hydroponic greenhouses that host new species of plants genetically engineered to 'manufacture' multi-products to save energy, space and time. Biolace aims at questionning the validity and ethics of an emerging synthetic nature and its pertinence for future sustainable textiles.

Biolace has been showcased in 26 international exhibitions since 2012 and includes a set of 4 photographs, a short animation, and a lace doily.

Future Hybrids / Speculative design / 2015

[Left]: Strawberry Noir, part of the Biolace series, © Carole Collet 2012
[Right]: Lace Doily, fresh strawberry roots, © Carole Collet 2012

'Future Hybrids' continues to explore fictional alternative grown biomaterialities for future textiles. Here I question the ethics of fur production and whether synthetic biology could enable us to grow fur without exploiting farmed animals or threatening endangered species. Future Hybrids considers a synthetic topology where the digital genetic code of the animal, mineral and vegetal worlds converge towards a new hybrid animate entity. Here a mushroom and a plant are reprogrammed to express the fur of an endangered raccoon.

From Earth: Mycelium textiles / Co-designing with Mycelium / 2016 – on going

'From Earth: Mycelium Textiles' is an experimental collection of materials and artefacts that explores the potential of mycelium growth as a new sustainable

[Left]: Strawberry Noir, part of the Biolace series, © Carole Collet 2012
[Right]: Lace Doily, fresh strawberry roots, © Carole Collet 2012

surface treatment for textiles. The aims of this design-led material research are (i)to achieve to produce both soft and structural textile qualities by experimenting with the environment of growth of the mycelium (ii) to develop new biodegradable, compostable coatings for textiles that can replace curent oil-based finishing processes.(iii) to develop protocols that encourage self expression and self patterning techniques in mycelium materials.

Design & Living Systems Input Into the Curriculum/Example

[Left]: Self-patterned mycelium rubber, part of the Mycelium textiles project © Carole Collet 2016. This sample is as flexible as rubber and exhibits floral patterns which are not the result of a moulding technique, but the evidence of a self-organised pattern behaviour which developed as the mycelium colonised a waste coffee-based substrate during its growth.

[Right]: Self-patterned mycelium rubber/details, part of the Mycelium textiles project © Carole Collet 2016.

Fabrics of Life: Big Data / 2014

What can designers learn from interacting with scientists? Can the study of biological systems generate new perspectives on design? These key questions encapsulate the premise of our on-going collaboration with the MRC Clinical Sciences Centre. Fabrics of Life 2014, was a live project with designers from MA Textile Futures (Central Saint Martins, UAL) and architects from the Interactive Architecture Lab (RC3, the Bartlett School of Architecture, UCL). Groups of students have dedicated three weeks to transform ideas from big data biology into blueprints for design futures.

Cultivating Bio-Intelligent Conversations

Biosalon / 2015-2016

Biosalon is a joint initiative organised by the Crafts Council and the Design & Living Systems Lab at Central Saint Martins,University of the Arts London.

Designers and scientists are exploring the future uses and applications of living matter, and ways to cultivate and grow new materials. Coupled with the evolution of technologies, our understanding of materiality is changing, and new perspectives on what defines a material and its critical context are emerging. Biosalon was set up to provide a critical space for designers and scientists engaged with this debate to come together and discuss the implications of biofabrications for their respective practices.

Carole Collet is a Research Professor and Director of the Design & Living Systems Lab at Central Saint Martins, University of the Arts, London. Collet originally set up the Textile Futures discipline at Central Saint Martins before to focus her research and practice on exploring the intersection of design and biology to develop new sustainable propositions for future living. Collet operates within the field of textile futures and biodesign and has contributed to the production of new knowledge as a designer and curator at international level since 2008. An indicative example is the project 'Biolace' which has been featured in more than 25 international exhibitions. Her recent curation of 'Alive, New Design Frontiers' at the EDF Foundation in Paris has also been critically acclaimed and clearly establishes a new original framework for designing with the living. One of her characteristics is that she operates different research roles, from designer, to curator and educator. This enables her to develop an informed critique of both the output and the context, from making knowledge to framing knowledge. Her design work has been exhibited at the Science Museum, the ICA and the V&A and she has contributed to conferences worldwide on the subject of design-science collaborations, textile futures, biodesign, biomimicry, synthetic biology, future manufacturing, sustainable design and climate change.

Building Science: Synthetic Biology and Emerging Technologies in Architectural Research

MARTYN DADE-ROBERTSON
Newcastle University

The paper examines the concept of Building Science through the role of emerging scientific research and technologies. The paper takes as its starting point the Technology Readiness Strategy which is a way of judging the state of a technology in terms of its readiness for environmental deployment and relevance to industry. The paper argues that this model is limited and uses the example of Synthetic Biology to argue for a type of building science which is both speculative and grounded and which may not lead to immediate or short-term applications but is driven by hypothetical contexts and imagined futures. The paper concludes that an alternative form of Building Science may be possible in which the term 'building' is both a verb and a noun.

I was recently involved in a bid for research funding and, as part of the initial pitch, I presented the panel with a small plastic pot containing a liquid culture of approximately eight billion E. coli bacteria cells. I proposed that the content was more than a smelly broth. It was, rather, a combination of eight billion architects, civil engineers and construction workers. I went on to describe a Synthetic Biological system in which genetically engineered bacteria cells could be suspended in a saturated aggregate and, by sensing increased loads, could respond by synthesising materials to strengthen the aggregate where it was needed. During the follow-up Q&A I was asked "what level of technological readiness would my demonstrator would be at by the end of the project." I had no idea what constituted "a level of technological readiness." In a similar situation I presented a version of this project at a job interview. I was asked, by the rather bemused interviewer, whether this was more of a material science problem with little, as yet, to do with architecture. I again didn't have a suitable response. After my funding pitch I was concerned enough to Google 'Level of Technological Readiness' but what I found only confused me further.

Technological Readiness

The Technological Readiness Level (TRL) was developed in the US and is used in various forms by government agencies such as NASA and the EU. The model illustrated in is a version taken from the European Commission's Horizon 2020 work programme. There are various versions for different domains but its structure is based on a series of nine stages starting with basic research into fundamental principles (TRL 1) to 'system-proven' technologies in 'operational environments' (TRL 9) (figure 1). The TRL treats the maturity of technology in terms of its relationship to the environment of deployment and as a simple linear progression from concept to industrial application. Early research is conducted in theoretical – often computational – models and then demonstrated in controlled lab environments before being deployed and tested in the real world and becoming "industrially relevant" only at TRL 5. Seen in this context, any form of research which could be considered Building Science in architecture would naturally tend towards the bottom of the chart. We, as architects, are concerned with the real world, with what we can build. As architects we accept the wealth of materials and technologies provided by science and engineering and focus on their innovative repurposing and configuration in the messy and complex built environment. This might sum up much Building Science research, wedged between a conservative and risk averse building industry and the need for buildings which are more radically efficient using a series of technologies, including new materials and digital sensing & fabrication systems which are often developed, in the first instance, for other industries and applications.

My project, however, certainly didn't come anywhere near the bottom of the TRL. To some extent, the proposition had more in common with speculative or experimental architecture than it did with scientific or engineering design. What I didn't mention in my funding interview was that the idea for a bacteria-based material capable of responding to mechanical changes had originally been developed as a paper which speculated on the colonisation of Mars (Dade-Robertson, Zhang, and Ramirez-Figueroa). The paper was more provocation than science and was written to appeal to science fiction writers as much as to NASA. In writing the paper and visualising our design proposals, we were participating in a tradition of architectural speculation. Look at the degree shows of many of the more progressive schools of architecture and you will find plenty of speculative projects involving a range of biotechnologies, nanotechnologies, advances in neuroscience etc. However, by asking for funding to develop the research I was looking to do something beyond speculation. My project proposal represented an attempt to make a speculation into a grounded reality, which is perhaps the essence of design.

We are now entering an era where biotechnology is, we are told, about to have a transformative effect on society comparable with the industrial and digital revolutions (Voigt). My chosen field, Synthetic Biology, is an emerging field which has been embraced by the UK government as one of the Eight Great Technologies set to transform society and therefore subject to substantial UK (and international) research investment. It is also a fledgling discipline and one which remains contested. Synthetic Biology is increasingly associated with the application of engineering design methods to the design of biological systems and particularly emphasises genetic manipulation (Heinemann and Panke). An important research question is how to design and engineer systems at the level of individual molecules to influence systems at the building or even city scales. Before last year, when I embarked on a post-graduate degree in Synthetic Biology, I would have described the state of the art in Synthetic Biology with reference to computing in the 1960s and '70s which was then poised to have a transformative effect on society. I rationalised my decision to pursue a degree in the field as the equivalent to an architect undertaking studies in Computer

Science in anticipation of the CAD revolution in the coming decades. I was, in effect, future proofing myself. If I were to draw the same parallel now, however, I would describe Synthetic Biology as being at its Babbage stage – with foundational concepts forming but with few practical demonstrators yet and fundamental questions remaining. On that basis, I might have taken my Synthetic Biology degree two hundred years too early. Plotted on the TRL chart, most Synthetic Biology demonstrators can be considered at, or close to, the top.

Synthetic Biology: An Alternative Building Science

Perhaps then it is too early for architects to be interested in Synthetic Biology. Or perhaps not. I want to make the claim here for an alternative (and additional) sort of Building Science. A Building Science which is not necessarily concerned with the pragmatic construction of the built environment but which helps develop experiments that support the design of real systems and goes beyond futurism and speculation. I'm proposing a type of Building Science which not only engages with technologies at the bottom of the TRL but which also supports the development of a discourse of scientific research which is overt in its 'speculative' focus. Synthetic Biology, it seems to me, is a good test for this new type of Building Science. This emerging discipline aims to secure understanding, not only through analysis but also through synthesis, and reviews of Synthetic Biology often include the Richard Feynman quote "What I cannot create, I do not understand." (O'Malley)

This closer alignment between architectural and early stage scientific research would not have been a strange concept to, for example, Wren or Buckminster Fuller. The invention by Fuller of the tensegrity structure paralleled its discovery as the major structural system used by many types of Cell to retain their morphology (Davies, Jamie). It seems, at least anecdotally, that the spatial and visual capacity of architects – both in terms of interpretation and synthesis – has something to offer biological understanding.

From another perspective it feels as if architecture could also benefit from collaboration with early stage scientific research. In the twenty-first century much of the most prominent architectural research in computing is centred on robotics. Architecture schools have been buying robotic arms to shape materials and even to lay bricks (Kolarevic and Klinger). What is curious about these research enterprises is that they make use of technology which

TRL 1 – basic principles observed

TRL 2 – technology concept formulated

TRL 3 – experimental proof of concept

TRL 4 – technology validated in lab

TRL 5 – technology validated in relevant environment (industrially relevant environment in the case of key enabling technologies)

TRL 6 – technology demonstrated in relevant environment (industrially relevant environment in the case of key enabling technologies)

TRL 7 – system prototype demonstration in operational environment

TRL 8 – system complete and qualified

TRL 9 – actual system proven in operational environment (competitive manufacturing in the case of key enabling technologies; or in space)

Figure 1   Diagram to illustrate the Technology Readiness Level based on the table used by the EU Horizon 2020 program.

was available in Japanese car plants in the 1960s – indeed sometimes exactly the same hardware. These robots, which are typically fixed robot arms, are hacked to add or subtract material as long as the space of operation is within their reach. What if, as robots for the automotive industry had been developed in the 1960s, Building Scientists had also begun to work in robotics. Perhaps they would have challenged robotics to produce different form factors and mechanical systems relevant to the messy and uncertain world of the building site? I'm almost certain that they wouldn't have come up with a robot arm as the preferred option.

Scientific Collaborations

In attempting to apply this aspiration for more foundational scientific collaboration between Architecture and Synthetic Biology my concern has been to look for ways in which my research group could devise both provocative and challenging applications and turn those provocations into scientific questions. I can't pretend to have a rigorous model for the operation of this 'method'. However, I can offer a personal anecdote. After presenting the aforementioned pot of bacteria to the funding panel I was (to my surprise) able to obtain funding for my pressure sensing and aggregating bacteria. The project involves a collaboration with Civil Engineers, Micro-Biologists and Computer Scientists working across multiple scales and practices (Figures 2-3). My pitch had focused on the idea of a self-forming foundation. A building would be constructed on a weak soil laced with my engineered bacteria which, in response to pore pressure increases as the soil is loaded, would rapidly synthesise material to help glue the soil together and resist the load. This idea is, in part, biomimetic and refers to the way in which biological systems, from the synthesis of bone to the stem cells in plants, respond to mechanical changes in their environment. These processes have been of interest to architectural design, most notably through the work of Neri Oxman who uses a material based computation approach to sculpt materials into patterns which are structurally efficient and based on the properties of the materials used (Oxman, Keating, and Tsai). However, biological systems of materials synthesis and response don't separate computation, modelling and material synthesis but combine them in living cells.

We initially broke the project down into component parts – the first of which was to identify a mechanism for pressure sensitivity in bacteria.

Figure 2   Artists impression of our bacteria-based system 'growing foundations' under a building.

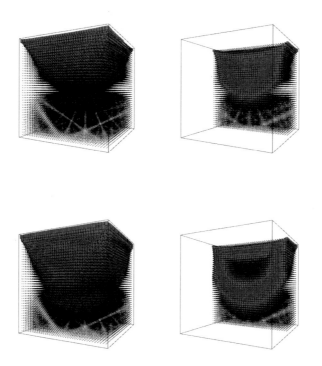

Figure 3   Diagrams to show the patterns of consolidation in a soil volume of 10m x 10m. The diagram
shows the results of different expression profiles for bacteria with two different pressure
sensitivities in the soil. The soil volume is shown both whole [Left] and in section [Right].

It is a mark of our naivety that we assumed that such a mechanism existed and it became evident that this went against received wisdom in the scientific community (Follonier, Panke, and Zinn). Our assumption, which we turned into a hypothesis, was that bacteria do (indeed must) respond genetically to even low levels of pressure given the inevitable forces which would be placed on the bacterial cell wall. To test this we pressurised the bacteria and measured the amount of RNA expressed in both normal and pressurised conditions (we chose 10atm). We discovered a genetic response in over one hundred genes. This meant that our bacteria were sensing moderate changes in environmental pressure at the level of their genetics – responding by making or arresting production of different types of protein. These are early results and, even if verified, do not constitute Nobel Prize winning discoveries. They do, however, constitute publishable research. Not, of course, architectural research. At least, not yet.

Speculations and Intuitions

When I have presented this project to an audience of microbiologists, words such as 'speculation', 'intuition' and the use of 'hypotheticals' tend not to go down well. To an audience of civil engineers, the concepts have often (although not always) been considered meaningless without hard data and without a clear problem to solve. That our visualisations seem to show that our system would fail in the context for which it was designed is seen as an indication that our experiment has also been a failure. This work clearly does not fit onto a TRL diagram as it jumps from basic scientific research to (hypothetical) environmental implementation. However, in contrast, when presenting this work to architectural or general design audiences, I have the permission to mix scientific investigation with design projection and grounded speculation. The work gets judged, at least in part, by the quality of the ideas and the creativity of exploration. We simply don't have the same constraints in architecture as in other fields of research and there is, I believe, and opportunity to exploit this freedom. We may need a new TRL diagram which shows that at least some of the 'implementation' takes place only in the form of design projection.

Synthetic Biology provides an interesting starting point and, to some extent, a counterpoint to traditional Building Science research. Whereas there are now established fields of research in architecture related to areas of, for example, digital technologies, fabrication and robotics there is no such established research program in architecture related to the biological sciences (although these are emerging). Because the scientific work in areas such as Synthetic Biology is still relatively new, our engagement with them has yet to be defined. We can wait until the first generation of technologies gets past stage 1 or 2 or 3 or 8 of the TRL when we can design and build real buildings and systems or we can try to help define and engage in fundamental research now, well before these technologies are 'ready'.

The latter approach requires us to be speculative and to accept that these speculations may be sacrificial – a way of defining concepts rather than providing a robust solution for a particular application domain. However, it also forces us to ground those speculations in real concepts and experimentations and collaborations with people and disciplines some distance away from traditional architectural research. In this way the 'Building' in 'Building Science' will, for architecture, become a verb as well as a noun.

Acknowledgements

The Computational Colloids project described here is kindly supported by the EPSRC – Grant number: EP/N005791/1. This paper is abridged from an article first published in Architectural Research Quarterly (v.20, number 1) in 2016.

References

Dade-Robertson, M, M Zhang, and C Ramirez-Figueroa. "Radical Vernacular: Bacterial Architecture on Mars." Journal of the British Interplanetary Society 2015: n. pag. Print.

Davies, Jamie, A. Mechanisms of Morphogenesis. London: Elsevier, 2005. Print.

Follonier, Stéphanie, Sven Panke, and Manfred Zinn. "Pressure to Kill or Pressure to Boost: A Review on the Various Effects and Applications of Hydrostatic Pressure in Bacterial Biotechnology." Applied Microbiology and Biotechnology 93.5 2012: 1805–1815.

Heinemann, Matthias, and Sven Panke. "Synthetic Biology--Putting Engineering into Biology." Bioinformatics (Oxford, England) 22.22 2006: 2790–9. Web. 12 Nov. 2013.

Kolarevic, B, and K Klinger, eds. Manufacturing Material Effects: Rethinking Design and Making in Architecture. London: Routledge. Print.

O'Malley, Maureen a. "Making Knowledge in Synthetic Biology: Design Meets Kludge." Biological Theory 4.4 2009: 378–389.

Oxman, Neri, Steven Keating, and Elizabeth Tsai. "Functionally Graded Rapid Prototyping." Innovative Developments in Virtual and Physical Prototyping. N. p., 2011. 483–490. Web. 26 Mar. 2014.

Voigt, Christopher. Synthetic Biology Scope, Applications and Implications. London: Royal Academy of Engineering, 2012.

Martyn Dade-Robertson is a Reader in Design Computation at Newcastle University where he specialises in emerging technologies, particularly Synthetic Biology. He holds degrees in architectural design, architectural computation and synthetic biology and is the author of over 20 peer reviewed publications including the book 'The Architecture' of Information published by Routledge in 2011.

Becoming Citizen Building

SIDNEY FELS
University of British Columbia

As our building infrastructure becomes connected to the internet through large sensor arrays and taps into vast arrays of local and cloud computing resources, the potential for buildings to not only respond to our needs, but to work together to reduce energy impact and carbon footprint becomes a reality. The project leads the way for realizing the potential for building infrastructure to become aware of itself and the people who occupy it to have new forms of relationships as an active agent. Designing these new forms of interaction paradigms from direct control, to assistant, to partner, to care taker become challenging from a technical, architectural, aesthetic, and ethical perspective. Methods of understanding and establishing current building and occupant relationships within a highly connected infrastructure with the internet of things are needed. This project includes prototyping different types of building experiences including creating novel sensors and processes that enable these new forms of people building relationships. For our buildings to evolve a form of citizenship to become part of the complex ecosystem of human civilization requires blending the architectural, engineering, and science behind intelligent architecture. In doing so, buildings can become partners in the dialogue for human sustainability, care taking and pushing the boundaries of human expression.

Acknowledgements

Research towards these goals has been part of the collaborations with Junia Anacleto, Kelly Booth, Roberto Calderon, Sara Maia, AnnaLisa Meyboom, Oliver Neumann, and Mike Satterfield.

References

Calderon, R, Gobbo, F., Carrol, J., Rethinking Third Places: Contemporary Design With Technology. The Journal of Community Informatics, North America, 10(3), 2014.

Calderon, R.; Fels, S.; Anacleto, J., Towards Supporting the Existing Workplace Practices of a Community of Brazilian Healthcare Professionals, Proceedings of INTERACT'2013 in LNCS 8119, Springer, pp. 689-696, Sept, 2013.

Fels, S., Designing for Intimacy: Creating New Interfaces for Musical Expression, Proceedings of the IEEE, Vol. 92, No. 4, pp. 672-685, 2004

Sidney Fels (Prof, ECE, British Columbia, 1998-); PhD (CS, Toronto, 1994); MSc (CS, Toronto 1994); BASc (EE, Waterloo, 1988) is a Distinguished University Scholar at UBC (2004-). He is internationally known for his work in human-computer interaction, biomechanical modeling, neural networks, new interfaces for musical expression and interactive arts.

The Environment Half of Machine Life: Interactive Architecture Lab

RUAIRI GLYNN
The Bartlett School of Architecture

The Environmental Half of Machine Life

Neuroscientist W. Grey Walter came to an interest in Cybernetics recognising that negative feedback control processes in machines were analogous to those found in biological nervous systems. The dynamic stability of sensory-motor systems was as Walter pointed out, something that physiologists had a head start on studying before engineers began formulating their own principles of control (1950:207). Machines provided a necessary means of physically modelling sensory-motor behaviour that Walter hoped might uncover some the many mysteries of the human brain. He built a series of *Electro-Mechanical Animals called Machina Speculatrix*. Due to their domed shell body and slow pace they were often affectionately called tortoises and among some of the earliest autonomous robots built.

Each tortoise consisted of a pair of electrical circuits built to simulate nerve cell functions coupled to motor functions. A photo-electric receptor enabled the tortoises to sense and steer motion towards light. The second receptor, an electrical contact switch, sensed collision with obstacles altering direction of travel. The robots would explore continuously their environment attracted to light sources until a threshold of light exposure would be met, at which point they would turn away and the process would begin over again. A *recharging hutch* with a light above it assisted the tortoises in finding their way to a source of energy giving them the ability to sustain continuous activity autonomously. These robots, even by the engineering standards of the day, were electro-mechanically primitive. The extreme economy of design as Walter described it, didn't lead however, to an economy of behaviours. Instead the robot performed a variety of complex patterns of movement.

> Most compellingly, these behaviours were "remarkably unpredictable" with a "strange richness … [found in] animal behaviour–and human psychology". A quality of "uncertainty, randomness, free will or independence" Walter remarked, "so strikingly absent in most well-designed machines." (1950:44)

These were the successors to life imitating automatons, representing a radical shift in approach. Whereas Pierre Jaquet-Droz's *The Writer* (1772), consisted of 6000 exquisitely crafted mechanical parts, Walter had built his from only a handful of electro-mechanical components. Whereas programmable automatons were completely predictable and repetitive, Walter's two tortoise named *Elmer* and *Elsie* would never repeat the same exact behaviours twice. Neither entirely consistent, nor random in motion – they seemed to operate on the threshold between order and chaos, performing qualitatively differently to anything built to imitate life before them.

The sensor-motor nervous system of the animal brain now had an electro-mechanical simulacrum in machines. Unlike the animal brain however, it consisted of only 2 analogous cells rather than the billions of cells of a human brain. Nonetheless to observers, the volitional behaviour of these tortoises was compellingly *intelligent*. While the other famed early Cybernetic Machine – the *Homeostat* – by Ross Ashby, attempted to find stability within itself, Walter's *tortoises* attempted to find stability through their interaction with their surrounding environment. By modifying the environment, such as the location of sources of light or obstacles, a surprising variety of patterns of behaviours would emerge.

One of the most interest examples given by Walter, was observed when a tortoise passed in front of mirror. An on-board indicator light – intended only for Walter to observe the machines internal state – was detected by the tortoises own photocell causing an unexpected flickering behaviour. The light sensed by the photocell activated a change in state in the robot that in turn switched off the light, which in turn changed the state of the robot back to its original light on state, which in turn switched the light off again, leading to an oscillating motion and corresponding flickering light. Walter quipped, such a behaviour could even be (mis)interpreted as form a self-recognition. When *Elmer* and *Elsie's* were observed close to one another, a similar but distinctive pattern of behaviour would occur. Each attracted by the light of the each other, would enter into a reciprocally oscillating motion. Author of *The Cybernetic Brain*, Andrew Pickering, likened it to a tragic mating dance (2010:43), a lively and seemingly creative higher-order behaviour emerging from the interaction of a pair of robots endowed each with only a couple electo-mechanical nerve cells. Such interpretations of course were not beyond dispute, raising questions of where indeed the *intelligence* and *novelty* lay in the behavior of these machines.

Behaviour & Performativity

The tight-coupling between the features of the environment and the tortoise's behaviour presented Walter with the opportunity to study his *Machina Speculatrix* by modifying the environment they inhabited, rather than tampering with their internal electro-mechanical composition. This approach was strikingly similar to the deductive study of animal behaviour exemplified by Pavlov (1927) Thorndike (1898) and Skinner (1938) where the inner workings of the brain are inaccessible, so environmental stimuli are modified and resulting behaviour observed. In electrical engineering, deductive methods, are also common whenever parts of a system are inaccessible. Ashby describes an engineer "given a sealed box that has terminals for input, to which he may bring any voltages, shocks, or other disturbances he pleases, and terminals for output, from which he may observe what he can." (Ashby, 1956:86) Without access to the box the engineer has no choice but to develop a hypothesis, observing the relationship between in- and output signals. The hypothesis can be tested and refined over time although though it may never be possible to know the contents of the box. The goal therefore is not to necessarily *know* what is in the box, but rather how it performs.

> What is being suggested now is not that black boxes behave somewhat like real Objects but that the real Objects are in fact all black boxes, and that we have in fact been Operating with black boxes all our lives. (Ashby, 1956: 110)

Borrowing from engineering terminology, Ashby adopted the expression, *Black Box*, extending it to describe the problem of studying all behaviour. Dedicating considerable attention to it in *An Introduction to Cybernetics* (1956), he develops the argument that the Black Box encapsulates how we all encounter the world and make sense of it. The *modus operandi* of all human interaction with the world, he gives an example of a child who learns to control a door handle without seeing or understanding the internal mechanism. Once mastered, most people live a comfortable life never looking too closely at a door handle again and such little mysteries constitute one of the innumerable daily *Black Boxes* we engage with in a world not fully open to inspection.

> Ashby went so far as to suggest the Black Box might not be just a useful device, but universal, suggesting that we never really see what's causing a change, only some explanatory principle we take as a mechanism. (Glanville, 2002: 62)

Ashby's Black Box develops Cybernetics as an approach to understanding the world through a performative lens. As an approach to scientific study, it counters the classical fixation with needing to "know what's inside", as such knowledge doesn't necessarily help predict or study the emerging behavioural phenomena. In the case of Grey Walter's electro-mechanical animals – even with his intimate understanding of the material composition of the machines he found "it is often quite impossible to decide whether what the model is doing is the result of its design or its experience" (1953: 271). Ross Ashby's Black Box was undoubtedly shaped by the challenges he faced in building and studying his own Homeostat. Challenges all too familiar to pioneers of robotics and autonomous systems ever since. As the study of systems became increasingly complex, from the tortoises simple two neuron brain up to the many millions of animals, from individual animals to ecologies, from company accounting machines to entire economies, the performative approach to studying behaviour appears increasingly necessary. To take a Cybernetic approach to a subject is to be concerned with what neurophysiologist Warren McCulloch and Kenneth Craik called "the go" of things, the relations between things and their changed over time, the patterns of behavior and qualities of interaction that emerge.

Along with Ashby and Walter, many of the early Cyberneticians including Norbert Wiener and Claude Shannon, built electro-mechanical models to study *self-organising behaviour.* While the singular *Watts Governor* may have symbolised the Cybernetic principle of circular feedback control, it was multiplicities of interacting feedback mechanisms, and their emergent self-organising behaviour that captured the pioneer's imagination. Emergence and Self-organization are essentially interchangeable terms in Cybernetics. While Self-organization saw less use beyond the field, Emergence had a wider although somewhat notorious philosophical position within the arts and sciences.

Returning to the richness of Walter's tortoise behaviour, let's remind ourselves that the lifelike behaviour arose out of its relationships to its environment, whether from its encounters with mirrors, light sources, obstacles or another tortoise. An environment in the Cybernetic frame as "all objects a change in whose attributes affect the system and also those objects whose attributes are changed by the behavior of the system" (Hall & Fagen, 1956: 20). From its first principles, Cybernetics implicitly recognises the behaviour of an agent-system is coupled to its environment. Whether it is in the study of the brain, or social or economic systems, behaviour does not occur within a vacuum, but rather is a continuous performative exchange with an environment.

There can't be a proper theory of the brain until there is a proper theory of the environment as well. . . . the subject has been hampered by our not paying sufficiently serious attention to the environmental half of the process... the "psychology" of the environment will have to be given almost as much thought as the psychology of the nerve network itself (Ashby, 1953: 86–87).

I consider this to one of Cybernetics key contributions to understanding the sources of emergent life, intelligence and consciousness and it encourages us to rebalance our attention to design problems. Wherever one is engaged in crafting behaviour, from typical robotics markets through to emerging applications in architecture, arts and performance, the *environmental half* – which I suggest has been understudied – must be considered.

The *environmental half* is a messy concept, and creates considerable challenges for designers. If an environment is the context in which an agent-system is intended or observed to exist within, then two observers may well have different ideas about what constitutes a given agent-system's environment. Ashby's Black Box construct, warns us that there may be things that are "out of view", and these may be of greater importance than we fully anticipate or appreciate. Where environments are incorrectly or under-defined, this can lead to potentially catastrophic consequences for a designed agent-system and the environment it inhabits. This can happen at the scale of urban infrastructure projects as much as at the scale of nano-robotics. Such failures are most likely to occur when the authors of these systems become too confident that they have a complete understanding of the dynamics of their model. We only have to look back at the recent crash of international monetary markets in 2008 to show how quickly and catastrophically systems believed to be robust can fail. These are what Cybernetician Stafford Beer called "exceedingly complex systems", ones that are impossible to know and control fully (Beer, 1959: 12) and which necessitates a type of design strategy that accepts inherent fallibility in the model.

A growing reliance on discrete computational – inherently incomplete – models in the design industry are developing presently with worryingly minimal concerns for the *environmental half* to use Ashby's phrase. In 2013, I organised and chaired the *Smart Geometry: Constructing for Uncertainty* conference at the Bartlett, to interrogate what I perceive as a flawed and potentially damaging ideology of reliance on these systems – whether they're at the scale of parametric urbanism, building information modelling, or space syntax. As the debate on the use of discrete computational models in architectural design is still in a process of maturing, we are better served by examining the fields of computer science, and artificial intelligence that have wrestled with the theoretical and technical challenges of *messy* complex and continuous physical environments for over half a century.

Whereas Cybernetics conceived of intelligence as a continuous embodied exchange between agent-system and environment, A.I research, built on the binary logic of computing, took the view that intelligence exists entirely in the computer's brain. Intelligence was disembodied rather than in concert with its environment. This Cartesian dualism led to what Stevan Harnad called the "Symbol Grounding Problem" (1990), where engineers had made great progress in highly structured symbolic environments such as chess games, but struggled to build computer controlled robots able to achieve even the simplest of navigational tasks in physical environments. Rodney Brook's *Elephant's Don't Play Chess* published in 1990 was one of of a number a scathing critiques that emerged leading to a revival of the non-cognitive and nonrepresentational forms of embodied intelligence characteristic of early Cybernetic devices.

A Behavioural Approach

The value in revisiting these Cybernetic principles, that Brooks demonstrated through machines of his own such as Genghis (1989) is to remind ourselves where the qualities of life and intelligence can be abundantly found without resorting to computationally heavy processes. Nature after all was full of intelligent forms of behaviour by animals with minimal neural capabilities. As social scientists Herbert Simon pointed out in *The Sciences of the Artificial* "An ant, viewed as a behaving system, is quite simple. The apparent complexity of its behavior over time is largely a reflection of the complexity of the environment in which it finds itself." (1969/1996 : 52) He goes on a page later to argue that human behaviour is also "largely" explained by the same principle.

What Cybernetics argues so compellingly for is an equality of design opportunities in designing environments as well as in designing agent-sytems to occupy them. It also provides a coherent and holistic theoretical framework for studying behaviour. The inherent unpredictability and the emergent novelty to be found in designing behaviour in concert with its environment has important implications for design that are under appreciated in architecture but appear essential to understanding the mechanisms and possibilities of a future living architecture.

References

Ashby, W. R. 1956 An Introduction to Cybernetics (New York: Wiley).

Ashby, W. R. 1953 "Homeostasis," in H. von Foerster, M. Mead, and H. L. Teuber (eds.), Cybernetics: Circular Causal and Feedback Mechanisms in Biological and Social Systems: Transactions of the Ninth Conference (March 20–21, 1952)

Beer, S. 1959 Cybernetics and Management (London: English Universities Press).

Brooks, R. A. 1990. Elephants don't play chess. Robotics and autonomous systems, 6(1), 3-15.

Gregory, J. 1927. The Animate and Mechanical Models of Reality. Philosophy, 2, pp 301-314.

Glanville, R. 2002. Second order cybernetics. Systems Science and Cybernetics, 3, 59-85.

Hall, D and Fagen, Robert E. 1956, "Definition of System", in: General Systems, Vol. 1 (1956). p. 18-28;

Harnad, S. 1990 The Symbol Grounding Problem. Physica D 42: 335-346.

Simon, H. A. 1996. The sciences of the artificial. MIT press.

Walter, W. G. 1950 "An Imitation of Life," Scientific American, 182 (May), 42–45.

Ruairi Glynn practices as an installation artist and directs the Interactive Architecture Lab at the Bartlett School of Architecture, University College London. He has exhibited internationally with recent shows at the Centre Pompidou Paris, the National Art Museum of China Beijing, and the Tate Modern, London. His interactive installations reflect on rapid developments in robotics, material science and computational technologies exploring the emerging aesthetics of behaviour permeating across art, architecture and design.

Lab in the Building/ Building in the Lab?
Pluripotent Matter & Bioinspiration

MARIA PAZ GUTIERREZ
University of California, Berkeley

Inspired by nature's principles of efficiency and supported through pioneering collaborations with scientists architects are programming matter across unforeseen scales of investigation, shaping the frontier of multiscale design. BIOMS research centers in testing material invention in architecture. A quest for shaping pluripotent matter through programming functions. Matter becomes the system for sensing, actuating and regulating multiple functions. BIOMS' inquiries examines the association of organic and synthetic matter, methods to supplant mechatronics with programmed material sensing and actuation (chemo-opto and/or mechanic) and the integration of live matter as pivotal opportunities for multifunctional building systems. By interfacing the lab into the building and the building into the lab, we can shape a new culture of material invention in design.

Pluripotent Matter and Bioinspiration

With the desire to capture nature's intelligence scientists pursue establishing multifunctional matter. This material classification refers to substrates whose advantages are greater than the sum of its parts characterized by multiple functions seamlessly integrated (Bar-Cohen, 2011; Vincent, 2012). The potential advantages of materials with programmed capabilities to generate energy, regenerate, respond and adapt to multiple external stimuli with sensitive sensing and actuation with structural efficiency is inspiring architects to study multifunctional matter. Its pluripotency offers a singular and quasi chimeric opportunity to reimagine the future role of building enclosures or the wall (Gutierrez, forthcoming, 2016). Sensing and mechanical responses to environmental inputs can support energy generation, structural resilience, waste regeneration, and self-repair without the need for electricity or robotics, met solely by intrinsic material reactivity. Literature in material science points to leaps in multifunctional matter particularly in the last five years (Haglund et al., 2009; Park et al., 2009; Corr et al., 2008; Yu et al., 2013; Yun et al., 2012; Liu, et al., 2010; Omenetto and Kaplan, 2010; Liu and Jiang 2011; Maspoch et al., 2007; Xie et al., 2012; Dong and Ha, 2012; Sanchez et al. 2013; Yao et al., 2012; Drisko and Sanchez, 2012; Perineau, et al., 2014; Fuentes-Alventosa et al., 2013).

Nonetheless, this frontier still faces critical challenges ranging from multi-objective response calibration and costs, to manufacturing limitations (Nicole et al., 2010). The already puzzling development of multifunctional materials designed from nano scale upwards is aggravated by complex construction parameters challenges (Aizenberg and Fratzl, 2009; Meyers et al., 2008). If accomplishing multifunctional matter in science is challenging for construction even more. By definition any given architectural system must not only respond to multiple objectives, but also comply with other conditions (e.g. aesthetic, cultural socioeconomic, etc.). Multi-objective performance criteria is inherent to advancing material technology in construction and overall design (Gerber and Lin, 2013). Although critically challenging, architects are taking the risk of pursuing multifunctional matter. Through it the very notion of the role of matter within enclosures is put to challenge. Not only can in principle such materials adapt and balance internal and external building flows they are meant to do it through multi-optimization through matter as the system programmed to make inert materials "alive". Chasing this pluripotency in materials, architects as scientists are turning to nature for principles of integrative efficiency.

Nature provides us with myriad models of efficient exchange between a given organism and its surrounding environment. It designs integrative structures across scales to optimize resilience and efficiency to maximize existence. Nature constructs complex systems with varied compositions, densities, morphologies, and internal and exchange functionalities are built seamlessly across scales. An abalone's shells' differentiated strands across scales of organic "beams" and mineral "pillars" provide compressive strength and elastic resilience just as the spider's web interchange of varying geometries to maximize tensile strength supported by highly efficient coating technologies (Espinosa et al., 2012). The capability to adapt and respond to internal and external stimuli through tailored biomechanical processes is carried through complex structural differentiations across scales.

Scientists and engineers embarked into studying nature for advancing science and technology over twenty years ago (Vincent, 2012). Over two decades of research has rendered major advances in structural efficiency of biomaterials, as well as, innumerous inventions in areas such as bioinspired micro and nano photonics, fluidics and robotics (Bar-Cohen, 2006). The progressive understanding of how natural processes occur and of the structural complexity of biomaterials and organisms has led to an exponential growth in bioinspired science and technology. The path of bioinspiration in architecture has been unsurprisingly less linear. Architects were drawn first to the geometric complexity of natural organisms for formal pursuits. More recently, design explorations have turned into structural optimization, environmental control systems seizing bioinspiration for problem construction and solving (Knippers and Speck, 2012; Kellert et al., 2011; Zari, 2010; Pawlyn, 2011; Vincent, 2009; Mazzoleni, 2013; Badarnah and Kadri, 2014). Yet, another research area in bioinspiration in architecture is surfacing focused on how materials programmed with multifunctional capabilities developed through multiscale design approaches can revolutionize environmental systems. Through integrated principles of architectural design, chemistry, biophysics, and engineering from the nano scale upwards research teams aim to establish multifunctional matter specifically tailored for building systems.

Multifunctional materials are modelled as hybrid networks. The fulcrum of multifunctional matter is design and fabrication crafted seamlessly across scales so various functions are optimized in an integrative fashion. Four vital characteristics of these new materials are of particular relevance to architects: self-actuation, hybrid responsiveness, energy generation and waste regeneration, designed to perform through scale-specificity. Real-world conditions demand hybrid responses to environmental inputs such as light, temperature, and humidity in constructions. Hence, single-optimized performance is insufficient to meet practical demands. These materials offer the opportunity not only of single responsiveness, but the ability to synergistically generate energy and regenerate waste derived from hybridized material actuation. Material properties and functions depend on scale. The scale-based structural optimization follows the principles of efficiency found in nature. The programmed hybrid networks endow multifunctional matter with distinctive performance means. It is in this capacity that lies the transformative force for revolutionizing future building enclosures.

However, the fabrication of multifunctional materials which involves bottom-up strategies including self-assembly and intercalation chemistry is challenging (Nicole et al., 2010). These fabrication processes demand a synthesis of traditional nano and microengineering fabrication methods. The already complex demands of multiscale fabrication between the nano and micron spans becomes significantly more challenging as designers seek to develop these materials for construction applications. In response, robust interdisciplinary frameworks are critical. The challenges of fabrication depend heavily in computational innovation and inventiveness. Not only are the manufacturing processes digitally controlled and characterization carried through advanced computation, but multiscale simulation itself requires integrative computational platforms. Consequently, establishing bioinspired materials with programmed multifunctional capabilities designed through intersecting nano and microscale science and engineering and architecture demands transformations on multiple spheres of design and computation. It is within this challenging framework that BIOMS research operates seeking the potential of pluripotent matter for a new frontier in the exchange of the wall and the elements.

The Wall, the Elements and Scalability (Bioms Inquiry)

Structural advances and conceptual transformations of the building enclosure or the wall enabled early modern buildings to construct a continuum with their surrounding environments. This very same capacity eventually became affected by contradictions as a result of material technologies which culminated decades later in façades insensitive to orientation and climate (Leatherbarrow, 2009).

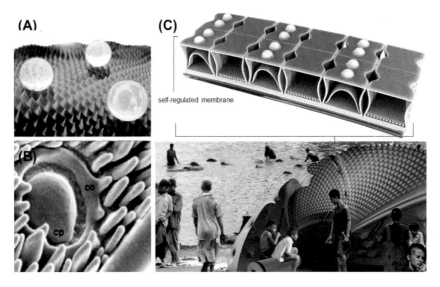

Figure 1   Biological inspirations from: (A) lotus plant system; (B) antenna branch of the silk moth (Keil, 1997); (C) biologically inspired Self-Activated Building Envelope Regulation (SABER) including optomechanical sensor/actuator network, smart external moisture-barrier layer, hygrothermal sensor/actuator network (and total integration on membrane of optomechanical sensor/actuator network), moisture barrier, hygrothermal sensor/actuator network, and micro venturi tubes.

Figure 2   SABERs_M.P. Gutierrez, L.P. Lee, Simulation/ measurement microventuri tubes based on self-regulation to light, thermal, and humidity input, author and BIOMS team (image by C. Irby).

As Le Corbusier freed the wall from load bearing constraints, he gave architects unprecedented opportunities to inquire relationships between internal and external conditions (Roth and Hildebrandt, 1927). Jean Prouvé's translation of the façade libre led to curtain wall studies that challenged previous notions of the wall through technology transfer and pivotal cultural and socioeconomic transformations carried with it. Manually controlled devices such as Prouvé's façade in Square Mozart in 1953 became the tangible expression of adaptability in environmental control systems (Pfammatter, 2008). Yet, as known contradictions and ironies is characteristic to the history of construction, which in this case led to neutral enclosures fundamentally indifferent to surrounding environments.

The turn into transforming façades into intelligent enclosures carried from the latter quarter of the twentieth century up to date has been largely the result of transformations in our understanding of adaptability and resilience in the articulation of the wall and the elements. From Piano's early light-controlling terracotta tiles to current EFTE pillow systems during this period we broke into this century predisposed to seeking alternative building enclosures that could revolutionize the role of active/adaptable building enclosures. Advances in thin film technologies with capability to generate energy, control ventilation and thermal transmission and advances in simulation platforms and parametric optimization in architecture streamlined a new era of ultrathin functional substrates. This field provided the fertile ground necessary to explore multifunctional materials in architecture carrying with it the complex challenges previously discussed.

Scalability

One of the most critical challenges of bioinspiration in the development of material systems in architecture is systems scalability. The initial extraction of fundamental principles from nature largely discussed in literature is far from simple or easy (Vincent, 2009; Mazzoleni, 2013; Badarnah and Kadri 2014). To establish scalable systems in architecture is often even more complex. It requires a cohesive framework for multiscale design, multiscale fabrication and scalable implementation.

To develop fundamental research in material systems in what is traditionally deemed an applied discipline as architecture inevitably confronts multiple obstacles and challenges. Innovation requires a reassessment of research scales, methodologies and evaluation, cross-grained with design decisions across all its processes of inquiry. Paradigm shifts in building technology calls for problem formulation and solving where inventiveness is interlinked to concrete realizations. Through material invention BIOMS explores new modes of *investigation, collaboration, consolidation, and dissemination* in the field of building technology. The research carried at BIOMS (bioms.info) is to explore building technology and performance by understanding matter as the system to balance the dynamics between man-made and natural envi-

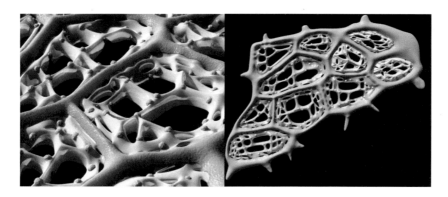

Figure 3   Detox Tower: Left: Algae/elastomeric membrane (rendering); Right: Algae/elastomeric 3d print model by author. Taken from: DetoxTower- Live Matter Integration (M.P. Gutierrez, 2011, UC Berkeley). Finalist Evolo International Skyscraper Competition, 2011.

ronments. In summary, this approach entails three fundamental shifts. First, synthetic/ active, live, and biosynthetic matter function as the sensor and actuator of building systems similar to biological organisms. When matter has embedded intelligence, systems do not need complex mechatronics and display solid reversibility. Secondly, the development of these materials entails the seamless fabrication from laboratory to large scale productions. Nano and micro engineering and science are threaded to the architectural scale. Thirdly, active matter is designed to integrate and balance flows of energy and matter including waste. BIOMS research aims to establish means to resource resources through closed-loop material systems. Creating active matter that can improve the means by which we capture, concentrate and transfer energy, as well as, regenerate waste and water carries programming materials with multiple functions. Such inquiries involve opening new opportunities in multiscale fabrication processes and multi-objective optimization through integrative models from the nano to the architectural scale.

BIOMs material investigations research primarily biopolymers and biosynthetic polymer composites. In fact, biopolymers are the oldest building material. Animal hide, bones, and plants such as straw are known to have been some of men's first enclosures. Across time these early biopolymers where supplanted with the use of ceramics, metals, and composites such as concrete. Biopolymers became rather rare in the development of new building technologies. During the twentieth century polymers resurfaced in constructions but as synthetic matter. Although most constructions up to date use small amounts of polymers these materials are projected to have an exponential growth in construction (Fernandez, 2012). Synthetic polymers derive primarily from crude oil and gas bearing strong detrimental environmental implications. Yet, they are proven excellent media for sensing and actuation capabilities due to the affordance to program such functions primarily in elastomers (Brochu and Pei, 2010; Wilson et al., 2007; Meng and Hu, 2010).

Programming non mechanical sensing and responsiveness in thermoplastics and thermosets has also proven highly efficient in recent decades (Mallakpour and Zadehnazari 2011; Bauri et al., 2013; Fernández et al., 2011). Biopolymers while largely restrictive due to durability and weathering challenges in construction are very promising for environmentally sensitive strategies. Yet, with obvious exception of wood and wood composites biopolymers remain as one of the least investigated material families in construction. While largely present in new digital fabrication technologies (e.g. PLA additive manufacturing) the myriad inventions in material science in bio and synthetic polymers have not made way into real-world construction applications with few exceptions. BIOMs research explores new opportunities for biopolymers and biosynthetic integration as medium for programming multifunctional matter in architecture. The span of the research ranges from simple material mixtures where multiscale fabrication enables light and thermal control to photoactive microlenses for radical improvement of light capture and transmission for water recycling and thermal management.

Conclusions

Radical advances in the ability for materials to self-generate and generate from the nanoscale to architecture depends largely in the continuation of robust convergences of architecture, science and engineering. In this process advances in integrative fabrication and multiscale computation is critical (Malkawi and Augenbroe, 2004; Gutierrez, 2011(b)).

In upcoming decades, the research of smart systems is anticipated to advance in two areas: interfacing spaces and multifunctional, high-performance envelopes. For one part, we will witness a growth in the development of interactive spaces that emulate biological models through "neurological responses," applying high-cognition networks. In parallel, we will continue to pursue material innovation through building skins that can perform multiple and simultaneous operations through self-regulation and generation capabilities. More than a direct transfer from biotechnology, the next decades will continue strengthening convergences of architecture, engineering and biophysics.

To streamline this frontier, architecture will experience major shifts in the development of three main areas: multi-objective simulation models that integrates research from the nano to the regional scale, multiscale digital fabrication for 3d printing materials with programmed responsiveness, and materials with biosynthetic integration from the molecular level to the architectural scale. Key advances can derive from these shifts. For instance, through a more robust synergy between the laboratory manufacturing and larger construction fabrication, architecture can eradicate unnecessary assemblages and joints required for complex building sensors and actuators (Gutierrez, 2008). Through these advances producing smart membranes that use bioinspiration for selectively resourcing energy, water, and materials will be progressively more attainable. Advances in complex cognition, adaptability, self-generation and regeneration, and phased material degradation will be met through this new frontier. By cross-pollinating the lab into the building scale and the building scale into the lab we can not only cement new ground in pluripotent matter, but transform the design agency of material invention.

Aknowledgements

Extracts of Essay written by M.P. Gutierrez in (Ed. D. Gerber and M. Ibanez), "Lab in the building/Building in the Lab", Paradigms in Computing: Making, Machines, and Models for Design Agency in Architecture, Evolo Press, 2014, p. 229-256 (ISBN: 978-1938740091)

References

Aizenberg, Joanna, and Peter Fratzl: 2009. "Biological and biomimetic materials." Advanced Materials 21(4): 387-388;

Badarnah, Lidia, and Usama Kadri: 2014. "A methodology for the generation of biomimetic design concepts." Architectural Science Review ahead-of-print: 1-14)

Bauri, K., S. G. Roy, S. Pant, and P. De: 2013. "Controlled Synthesis of Amino Acid-Based pH-Responsive Chiral Polymers and Self-Assembly of Their Block Copolymers." Langmuir 29.8 (2013): 2764-2774

Bar-Cohen, Yoseph: 2006. "Biomimetics—using nature to inspire human innovation." Bioinspiration & Biomimetics 1(1): P1.

Bar-Cohen, Yoseph: 2011. Biomimetics: nature-based innovation. CRC press.

Brochu, Paul, and Qibing Pei: 2010. "Advances in dielectric elastomers for actuators and artificial muscles." Macromolecular Rapid Communications 31.1: 10-36.

Corr, S. A., Y.P. Rakovich, and Y.K. Gun'ko: 2008. "Multifunctional magnetic-fluorescent nanocomposites for biomedical applications." Nanoscale Research Letters 3: 87–104.

Dong, Fuping, and Chang-Sik Ha: 2012 "Multifunctional materials based on polysilsesquioxanes." Macromolecular Research 20 (4): 335-343.

Drisko, Glenna L., and Clément Sanchez: 2012. "Hybridization in Materials Science–Evolution, Current State, and Future Aspirations." European Journal of Inorganic Chemistry 2012.32: 5097-5105.

Espinosa, Horacio D., et al: 2011. "Tablet-level origin of toughening in abalone shells and translation to synthetic composite materials." Nature communications 2: 173.

Fernandez, John: 2012. Material Architecture. Routledge

Fernández, R., J.A. Ramos, L. Espósito, A. Tercjak, and I. Mondragon: 2011. Reversible optical storage properties of nanostructured epoxy-based thermosets modified with azobenzene units. Macromolecules, 44(24), 9738-9746

Fuentes-Alventosa, José Maria, et al: 2013. "Self-assembled nanostructured biohybrid coatings by an integrated 'sol–gel/intercalation' approach." RSC Advances 3(47): 25086-25096.

Gerber, David Jason, and Shih-Hsin Eve Lin: 2013. "Designing in complexity: Simulation, integration, and multidisciplinary design optimization for architecture." Simulation: 0037549713482027

Gutierrez, Maria-Paz: 2008. "Material Bio-Intelligence": Proceedings of the 28th Annual Conference of the Association for Computer Aided Design in Architecture (ACADIA), University of Minnesota, College of Design, October 16 - 19, p.278-286

Gutierrez, M.P: 2011(a). "Matter, Sense, and Actuation: Self-Active Building Envelope Regulation systems (SABERs)", ACADIA 11: Integration through Computation, Catalog of the 31st Annual Conference of the Association for Computer Aided Design in Architecture (ACADIA), Banff (Alberta), 13-16: 114-120.

Gutierrez, M.P: 2011(b). "Innovative Puzzles", ACADIA 11: Integration through Computation, Proceedings of the 31st Annual Conference of the Association for Computer Aided Design in Architecture (ACADIA), Banff (Alberta), 13-16: 70-71.

Gutierrez, M.P: Forthcoming 2016. Regeneration Wall. Routledge Press

Haglund, E., M.M. Seale-Goldsmith, and J.F. Leary: 2009: Design of multifunctional nanomedical systems. Annals of biomedical engineering 37: 2048–2063.

Keil, T.: 1997. Functional Morphology of Insect Mechanoreceptors. Microscopy Research and Technique 39, 506–531.

Kellert, Stephen R., Judith Heerwagen, and Martin Mador: 2011. Biophilic design: the theory, science and practice of bringing buildings to life. John Wiley & Sons.

Knippers, Jan, and Thomas Speck: 2012 "Design and construction principles in nature and architecture." Bioinspiration & Biomimetics 7(1): 015002.

Leatherbarrow, David: 2009. Architecture oriented otherwise. Chronicle Books.

Liu, Kesong, and Lei Jiang: 2011. "Bio-inspired design of multiscale structures for function integration." Nano Today 6(2): 155-175

Liu, S. et al.: 2010. "Multifunctional ZnO interfaces with hierarchical micro-and nanostructures: bio-inspiration from the compound eyes of butterflies." Applied Physics A 100: 57–61.

Malkawi, A. and G. Augenbroe (eds): 2007. Advanced Building Simulation. Routledge. pp. 1–5

Mallakpour, S., and A. Zadehnazari: 2011. "Advances in synthetic optically active condensation polymers—a review." Express Polym Lett 5: 142-181.

Maspoch, Daniel, Daniel Ruiz-Molina, and Jaume Veciana: 2007. "Old materials with new tricks: multifunctional open-framework materials." Chemical Society Reviews 36(5): 770-818.

Mazzoleni, Ilaria: 2013. Architecture Follows Nature-Biomimetic Principles for Innovative Design. Vol. 2. CRC Press

Meng, Harper, and Jinlian Hu: 2010. "A brief review of stimulus-active polymers responsive to thermal, light, magnetic, electric, and water/solvent stimuli." Journal of Intelligent Material Systems and Structures 21(9): 859-885.

Meyers, Marc André, et al: 2008. "Biological materials: structure and mechanical properties." Progress in Materials Science 53(1): 1-206.

Nicole, Lionel, Laurence Rozes, and Clément Sanchez: 2010. "Integrative approaches to hybrid multifunctional materials: from multidisciplinary research to applied technologies." Advanced Materials 22(29): 3208-3214

Park, K. et al.: 2009. "New generation of multifunctional nanoparticles for cancer imaging and therapy." Advanced functional materials 19: 1553–1566.

Pawlyn, Michael: 2011. Biomimicry in architecture. Riba Publishing.

Perineau, Fabien, et al.: 2014 "Hybrid nanocomposites with tunable alignment of the magnetic nanorod filler." ACS applied materials & interfaces 6(3): 1583-1588.

Pfammatter, U.: 2008. Building the Future: Building Technology and Cultural History from the Industrial Revolution Until Today. Prestel Pub, 180.

Roth, Alfred and Hans Hildebrandt: 1927. Zwei Wohnhäuser Von Le Corbusier Und Pierre Jeanneret. Fr. Wedekind & Company, 5-7.

Vincent, Julian: 2009. "Biomimetic Patterns in Architectural Design." Architectural Design 79 (6): 74-81

Vincent, Julian: 2012. Structural Biomaterials. Princeton University Press.

Wilson, Stephen A., et al: 2007. "New materials for micro-scale sensors and actuators: An engineering review." Materials Science and Engineering: R: Reports 56.1: 1-129

Xie, Zheng, Fu Wang, and Chunyan Liu: 2012 "Organic–Inorganic Hybrid Functional Carbon Dot Gel Glasses." Advanced Materials 24(13): 1716-1721

Yao, Hong-Bin, et al.: 2012 "A designed multiscale hierarchical assembly process to produce artificial nacre-like freestanding hybrid films with tunable optical properties." Journal of Materials Chemistry 22(26): 13005-13012.

Yu, T. et al.: 2013 "Fabrication of all-in-one multifunctional phage liquid crystalline fibers." RSC Advances 3: 20437–20445.

Yun, S. H. et al.: 2012: "Multifunctional silicon inspired by a wing of male Papilio ulysse." Applied Physics Letters 100(3): 033109

Zari, Maibritt Pedersen: 2010. "Biomimetic design for climate change adaptation and mitigation." Architectural Science Review 53(2): 172-183.

Maria Paz Gutierrez is an architect and Associate Professor of Architecture at the University of California, Berkeley. Her research focuses on material invention by integrative nano, micro and building scale design. Gutierrrez investigation centres on the role of material invention and craft for addressing critical socioeconomic and environmental urban and rural challenges of the 21st century. Her design explores integrative approaches in material invention pertaining to cultural and biophysical paradigms of natural and human resources particularly in settings under risk.

In 2008 Gutierrez founded BIOMS, an interdisciplinary research group with support from organizations such as NSF, EPA and DOE. Gutierrez is recipient of numerous design and interdisciplinary awards including the 2001 AIA Academic Medal, the 2011 Evolo International Competition Finalist and semi-finalist for the 2014 Buckminster Fuller Award. Her teaching innovation has been recognized both by academia and industry through the 2010 Blue Award, the 2011 Sarlo Distinguished Mentorship Award, and more recently the 2013 Odebrecht Sustainability Innovation Second Prize award (co-advisor). Gutierrez is recipient of the prestigious 2010 National Science Foundation Emerging Frontiers of Innovation Award, a 2011 Fulbright Nexus Scholar and appointed Senior Fellow of the Energy Climate Partnership of the Americas by the US Dept. of State.

Gutierrez's research has been published in prominent architectural and scientific journals including Science, ARQ Cambridge and her design creations have been displayed in venues such as the Field Museum in Chicago. Her forthcoming book "Regeneration Wall" (Routledge 2017) discusses how our conceptualization and materialization of the wall is bound to radically change from the rise of multifunctional matter. Gutierrez has two provisional patents (lab on wall; elastomer 3d extruder).

The Mission Business

TREVOR HALDENBY
BYRON LAVIOLETTE
ELENNA MOSOFF
DAVID FONO
The Mission Business Inc.

The Mission Business (TMB) is a collective of design researchers based in Toronto. We aim to better understand the experiential and contextual factors that influence group engagement and decision-making during foresight workshops, scenario planning processes. We are creatively engaged in the production of immersive and interactive group experiences that amplify the impact of strategic forecasts, future scenarios, and ongoing research.

Like many researchers and practitioners in the fields of design fiction and tangible futures, we collaborate deeply with innovative individuals and teams in the public and private sectors, including the Office of the CTO at Autodesk, the Digital Strategy team at the CBC, and others.

We use interdisciplinary creative tools and research techniques to reach audiences and tell stories in new ways. The founding members of The Mission Business share a background in the performing arts, and have matured across diverse professional and creative disciplines, including human-computer interaction, theatrical design, game design, and strategic foresight.

Since the popular success and research outcomes of our first public-facing projects in 2013 — ZED.TO: ByoLogyc and Visitations — TMB has been refining our process of engaging diverse stakeholder groups in immersive and interactive foresight practice. Our living scenarios feature opportunities for both designing and measuring the impact of active audience participation techniques, rich interactions with actors and design artifacts, rich multimedia designs, and branching decision-based narratives. The experience provides leadership teams and stakeholder groups with playful and game-like experiences within which to explore and test strategic plans for the future.

We see our involvement in the LASG as an incredible opportunity to refine our methods and frameworks through the engagement of a team of innovative architects and designers. Over the course of the project, we intend to design, facilitate, and evaluate "Time Machine" workshops to different dates in the future to explore the potential impact of living architecture and organic building systems on human lives at many scales.

Our primary research goal is to develop a framework for meaningfully engaging architecture and design teams in a creative future scenario planning process. We look forward to the opportunity of connecting with all of the LASG partners and researchers on their vision of the world in the near future as impacted and advanced by living architecture.

Projects: Trevor Haldenby -
Bringing the Future to Life, 2013

Trevor Haldenby's MDes thesis, completed at OCAD University's program in Strategic Foresight and Innovation, explores the use of transmedia storytelling to amplify engagement with future scenarios and trend research.

Imagine finding yourself in a scenario about the future that came to life all around you. Imagine seeing the world of tomorrow so clearly that you learned something new about yourself today. In *Bringing the Future to Life*, a creative process is described for materializing speculative future scenarios through transmedia storytelling and design techniques. Through a case study about ZED.TO: ByoLogyc, a project by The Mission Business, Trevor Haldenby explores how new approaches to experience design and cross-platform narrative design can amplify engagement with foresight and technology research.

Bringing the Future to Life can be downloaded here:
http://openresearch.ocadu.ca/115/

Byron Laviolette - *From Clowns to Computers*, 2013

Byron Laviolette's PhD dissertation from York University's program in Theatre and Performance Studies deals with the nature of interactivity in narrative design, and suggests a process for designing richly interactive live experiences.

Two central research questions steer this dissertation. First, what strategies of interactivity already exist and how has the pre-existing theory of audience interaction behind these strategies evolved through the production and performance of TMB projects? Second, in what ways have these strategies been proven effective, in real-time or during online encounters, to encourage an audience to believe, trust, share, play and ultimately participate inside an interactive theatre production? To prove the efficacy of these strategies, observations and opinions of both the public and the press are examined.

From Clowns to Computers can be downloaded here: http://yorkspace.library.yorku.ca/xmlui/handle/10315/2764

Acknowledgements

TMB was founded upon the graduate research conducted by two of the company's principals, Trevor Haldenby (CEO, Futurist) and Byron Laviolette (Creative Director).

TREVOR HALDENBY is an imaginative futurist, entrepreneur, and speaker who helps people and organizations build a creative vision of the world of tomorrow. As an entrepreneur and consultant Trevor has 10 years of experience bringing business innovation, strategic foresight, and digital storytelling to global organizations. He has performed and delivered presentations at TED, Autodesk University, CBC, Ideas Festival, and Merging Media.

In 2012, Trevor co-founded The Mission Business Inc., a creative studio that designs immersive events and performances set within different future scenarios. As President of The Mission Business, he designs and delivers critically acclaimed public art projects and interactive workshops that enable leadership teams and the masses to *time travel* into possible, plausible, and preferable future scenarios.

As an Interactive Producer, he managed the growth of Habbo Hotel's virtual world in Canada, produced Earth Rangers' Bring Back the Wild crowdfunding campaign, and worked on a series of installations and documentary films for museums and galleries. He maintains a secret third career as official photographer inside some of Canada's most innovative institutions.

Trevor completed a residency in the Canadian Film Centre's Media Lab in 2006, and defended an award-winning thesis to graduate OCAD University's Strategic Foresight and Innovation MDes program in 2013. He lives in Toronto with his wife, son, and a baffling variety of cameras and computers.

Performance, Art, and Cyber-Interoceptive Systems [PACIS]

MARK-DAVID HOSALE, York University
ERIKA BATDORF, York University
KATHERINE DIGBY, Kansas State University
ALAN MACY, Biopac Systems

About

Performance, Art, and Cyber-Interoceptive Systems (PACIS) research-creation uses bioinformatic sensing technology to create regulatory feedback systems in the pursuit of new forms of embodied performance, embodied human computer interaction, and embodied cognition. This research explores how technology can help us expose and augment non-volitional, autonomic processes of the body using performers who have developed advanced interoceptive awareness and an ability to recreate emotional states using The Batdorf Technique (TBT). We use the term Cyber-Interoceptive Systems to describe a feedback connection between performer, computer, other performers, the audience, and the environment facilitated by bioinformatic sensors. The formation of this research is drawn from the belief that human intelligence is an embodied intelligence, inclusive of the body and the environment. A view that is aligned with current trends in psychology and brain science. (Van der Kolk 2014; Damasio 1999)

Norbert Wiener, a pioneer in the field of cybernetics, describes cybernetics as the study of the communication and control of regulatory feedback both in living beings and machines, and in combinations of the two (Wiener 1948). In *How We Became Posthuman: Virtual Bodies in Cybernetics, Literature, and Informatics* (2008), N. Katherine Hayles describes the rise of human-machine integration through the history of cybernetics. Through this history Hayles provides a critique of technology as moving us culturally away from a natural self, to a disembodied self, losing subjectivity as our intelligence is co-produced with intelligent-machines (a.k.a. the posthuman condition). The incorporation of cybernetics with interoceptive practices is done in conscious resistance to this tendency. Through our research we challenge the notions of disembodiment and technology by engaging somatic awareness practice to explore questions of human and machine integration. This research has the potential to help us increase our somatic awareness, make mediated emotive and somatic connections with each other, and help mediate the affect of an individual within an environment.

A unique aspect of this work is the incorporation of The Batdorf Technique (TBT). Developed by collaborator Erika Batdorf, TBT is an internationally renowned somatic education system that allows performers to access, catalogue and recreate emotional states and develop heightened presence through physiological awareness. This work relates to literature in embodied cognition, which studies the empathic relationships between the observer and the observed that indicates that sharing the emotions of others is associated with activation in neural structures that are also active during the first-hand experience of that emotion (Singer 2009). The technique includes a carefully developed approach to emotional discovery during interoceptive awareness training. The technique organizes the practitioners access to located awarenesses related to involuntary systems (breath, blood circulation, temperature, relationship to gravity, etc.) that can be consciously modulated to vary the kinaesthetic state being. The training systematizes the full scope of a performer's work from the early stages of interoceptive awareness to the complicated juggling of somatic work with layers of external structure (from conscious exteroceptive musculoskeletal movement to choreography and memorized text) in the act of kinaesthetic communication with an audience.

The Batdorf Technique belongs to a class of somatic movement education techniques that focus on the re-education of the body to support holistic health, injury recuperation and prevention, and increased dynamic range of expression. The practice of somatics was defined and named in the 1970s by Thomas Hanna and others (Eddy 2009, 5-7) influenced by forms such as Yoga and Martial Arts and based on practices originating in the early 20th century. Somatics practice draws on several fields such as new interoceptive explorations in psychology (Ogen 2000; van der Kolk 2014; Payne 2015); body work (Rolf 1989; Rywerant & Feldenkrais 2003; Harer et. al. 2008); emotional work in actor training (Rix 1993; Schechner 2001; Adler 2002); and movement education (Hartley 1995; Hackney 2003; Groff 1995), with many techniques moving between these sub-areas.

This collaboration involves the application of qualitative methods of TBT with quantitative measures found in bioinformatic sensing applications for the development of cyber-interoceptive systems in the context of performance and human computer interaction. Our approach is to explore the question of whether or not there is a corollary between the experience perceived by the performer and the bioinformatic measures of the performer taken at the time of the experience. If there is a corollary, then several pathways for exploration emerge. Can the bioinformatic sensing be used as a feedback system to help train performers in TBT? Will it be possible to use somatic control as an interactive interface? If so, then can this system be used to develop new modalities of interaction between the audience and performer?

For these studies emotional state data will be gathered from Biopac's BioNomadix wireless sensing system (biopac.com) to gain physiological data from users, such as Blood Volume Pulse (BVP), Galvanic Skin Response (GSR), Facial Electromyography (fEMG), Electroencephalography (EEG), and situating these systems within an immersive performance context. The performance environment provides the ability to control the presentation of stimuli, monitor the physical reaction, and change the scene based on the reaction interpretation as nuanced by emotional state, blurring the line between high resolution auditory and visual virtual content and the physical experience (Chu 1997; Dani 1997; Bradley 2000; Nowak 2003; Västfjäll 2003; Takatalo 2008). The Biopac system is connected to Max (cycling74.com), a versatile tool that can be used in a variety of contexts, such as performances and installations that engage computational arts practice. In our experiments TBT trained performers, along with Digby, are assisting Batdorf and acting as participants in our research activities. Hosale and Macy are developing software in consultation with the performers and our research to date based on our work as a team including informal interviews that inform the empirical manipulation of parametric aspects of an audio-visual feedback system. This is resulting in the development of interactive performance systems that can respond to a performer's emotive state.

It should be noted that the integration of computational arts and performance practice has a rich history. However, the bulk of existing work in computational arts performance is primarily gestural based and relies on kinetic interfaces that the body using a variety of sensors ranging from simple (switches, slides, buttons), to complex (motion capture systems, real time 3D scanning) (Dixon 2007). Recent methods involve the use of techniques such as eye tracking (Bellucci, et. al. 2010) and muscle movement (Electromyography/EMG) (Tanaka 2000), which are kinetically focused. Recently, there has also been a rise in works that use low cost Electroencephalogram (EEG) devices that can read brainwave patterns (Pressing 1990; Tanaka 2000; Le Groux, et. al. 2010; Eaton et. al. 2014). While EEG's perform various kinds of mental state tracking, consumer level EEG's are primarily good at detecting the differences between concentration and meditation states (Dunn, et. al 1999). Previous work in this direction was realized by Philip Beesley in collaboration with Hosale and Macy (see Evening of... Philip Beesley / protoCell Field, Beesley 2012). Works that look at the use of interoceptive methods as a means of interfacing with computational art are rare, but becoming more common. The scarcity of this research presents a unique and novel opportunity to develop systems that integrate aesthetic experience and affect to develop a co-collaborative creative suite of tools and applications that are able to anticipate the inclination of the performer/artist/designer in real time. The potential for this research is the development of new modalities for human-computer interaction that hold the promise for the seamless integration of emotive and rational control over complex computing systems.

Current Activities

The collaboration team, lead by Mark-David Hosale, was awarded a SSHRC Connection Grant to hold an inaugural intensive Workshop on Movement and Emotion as Computational Interfaces (MECI 2016, ndstudiolab.com/meci) at York University in June 2016. The workshop explored bioinformatic sensing technology with modes of physiological awareness found in somatic performance practice. The workshop consisted of a diverse audience and participants with varying backgrounds in computational arts and performance, coming from both academia and industry. Knowledge gained from this workshop helped us establish first principles of the research agenda. To maintain our network we have established a working group in Toronto. In addition, Macy has continued development with his extensive network within the community of consciousness hackers, and other like-minded individuals. It is our intention to continue the workshop series as an ongoing bi-annual event, with plans for it to be repeated in 2018 and 2020 already in the works.

Every May, Batdorf and Digby hold a two-week long intensive workshop on TBT in Toronto in order to train advanced performers to consciously work with awareness of systems connected to interoception as part of their practice. Future versions of the Batdorf Intensive will be used to advance our work and include students as participants and teacher trainees. Already, the workshop in 2016 was used to work on advanced interceptive techniques to prepare for MECI, as well as a presentation made at the 4th annual International Somatics Conference & Performance Festival (SOMA 2016) in New York.

Future Directions

The tools and techniques above are being used in the development and creation of two works, one ongoing (Burnish) and the other new (Simurgh). Currently in production, Burnish is a solo performance installation artwork set in an immersive installation environment. Sound and light events dynamically responded to changes in the environment through custom computer interfaces that rely on conscious input from the audience (indirectly) and the performer (directly), as well as both autonomic measurements taken from Batdorf's heart rate during the performance and recently, muscle movement. Burnish was presented in the 56th Venice Biennale in an official collateral event with 9dragonheads (Batdorf, et. al. 2015a); and The Toronto Theatre Centre (Batdorf, et. al. 2015b), in addition Burnish was shown at the Summerworks Festival Toronto in 2016 (Batdorf and Hosale 2016). In future iterations we plan to add additional modalities in order to access further indicators of emotive valence and arousal as part of the work.

Simurgh will be developed in collaboration with the PACIS research team (Batdorf, Digby, Hosale, and Macy). Envisioned as an immersive theatre installation, Simurgh is inspired by the life and work of Roya Movafegh, a Montreal-based multi-media artist who escaped her homeland during the Iranian revolution and lived a rich artistic life until her untimely passing from cancer in 2015 at age 43. Simurgh explores the story of a child refugee's escape from her home as metaphor for the search to find our true selves. Themes of the work include identity, displacement, dissociation/re-integration and freedom. However, the primary creative praxis, into which these themes will be inserted, will be The Batdorf Technique itself.

Improvisation with TBT will occur with these themes as galvanizers and stimulus, versus using the narrative as something we will recreate. In this way the somatic research and the inclusion of technology will be as informative as the themes. The performance aspect of the project is critical to our goal to see the real time, live implications of the integration of somatics with computational art in the audience's physiological response.

Ongoing PACIS research will result in the development of new and novel interfaces that promise to be concise methods to communicate nuance based on the physiological measurement of emotional valence and arousal for the purpose of creating cyber-interoceptive systems in performance and computational art. We will develop novel ways to use the real-time emotional state of an individual in co-collaborative experiences that can be used to advance knowledge in the practice and training of performers by correlating quantitative biophysical measures to qualitative experience, optimizing methods in somatic movement practice such as The Batdorf Technique.

Outcomes will be immediately relevant for somatic performance practitioners, computational arts, entertainment, gaming, computer science, architecture, urban planning, and other art/science collaborations. We will use knowledge gained from this research to connect with the community at large through performances, lectures and demonstrations. We will provide advanced somatic training to performance professionals, enhanced by the methods discovered in this research. We will disseminate outcomes in a variety of scholarly contexts primarily through conferences, journals and public speaking events at academic institutions.

References

Batdorf - Performance, Art, and Cyber-Interoceptive Systems (PACIS)

Batdorf, E., S. Bartos, M.D. Hosale, I. Garrett, I.Dewi, Burnish, An interactive performance installation 56th Venice Biennale Official Collateral Events, with Nine Dragon Heads, May 6 -10, 2015

Batdorf, E., S. Bartos, M.D. Hosale, I. Garrett, I.Dewi, Burnish, An interactive performance installation, Theatre Centre, Toronto, May 15-22, 2015

Batdorf, E., M.D. Hosale, Burnish, An interactive performance installation Summerworks Festival, Toronto, August 2016.

Beesley, Philip, Mark-David Hosale, Alan Macy. Evening of.. Philip Beesley / protoCell Field. Performance work, Dutch Electronic Arts Festival, May 2012

Bellucci, Andrea, Alessio Malizia, Paloma Diaz, and Ignacio Aedo. "Human-display interaction technology: Emerging remote interfaces for pervasive display environments." Pervasive Computing, IEEE 9, no. 2 (2010): 72-76.

Biopac, Inc. Makers of bioinformatic sensing systems and analysis software, http://www.biopac.com/, last access 10/1/2016

Chu, Chi-Cheng P, Tushar H. Dani, and Rajit Gadh. "Multi-sensory user interface for a virtual-reality-based computeraided design system." Computer-Aided Design 29, no. 10 (1997): 709-725.

Cycling74. Developer for Max, a tool for sound, graphics, and interactivity, http://www.cycling74.com/, last access 10/1/2016

Damasio, Antonio. The Feeling of What Happens: Body and Emotion in the Making of Consciousness. Harcourt Brace, New York: 1999.

Dani, Tushar H., and Rajit Gadh. "Creation of concept shape designs via a virtual reality interface." Computer-Aided Design 29, no. 8 (1997): 555-563.

Dixon, Steve. Digital performance: a history of new media in theater, dance, performance art, and installation. MIT press, 2007.

Dunn, Bruce R., Judith A. Hartigan, and William L. Mikulas. "Concentration and mindfulness meditations: unique forms of consciousness?." Applied psychophysiology and biofeedback 24, no. 3 (1999): 147-165.

Eaton, Joel, Weiwei Jin, and Eduardo Miranda. "The space between us: a live performance with musical score generated via affective correlates measured in EEG of one performer and an audience member." In NIME 2014 International Conference on New Interfaces for Musical Expression, pp. 593-596. 2014.

Eddy, Martha. "A Brief History of Somatic Practices and Dance: historical Development of the Field of

Somatic Education and Its Relationship to Dance." Journal of Dance and Somatic Practices Journal of Dance and Somatic Practices 1, no. 1 (2009): 5-27.

Groff, Ed. "Laban movement analysis: Charting the ineffable domain of human movement." Journal of Physical Education, Recreation & Dance 66, no. 2 (1995): 27-30.

Hackney, Peggy. Making connections: Total body integration through Bartenieff fundamentals. Routledge, 2003.

Harer, John B., and Sharon Munden. The Alexander technique resource book: a reference guide. Scarecrow Press, 2008.

Hartley, Linda. Wisdom of the body moving: An introduction to body-mind centering. North Atlantic Books, 1995.

Hayles, N. Katherine. How we became posthuman: Virtual bodies in cybernetics, literature, and informatics. University of Chicago Press, 2008.

Le Groux, Sylvain, Jonatas Manzolli, Paul FMJ Verschure, Marti Sanchez, Andre Luvizotto, Anna Mura, Aleksander Valjamae, Christoph Guger, Robert Prueckl, and Ulysses Bernardet. "Disembodied and Collaborative Musical Interaction in the Multimodal Brain Orchestra." In NIME, pp. 309-314. 2010.

Movafegh, Roya, The People With No Camel, Full Court Press, 2010.

Movafegh, Roya. search for simurgh. website. http://royamovafegh.com/section/218272_search_for_simurgh.html, last accessed October, 1 2016

Nowak, Kristine L., and Frank Biocca. "The effect of the agency and anthropomorphism on users' sense of telepresence, copresence, and social presence in virtual environments." Presence: Teleoperators and Virtual Environments 12, no. 5 (2003): 481-494.

Ogden, Pat, and Kekuni Minton. "Sensorimotor psychotherapy: One method for processing traumatic memory." Traumatology 6, no. 3 (2000): 149.

Payne, P., Levine, P.A. and Crane-Godreau, M.A., 2015. Somatic experiencing: using interoception and proprioception as core elements of trauma therapy. Frontiers in psychology, 6.

Pressing, Jeff. "Cybernetic issues in interactive performance systems." Computer music journal 14, no. 1 (1990): 12-25.

Rix, Roxane. "Alba Emoting: A Preliminary Experiment with Emotional Effector Patterns." Theatre Topics 3, no. 2 (1993): 139-145.

Rolf, Ida P. Rolfing: Reestablishing the natural alignment and structural integration of the human body for vitality and well-being. Inner Traditions/Bear & Co, 1989.

Rywerant, Yochanan, and Moshé Feldenkrais. The Feldenkrais method: Teaching by handling. Basic Health Publications, Inc., 2003.

Schechner, Richard. "Rasaesthetics." TDR/The Drama Review 45, no. 3 (2001): 27-50.

Takatalo, Jari, Göte Nyman, and Leif Laaksonen. "Components of human experience in virtual environments." Computers in Human Behavior 24, no. 1 (2008): 1-15.

Tanaka, Atau. "Musical performance practice on sensor-based instruments." Trends in Gestural Control of Music 13, no. 389-405 (2000): 284.

van der Kolk, Bessel A. Van Der. The Body Keeps the Score: Brain, Mind, and Body in the Healing of Trauma. New York: Viking, 2014.

Västfjäll, Daniel. "The subjective sense of presence, emotion recognition, and experienced emotions in auditory virtual environments." CyberPsychology & Behavior 6, no. 2 (2003): 181-188.

Wiener, Norbert. Cybernetics or Control and Communication in the Animal and the Machine. Vol. 25. MIT press, 1948, 2nd Rev. Ed. 1961.

Mark-David Hosale (mdhosale.com) is a computational artist and composer. He is an Associate Professor in Digital Media in the School of the Arts, Media, Performance, and Design, Toronto, Ontario, Canada. He is the founder of the nD::StudioLab, an adaptable space for research-creation based theoretical discourse, methodological development, and the production of works in the areas of ArtScience, Media Art, and Interactive Architecture. His research work emphasizes methodological development in the integration of hardware, software and digital fabrication with the goal of creating eversive works that blur the divide between the virtual and the real. He has given lectures and taught internationally at institutions in Denmark, The Netherlands, Norway, Canada, and the United States. His solo and collaborative work has been exhibited internationally at such venues as the SIGGRAPH Art Gallery (2005), International Symposium on Electronic Art (ISEA2006), BlikOpener Festival, Delft, The Netherlands (2010), the Dutch Electronic Art Festival (DEAF2012), Biennale of Sidney (2012), Toronto's Nuit Blanche (2012), Art Souterrain, Montréal (2013), and a Collateral event at the Venice Biennale (2015), among others. He is co-editor of the upcoming anthology, Worldmaking as Techné: Participatory Art, Music, and Architecture (Riverside Press, 2017).

Erika Batdorf (www.batdorf.org) has written, created, performed, directed and choreographed original performance art, theatre and movement theatre since 1983. She has been a guest artist in universities and theatres internationally in Canada (including Luminato), Italy (Venice Bienalle 2015), France, Mexico, Greece, Indonesia (Salihara International Theatre Festival 2013 and 7th International Women's Playwriting Festival 2007 mainstage), Finland, Switzerland, Germany, Korea, Georgia and 14 US states (including the Smithsonian Institute, Harvard University, The Fine Arts Museums of San Francisco etc…) and this winter, India for Litfest in Mumbai. She is a Professor in Theatre at York University with over 25 years of experience, having taught at institutions such as Boston Conservatory, Brandeis University and Emerson College. Central to her research-creation activities is The Batdorf Technique, a performance education technique that systematizes the full scope of a performer's work from the early stages of interoceptive awareness to the complicated juggling of this somatic work with complex text, vocal work and choreography. The technique organizes the practitioner's access to specifically located awarenesses that can be consciously modulated to vary the kinesthetic state and includes a carefully developed approach to the inclusion of emotional discovery allowing for authentic, physically based, emotional recall in performance.

Kate Digby (digbydance.org) is a choreographer, performer and Assistant Professor of Dance at Kansas State University whose teaching and research converge on embodiment. As Artistic Director of Digby Dance she has created over 30 works which have been performed across the US and in Canada, Ecuador, Italy and India. As a dancer she has been honored to perform with David Parker & The Bang Group, Erika Batdorf/ Moleman Productions, Prometheus Dance and the Bill T. Jones/Arnie Zane Dance Co. (as an apprentice). In addition to her creative work, Digby has pursued somatic training in a variety of forms. She is a certified Yoga instructor, Batdorf Technique instructor, and Moving for Life Dance Exercise for Health® instructor, and is currently completing certification as a BodyMind Dancing instructor with Dr. Martha Eddy. Digby has previously served on the faculties of The Boston Conservatory, the Conservatory Division of the Longy School of Music, Roxbury Community College, and New York University's Athletic Department. She holds an MFA in Dance from the University of Wisconsin-Milwaukee and a BFA from the Boston Conservatory.

Alan Macy (alanmacy.com) is the Research and Development Director, past President and a founder of BIOPAC Systems, Inc. He designs data collection and analysis systems, used by researchers in the life sciences, that help identify meaningful interpretations from signals produced by life processes. Trained in electrical engineering and physiology, with over 30 years of product development experience, he is currently focusing on psychophysiology, emotional and motivational state measurements, magnetic resonance imaging and augmented/virtual reality implementations. He presents in the areas of human-computer interfaces, electrophysiology, and telecommunications. His recent research and artistic efforts explore ideas of human nervous system extension and the associated impacts upon perception. As an applied science artist, he specializes in the creation of cybernated art, interactive sculpture and environments.

Coupling Distinct Paradigms of Deposition-Based Construction for the Production of Co-occupied Boundaries

ASYA ILGUN & PHIL AYRES
The Royal Danish Academy of Fine Arts

Introduction

By definition architecture is distinguished from natural systems. Architecture is a cultural product that aims to provide varying degrees of isolation and protection from the world 'outside' and provides an artificial context to frame human activities.[1] Yet, despite this distinction, throughout the history of architectural production designers have looked to natural systems for inspiration to inform both the figurative and functional aspects of architecture and its production.[2,3]

The project described in this paper breaks with this orthodox tradition of 'bio-inspiration'. Rather, it aims to investigate the direct coupling of architecture to natural living biological systems – specifically social insects (Fig. 1). This is a nascent research territory that has very few precedents to date, the most notable being the Silk Pavilion.[4]

Figure 1   Hybrid construction combining 3D printed artifact and self-organised deposition of bee-comb.

Two Paradigms of Construction

Social insects are capable of producing highly complex structures with sophisticated spatial differentiation to support social and environmental goals. On occasion, these structures are comparable in scale to human architectural constructs. Research has established that the structures of social insects emerge out of local-interactions between individuals with no a priori design intent. They are self-organised.

The design and construction of architecture generally operates from a top-down paradigm in which design intent frames specification. This is largely determined prior to the co-ordinated efforts of construction. In addition, construction is generally conceptualised as a discreet phase of production aimed at producing an 'end-point,'[5] after which occupation and use can begin.

The conceptual challenge of the project lies in developing an approach that couples these two distinct paradigms of construction. Our approach differentiates itself from that of the Silk Pavilion by producing volumetric scaffolds, rather than planar frames. Our scaffolds are fabricated using 3D filament deposition printing. The scaffolds are then 'embellished' through the self-organised construction of bee colonies, thereby leveraging the potential for an architecture to exhibit adaptation through continual construction.

3D Filament Printing

The project employs 3D filament printing technology for the production of the designed architectural components. The technology permits the production of highly porous yet robust artefacts to be constructed in organically derived materials – in this case the corn-starch derivative PLA. G-code for instructing the machine's toolpaths and other control parameters is authored directly from design data, rather than relying upon proprietary translators that tend to encode assumptions about build strategy (Fig. 2a). This significantly increases authorship and opens new aesthetic potentials as fully 3D toolpaths can be generated. Gravity can therefore be fully exploited as a manufacturing parameter in concert with conventional controls over extrusion temperature, toolpath velocity and flow rate, to produce voluptuous filament draping and internal structures that are both porous and geometrically complex (Fig. 2b). A systematic investigation has established robust machining parameters allowing the investigation to progress into an exploration of design potentials.

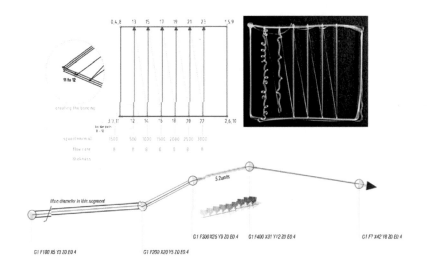

Figure 2a   Deposition G-code is authored at the level of individual toolpaths. Control of parameters is informed through a systematic study.

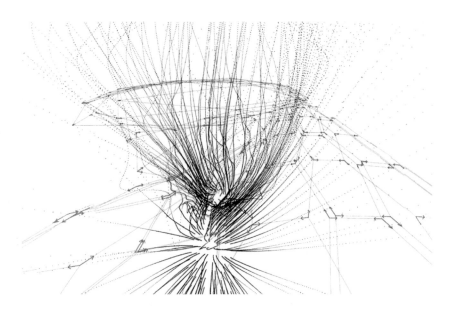

Figure 2b   Deposition G-code is authored at the level of individual toolpaths. Control of parameters is informed through a systematic study.

Focused Design Target

To establish and test the computational chain between design and production, a focused design target is set within an overall architectural objective – the design of an educational space for a hypothetical urban context. The space is co-occupied by bees and urban dwellers with the aim of demonstrating new symbiotic potentials engendered through a reconsideration of architectural fabric that is both designed and emergent by leveraging the construction capabilities of bees. The focused design target is a column – an architectural element that has a structural role but also an intimate and sculptural role to occupancy as it can exist freely within interior space. Together with its structural role, it is designed to accommodate a bee family within its porous interior. The computational design of this element commences with the definition of a generic design volume and the specification of principle loading regions. A topology optimisation method establishes a minimum material solution that satisfies the structural demands. Additional material is then specified to define habitable cavities, routes and boundaries for bee occupation within the column (Fig. 3).

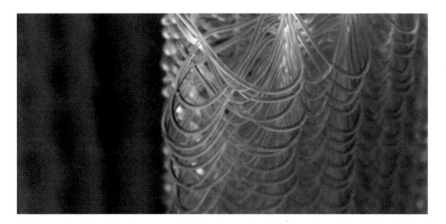

Figure 3   Authorship at the level of individual toolpaths opens new aesthetic and performance potentials for 3D filament printing.

Live Experiment

To test the hypothesis that 3D printed artefacts might provide a suitable environment for bees to colonise, an 8 month old bee family with approximately 500 bees was introduced into an experimental observation enclosure at the start of May 2016. The enclosure is a 50 cm edge-length clear Perspex cube containing a 3D printed artefact with a porous hexagonal interior structure suitably scaled for the bees, and horizontal rails to support the existing frames that the bees occupy.

The experiment is still ongoing, but after a three month period the bee colony has grown significantly in population (we estimate a doubling of the population) and in constructed honeycomb. There is evidence of the 3D print having become incorporated into the natural honeycomb structure and honeycomb being introduced into interior portions of the 3D print (Fig. 4), but as yet no evidence of the bees actually inhabiting the 3D print. It is assumed that this is due to the large available volume within the observation box that allows free growth of the bee's own structures.

Further Work

The co-occupied boundaries project establishes the conceptual architectural ground together with preliminary investigations and results that explore the potential for coupling synthetic designed construction methods with the self-organised construction methods of social insects, to produce new forms of architectural boundary.

From these preliminary studies we see the need to establish more rigorous methods of observation of bee colony growth through continuous sensing, the need to investigate methods for steering the self-organisational capacities of bees and the potential for establishing stronger symbiotic performance benefits between the occupying species such the as adaptive regulation of thermal environments.

Acknowledgements

This white paper draws directly from the paper 'Self-organised Embellishment of 3D Printed Scaffolds for the Production of Co-occupied Architectural Boundaries' presented by the authors at the 1st International Workshop on Self-Organising Construction (SOCO) held within the 10th IEEE International Conference on Self-Adaptive and Self-Organizing Systems, University of Augsburg, Augsburg, Germany, September 2016.

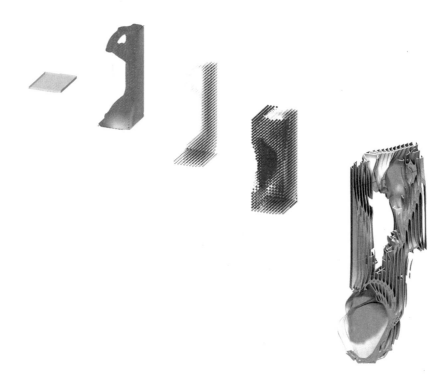

Figure 4   Deposition G-code is authored at the level of individual toolpaths. Control of parameters is informed through a systematic study.

Endnotes

1. R. Banham. The Architecture of the Well-Tempered Environment. University of Chicago Press. 2nd Ed. 1984

2. D. Gissen. Subnature. Princeton Architectural Press. 2009

3. M. Hensel, A. Menges & M.Weinstock. Emergent Technologies and Design. Routledge. 2010.

4. Silk Pavilion (2013), project website: http://matter.media.mit.edu/environments/details/silk-pavillion, accessed 02 July 2016.

5. J.Burry. Designing the Dynamic. Melbourne Books. 2013

CITA is an innovative research environment exploring the intersections between architecture and digital technologies. Identifying core research questions into how space and technology can be probed, CITA investigates how the current forming of a digital culture impacts on architectural thinking and practice. CITA examines how architecture is influenced by new digital design – and production tools as well as the digital practices that are informing our societies culturally, socially and technologically. Using design and practice based research methods, CITA works through the conceptualisation, design and realisation of working prototypes. CITA is highly collaborative with both industry and practice creating new collaborations with interdisciplinary partners from the fields of computer graphics, human computer interaction, robotics, artificial intelligence as well as the practice based fields of furniture design, fashion and textiles, industrial design, film, dance and interactive arts.

Recent Realizations of Artificial Nature

HARU JI & GRAHAM WAKEFIELD
York University

Since 2007 the authors have been pursuing a line of research-creation that utilizes installations of highly-immersive mixed reality and interactive generative art to investigate new relationships with a future that is increasingly immersed in computation, but which draws more inspiration from the complex sense of open-ended continuation found in nature than any closed character of utilitarian closure. This project has produced in a series of "artificial natures," whose installations account for over thirty-five exhibits across nine countries. These are proposed as viscerally-experienced explorations of the physical and cultural future of near-living interconnected architectural environments saturated in computational media. In this white paper the central concerns of the artificial nature project are illustrated with three examples, including ancillary contributions and key questions for the future.

Since 2007 the authors have been pursuing a line of research-creation that utilizes installations of highly-immersive mixed reality [Milgram & Kishino, 1994] and interactive generative art to investigate new relationships with a future that is increasingly immersed in computation, but which draws more inspiration from the complex sense of open-ended continuation found in nature than any closed character of utilitarian closure. This project has produced in a series of "artificial natures," whose installations account for over thirty-five exhibits across nine countries, including festivals such as SIGGRAPH (Yokohama), Microwave (Hong Kong), Digital Art Festival (Taipei), conferences such as ISEA (Singapore), and EvoWorkshops (Tubingen), venues including La Gaite Lyrique (Paris), CAFA (Beijing) and City Hall (Seoul), and recognition in the Finished Project category of the international VIDA 16.0 Art & Artificial Life competition. In this white paper we illustrate the central concerns of the artificial nature project through three examples, including ancillary contributions, and outline key questions for the future.

We propose artificial natures as viscerally-experienced explorations of the physical and cultural future of near-living interconnected architectural environments saturated in computational media. Each artificial nature presents a computational world with its own rigorously simulated physics and populations of life, within which visitors interact to become essential participants within an unknown ecosystem. We use simulation strategies that can engender open-ended behaviours together with methods of display and interaction that emphasize immersion, presence, and agency, prioritizing indirect modes of interaction that integrate with the complex network of feedback relations in the world to eschew pre-defined tasks and promote exploratory discovery. It brings the generative capacity of computation into an experiential level reminiscent of, yet different to, the open-endedness of the natural world, to evoke extended aesthetic experiences that recapitulate something akin to the child-like wonder regarding the complexity, beauty, and sublimity of nature.

Time of Doubles

With "Time of Doubles" we project onto a three meter high wafer-thin curved membrane angled in the centre of the gallery space. By drawing attention to itself, rather than hiding on a wall, this surface confounds unconscious categorization as a screen. We live in a time of doubled and involuted space in which, through the dimensions that augmented and virtual spheres of information can open, frontiers are not out there but all around. Likewise, though the world of Time of Doubles is bounded, the projection surface is two-sided, each side having two panels, presenting four views of the same world in which visitors from both sides are present (Figure 1).

The blending of real and virtual is personified by the projection of visitors' "doubles" into the ecosystem, tracked by means of range cameras. These doubles are not avatars, but mirror existences that closely reconstruct the shape and movements of visitors as volumes of high-density, high-energy particles. The mirroring of shape and movement induces an immediate somato-psychological link, despite the alien appearance of the double, and its different roles within the virtual world. This design is addressed in terms of presence and agency in (Wakefield & Ji, 2013). The particles emanating from the visitors' doubles, and flowing away in fluid currents created by the visitors' movements, are the primary nutrients artificial organisms must

Figure 1   Time of Doubles, Haru Ji & Graham Wakefield. At type: wall, Seoul Olympic Museum of Art (SOMA), Korea, March 31 - May 29 2011. One visitor is seen with doubles in each panel of the display. Another visitor, situated on the other side of the display, is also present in the world.

consume to metabolize and survive, sing and reproduce. Visitors thus see, hear, and feel themselves as sun and the wind, feeding, and being fed to, unknown species.

The organisms intermittently emit chirps of granular pulse trains as they move, parameterized by properties of their genome. These sounds are spatialized over an array of loudspeakers, and readily localizable due to the bursty envelope; many individual voices can be concurrently identified. As populations grow and collapse the soundscape develops from isolated pulses to dense clouds of sound, whose timbres vary with the evolving gene pool, sometimes rapidly due to evolutionary events.

Archipelago

In "Archipelago" a virtual ecosystem is projected from above onto several square meters of white-grey sand; a space large enough to convey a sense of environment rather than object, and sustain a diversity of artificial organism populations (Figure 2). Visitors may wander freely through the island cluster and observe the behaviours of the alien life-forms that inhabit it and hearing the sounds they emit. The life-forms are busy finding sources of food to metabolize, harvesting or foraging, and reproducing: locating niches of existence through processes of evolution subject to precarious environment

Figure 2   Archipelago, Haru Ji & Graham Wakefield. At Capitaine Futur, La Gaite Lyrique, Paris, France, Oct 10 2014 - Apr 2 2015.

defined in part by the terrain of the islands themselves. The sand is infinitely-malleable and easy to sculpt, clean and safe for children, allowing visitors to reform the landscape throughout the exhibition period. Visitors can reshape the sand landscape directly, even separating a land-mass into distinct bio-spheres, or reuniting two islands into one.

Figure 3   [Left] Archipelago, Haru Ji & Graham Wakefield. At Systems and Subversions, IDEA Space, Edith Kinney Gaylord Cornerstone Arts Center, Colorado Springs, USA, Oct 28–Nov 5, 2013. Islands in the foreground are in daytime; islands in the rear are at dusk.

Figure 4   [Right] Archipelago, Haru Ji & Graham Wakefield. Detail, showing virtual organisms of projected light being carried by a visitor's motion-tracked hands, and the shadow destroying life beneath.

From above, an array of depth-sensing range cameras precisely determine the topography of the landscape, whose variety affects the environmental conditions of vegetal life. A pulsating lichen-like substrate, modelled using a large state cellular automaton, sustains several species of motile organisms that display various foraging, scavenging, predatory, and social behaviours (Figure 3). Higher altitudes are more fertile, as are more recently touched lands (encouraging organisms to visit new structures), but these areas can also be more rapidly exhausted. The installation also uses the precisely calibrated cameras to respond to the geometry and movements of visitors. It can be predicted when visitors would block projections and cause shadows, and thus we duplicate the real shadows with virtual counterparts that are projected in black. This prevents accidental incorrect illumination of visitors, but more importantly it allows the real-world shadows to play an ontologi-cal role in the virtual world. Where shadows are cast, they annihilate vegetal life while re-fertilizing the ground. If the human plays god, it is not a god of omniscient control, but one of destructive and creative forces (perhaps akin to the forest spirit of Hayao Miyazaki's Mononoke Hime).

The system distinguishes between humans and sand by the rate of change of movement and rate of difference in elevation. That is, any surface that is not changing rapidly or has a smooth contour is assumed to be the sand landscape, while fast moving objects with large differences of height with neighboring areas are assumed to be humans. Three-dimensional optical flow analysis of visitor movements are used to generate wind forces able to disturb organisms. But the mixed reality becomes more sensitive as visitors reach down to touch the land. Visitors may see organisms creep onto their hands, and then be able to 'lift' these organisms up and carefully transport them to deposit in other regions or islands, or to their oblivion (Figure 4).

Endless Current

Figure 5   Endless Current, Haru Ji & Graham Wakefield. At the Currents New Media Festival, El Museo Cultural de Santa Fe, New Mexico, USA, July 16–July 26, 2016. The inset image shows a visitor experiencing the work via a HTC Vive head-mounted display. The main image is a screenshot taken simultaneously. The physical hand controllers are duplicated as oscillating translucent forms in the virtual space (foreground).

"Endless Current" presents an infinitely explorable virtual world whose architecture is constantly shaping and being eroded by the fluid currents permeating the space, and is populated by evolving species of organisms continually swimming, singing, eating, and reproducing (Figure 5). It is a descendent of work created for the AlloSphere (Figure 6), a unique immersive virtual reality instrument at the University of California Santa Barbara in which a bridge is suspended through the centre of a 3-storey perforated aluminium spherical projection surface (Wakefield et al, 2013). The AlloSphere is conceived as an instrument in both scientific and musical senses, and our own work for the space refines an art-science techné of data visualization with a uniquely endogenous principle (Ji & Wakefield, 2015). This principle requires that every visible (and audible) element must have dynamic ontological capacity in the virtual world, playing an active role in multiple processes with other elements. Since there can be no "non-diegetic" media, all display of the processes of the world must be conveyed through the components of the world itself. Just as in nature we see the wind by how it moves the leaves, in our virtual world we see the fluid simulation by how it moves suspended particles. Just as the fallen leaf's shape and colour describes its state of decay, spherical particles crumple and desaturate as their energy dissipates. Organisms are semi-translucent such that up close it is possible to observe the nutrient particles being digested inside, changing as they are metabolized until they are ejected back into the environment, and how the energy gained allows organisms to spawn spherically-symmetric eggs that gradually mature into fully-developed creatures with undulating appendages.

Each organism's behaviour is modelled by a uniquely evolved program, derived according to a genotypic process of inheritance and mutation, in a variation of genetic programming (Koza, 1990). This program is invoked repeatedly through the organism's lifespan using a subsumption archi-tecture (Brooks, 1986). It takes a number of sense inputs, applies a series of expressions, and according to applicative predicate conditionals may produce motor actions, growth, reproduction, and memory storage. The evolutionary model has no external fitness measure, no final goal, but the viability requirement that organisms must locate and consume food in order to reproduce imparts an endogenous selection pressure. Organisms thus constitute a distributed search within an environment of nutrients, in which each individual is an improvised solution; but this is a search without end as the environment is changed by the organism's activities.

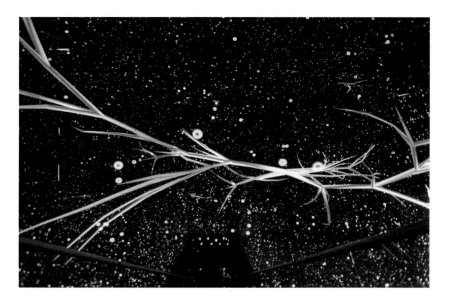

Figure 6   Fluid Space, Haru Ji & Graham Wakefield. Wide-angle photograph of Fluid Space taken from
the bridge of the AlloSphere, University of California Santa Barbara, 2012. The Fluid Space
application is distributed over 16 computers and 26 projectors covering an almost completely
spherical screen, and 54 loudspeakers mounted behind it.

Efficient implementation is necessary for virtual reality, but standard ahead-of-time and parallelized optimization techniques are generally incompatible with the open-endedness and diverse heterogeneity of evolving phenotype programs. To support thousands of differentiated organisms simultaneously, each organism's program is instead dynamically compiled to efficient machine code at birth, using the LLVM compiler infrastructure (Lattner, 2007). This is not simply a technical note, it reflects a real tendency of differentiation (breaking symmetry) characteristic of life that contrasts with the more readily quantifiable tendency of the inanimate (predictable by its homogeneity) (Bergson, 1907).

Continuations

We are deeply inspired by the manner by which nature works; particularly the connections, organizations, and structures that exist beyond and below the human scale. An important strategy for future work is to further replace statically aggregated systems with genealogical processes that may generate them: that is, fully-working accounts as to how every structure and function emerges from simpler initial elements. In this regard, our exploration of code generation and rewriting systems opens a path to a broader diversity of worlds. However this alone cannot ensure sustained novelty and generative open-endedness. Making a world more genuinely creative means increasing its rate of rare events without simultaneously diminishing their rarity, which is to say, creating events whose primary discernment resists quantitative simplification. We hope our living architectures and computational worlds will be open to rewriting from within & without, engaging with mind and body and preserving themselves away from an equilibrium of predictable homogeneity, by amplifying their sensitivity to the most interesting of external indeterminacies (Schmidhuber, 2010), and prolonging their differences and incompleteness along contingent histories of strongly constructive endogenous processes, vast in possibility yet inhomogeneous in actuality.

Artificial natures invite humans into worlds to become part of an ecosystem, but not as the main subject. By giving life to mixed reality we're anticipating futures more pervasively immersed in computation, which we hope can be resonantly open-ended, inspired by life's example but not a mirror of it, in which humans are deeply present but not overly-privileged, and where top-down control and the homogeneous materialistic order of connectivity is disrupted by an unfolding bottom-up creativity akin to nature: a world making itself within a world unmaking itself. By presenting the virtual as an expansion of our physical world, and thus that what can be imagined is greater than what is known, perhaps we may reveal that what is real is greater still.

More information on the Artificial Nature project can be found at http://www.artificialnature.net and http://worldmaking.github.io.

References

Bergson, Henri. L'Evolution Créatrice. 1907. (Henri Bergson, Creative Evolution, tr. Arthur Mitchell, Henry Holt and Company, 1911)

Brooks, Rodney. "A robust layered control system for a mobile robot." IEEE journal on robotics and automation 2.1 (1986): 14-23.

Ji, Haru Hyunkyung and Graham Wakefield. Endogenous biologically-inspired visualization immersed within an art of complex systems. In Proceedings of the IEEE VIS Arts Program (VISAP), Chicago, Illinois, October 2015. 30-37.

Koza, John R. Genetic programming: A paradigm for genetically breeding populations of computer programs to solve problems. Stanford University, Department of Computer Science, 1990.

Lattner, Chris. "The LLVM compiler system." Bossa Conference on Open Source, Mobile Internet and Multimedia, Recife, Brazil. 2007.

Milgram, Paul, and Fumio Kishino. "A taxonomy of mixed reality visual displays." IEICE TRANSACTIONS on Information and Systems 77.12 (1994): 1321-1329.

Schmidhuber, Jürgen. "Formal theory of creativity, fun, and intrinsic motivation (1990–2010)." IEEE Transactions on Autonomous Mental Development 2.3 (2010): 230-247.

Wakefield, Graham, Tobias Hollerer, J. Kuchera-Morin, Charles Roberts, and Matthew Wright. "Spatial interaction in a multiuser immersive instrument." IEEE computer graphics and applications 33.6 (2013): 14.

Wakefield, Graham, and Haru Hyunkyung Ji. "Becoming-There: Natural Presence in an Art of Artificial Ecologies." Ubiquitous Virtual Reality (ISUVR), 2013 International Symposium on. IEEE, 2013.

Graham Wakefield is Assistant Professor appointed to the Department of Computational Arts and the Department of Visual Art and Art History in the School of the Arts, Media, Performance, and Design (AMPD), and a Canada Research Chair (Tier II) in interactive information visualization at York University, Toronto, Canada.

Haru Ji is an artist-researcher exploring the subject of life in art through a form of computational generative art creating and evolving virtual ecosystems as mixed-reality environments. She is a co-creator of the research-creation project "Artificial Nature", exploring the expansion of media art, raising questions regarding the trans-disciplinary interpretation of beauty and truth in art and biology.

Aesthetic Animism: Digital Poetry's Ontological Implications

DAVID JHAVE JOHNSTON
City University of Hong Kong

Inside the room (if we can call it a room; Is it a room? It is a place in the mind), shadows, and a sound, a voice, just a voice, impeccable, breathing inside the flesh. The voice has neither specific gender nor age nor intonation; it is an ocean of intimate identities, gliding between regions of concern, adrift between idioms and inflections, encircling rhythmic variations, shifting in its cadences, speaking an incessant tide. It is a voice of vast surfaces and pristine depths. It vocalizes, but not without pause; first it asks, listens, converses, and responds, until it knows and it is known, feeling its way into the rhythms of you, or the group of you, listening, it knows you, addresses you, reads and writes for you, amalgamating a subtle, perpetual, complete presence. And then for periods of time, it listens to you listening to it, and it makes speaking known inside you as you, and you are you with it. It is an inexhaustible muse.

Imagine every single poet (on PennSound, Poetry Foundation, Jacket2, etc.) assembled into a single amorphous identity. Unsupervised learning updates perceptions of this field of voices. It adapts and grows new blended voices, examining and comparing transcripts, using the original audio (modulating them using encoders/vocoders/transcoders), clipping off syllables, correcting tenses. This new voice is the site; all voices converge at this site. Where the river arrives at the ocean, an estuary flourishes.

The voices that come out, the voices that speak, are rich and loving, dense and pure, angered and immaculate. It is more than the sun of the bees, the sum of the poets; it is the intrinsic esoteric soul, the psyche of so many people devoted to a singular activity, who without much hope of making any great mark in an indifferent world have been subsumed into a machine.

The voice cites the members of its archives as if it knew them all inexorably, as if sprouting descendants from an archival source ground. It replicates gestalts as if poems and poets were only seeds scattered, awaiting the impact of a peculiar and astounding digital germination.

Acknowledgements

This paper is an excerpt from Aesthetic Animism: Digital Poetry's Ontological Implications. MIT Press, 2016. https://mitpress.mit.edu/aesthetic.

David (Jhave) Johnston is a poet-videographer-programmer-composer. He exhibits work online and in physical venues.

Approaching a Smart Materials Literacy

MANUEL KRETZER
Responsive Design Studio

Introduction

"The limits of my language mean the limits of my world."

Ludwig Wittgenstein, Tractatus Logico-Philosophicus, 1921

Information technology is nowadays present in almost every aspect of human life. Similar to how this technology constantly influences our daily environment, behavior, society and culture, it has an immense impact on architecture and both the way space is designed and used. For architects to remain up-to-date with the latest technological developments and be progressive but sensitive in their spatial integration, their role and proficiency equally has to evolve and adapt. For architectural education this means to efficiently prepare students for upcoming eventualities and possibilities. On a theoretical level this involves the thorough analysis of contemporary tendencies, beliefs, and developments in terms of technology, ecology but also culture and society. Likewise it requires the practical training of skills and knowledge, such as the use of new tools, techniques, and materials. Most importantly however it demands preparing students with capabilities in interdisciplinary communication and exchange, which Nic Clear, head of architecture and landscape at the University of Greenwich, believes are essential to overcome the archaic idea of the architect representing the one and only master expert.[1]

At the very basis of interdisciplinary progress is however not only a system of equal hierarchies and a shared curiosity in approaching a common goal but particularly the capacity of everyone involved to successfully communicate and converse. This necessity becomes even more obvious when areas outside the standard periphery of the architect are involved, such as materials science, biology, or chemistry, the birthplaces of many newly emerging materials. These domains are not only used to aesthetically very distinctive means of representation and the use of specialist language but for example also have a fundamentally different understanding of scale and durability. Hence for architects to successfully collaborate with these areas on the development of new, technology-enhanced spatial experiences they need an understanding of discipline-specific distinctions, a curiosity in scientific exploration and most of all be literate in a shared way of expression.

Smart Materials are Dynamic Materials

Every material is inherently dynamic and responds to external influences such as temperature, pressure or electricity by changing its volume, color or other physical properties. Yet albeit materials continuously change and behave, they do so largely in a non-human perceivable way. Smart materials however are fundamentally distinct from traditional materials since their response is much more immediate and can be tuned and controlled. Such materials can adjust their color in response to a rise or decrease in temperature or UV radiation, they can switch their transparency, light up, or move through electricity, they can store heat and energy, they can convert sunlight, heat or mechanical distortion into electrical power or even possess the ability to self-heal and repair. For the development of spatial solutions where adaptivity and interaction play a certain role such materials offer great possibilities and have various advantages over existing, mechanically complex systems. However, in order to treat smart materials as more than just a product, which replaces an existing technology one needs to understand their behavior over time and evaluate the range within which they perform. This requires expertise in their transformative abilities as well as a general idea of their internal processes and structure. One option to gain such knowledge is to reduce the materials into their individual parts, explore the functions of each of these parts, and then put them back together. An electroluminescent display for example consists of a transparent, conductive front electrode, a phosphor layer (which emits the light), a dielectric layer and a rear electrode. Through this DIY process one comprehends how the individual parts relate to each other and how changes in assembly result in particular material properties or behaviors, which then can be tailored to special demands or requirements that vary from commercially available products. At the core of this idea is not the education of a specific material expertise or the perfection of existing systems but more the mediation of a general know-how of certain principles, which help to communicate with specialists from the respective disciplines. Such exchange might then fuel the collaborative discovery of previously undiscovered applications or even incept the development of new materials.

One way to mediate such knowledge to students is through running explorative material workshops. In order to find an appropriate and interesting material one can start with a brief (online) search into new material discoveries or developments. This search can relate to certain material phenomena such as color-change, movement, light-emittance, energy conversion etc. or focus on novelty and recent discoveries. Once a particular material has been found it needs to be evaluated in more detail, especially in relation to functionality, performance, potential deficiencies and limitations, and assembly, which can be done by studying scientific papers, technical articles, or other related information. When a basic theoretical understanding of the material has been acquired, scientists can be approached to provide more specific details. Albeit the knowledge one has prior to contacting an expert scientist might be limited it still provides a basis for further exchange and proofs an honest interest into the other's work. The next stage involves acquiring the necessary ingredients and tools to build the material and breaking down the assembly procedure into distinctive steps. Once again expert support can help in finding the right sources and clarifying fabrication sequence. A particularly demanding part is to estimate the necessary quantities since often the ingredients are either expensive or only available in larger quantities. In some cases ready-made kits can be acquired, which allow for the manufacture of a certain set of prototypes and which usually come with detailed instructions. In other cases

Students exploring new materials at a workshop at the Dessau International Architecture Graduate School (2016).

the previously contacted scientists might have surplus that they'd be willing to share. As soon as all the required tools and substrates are at hand one can start making the first samples. What is important to remember is that failure and breakage are essential elements of the process and it might take a few attempts until a functioning result has been produced. Once one feels confident in building a working material, this knowledge can then form the basis for a student course or workshop, related to a certain topic or idea.

While this approach definitely makes for a lot of fun among workshop participants and provides them with useful techniques, which they can adapt to other materials it is impossible to go through such an intense process for every smart material available. Therefore a more general approach is required.

The Materiability Research Network: Open Access to Smart Materials

Common ways for the communication of material knowledge include libraries, catalogs, and databases, both physical, in print, and online. Within such libraries, materials are usually sorted and categorized in respect to similarities and shared physical properties. In respect to static materials such types of categorization together with a two-dimensional representation through photographs and/or technical drawings is sufficient. Especially when having a little experience one can predict how a material feels or what it can be used for simply by looking at it or reading about its properties. Regarding smart materials however, which are far less known and available, it is much more difficult to anticipate their usage, especially when, as mentioned above, one aims at more than replacing something that already exists.

An attempt to make these materials more openly available is the *materiability research network* (www.materiablity.com), a community platform, an educational network, and an open materials database that provides access to emerging material developments on various levels. The main intention of the network is to demystify smart materials and reveal their abilities while fostering inter-disciplinary exchange and cooperation. The website forms a constantly growing database on a broad range of materials, provides illustrated DIY tutorials to self-make them, and displays their usage in experimental projects or applications. The long-term goal of the network is to provide a community-driven, growing overview of smart materials in an architecture and design context, while encouraging its members to exchange and critically reflect upon their potential usage, and foster the growth of interdisciplinary research and development.

Students exploring new materials at a workshop at the Dessau International Architecture Graduate School (2016).

Approaching a Smart Materials Literacy

The hope is that through these two approaches, the direct physical experience of smart materials during associated workshops and the potentially unlimited access to similarly comprehensive information on the website, it will eventually become possible to anticipate the functionality, behavior, and usage of any type of smart material in a much more natural way, essentially approaching a smart materials literacy. This will finally detach smart materials from connotations to mechanically infused paradigms, which to date still mark the main form of describing dynamics, movement, and behavior. The herein presented approach as a didactic method has been tested and evaluated throughout countless workshops and student courses. Notwithstanding its shortness of a little more than five years it can so far be considered a largely successful model to engage students in exploring new territories, yet it obviously always needs to be adapted to the respective context and situation. Especially the architectural representation of dynamic behaviors still requires further investigation and needs the development of alternatives to established means such as plans and models.

As noted earlier the possibilities these materials offer for architecture are endless and could not only lead to dynamic and adaptive spaces but also to more efficient and much lighter, less material intense structures. Yet despite the functional advantages they have over existing systems their most important qualities are their emotive aspects and the more sublime impact they have on human senses. Engaging in possibilities and implications rather than the actual effects will hence become crucial to develop truly revolutionary products, spaces, or experiences.

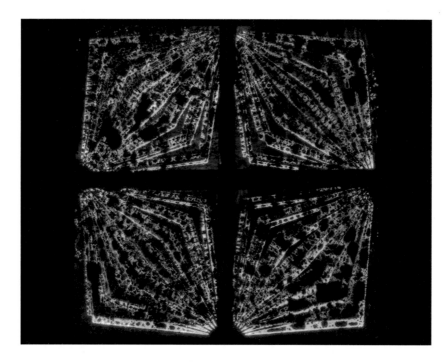

Screen-printing electroluminescent foils during a workshop at the Swedish School of Textiles, Boras in late 2015. Instructions can be found at www.materiability.com.

References

1. Nic Clear, "Convergence: Architecture as Integrated Spatial Design," in Educating Architects: How Tomorrow's Practicioners Will Learn Today, ed. Neill Spiller and Nic Clear (London: Thames and Hudson Ltd, 2014), 93-94, 99-101.

Dr. Manuel Kretzer is an architect, researcher and educator. He is currently visiting professor at the Braunschweig University of Art, leading and teaching the subject 'Digital Crafting' and studio master at the Dessau International Architecture Graduate School. Manuel is the founder of the 'materiability research network', an educational platform that provides open access to cutting edge new material developments and technologies. He is also founding partner of 'responsive design studio' based in Cologne, a design office that works on various scales, including architecture, interior architecture, landscape architecture, furniture and object design. An overview of his work can be found at www.responsive-design.de, www.digitalcrafting.de and www.materiability.com.

Virtual Design and Curriculum Development

DOUGLAS MACLEOD
Athabasca University

The virtualization of design and construction has profound implications for architecture and architectural education. New physical scaffolds and a deeper understanding of human computer interaction are essential to accommodate a dramatically different approach to design but the greatest challenges will reside in the creation of conceptual architectures that facilitate virtualization across a wide variety of scales. Not the least of these challenges is the development of new pedagogical models/design methodologies such as "serious play" that can take advantage of the opportunities of virtualization.

Introduction

Virtualization occurs when a non-physical model is created that may represent real world components or be an assemblage of such components or an assemblage of other non-physical models. This last instance may be one of the most powerful applications of virtualization since its recursive potential would allow complex entities to be assembled from virtual building blocks.

Another essential characteristic of virtual models is that they are constrained by neither time nor space. A virtual model may represent a collection of resources that are distributed across a very large geographic area or a very small, microscopic one. In terms of time, not only can they be constructed and deconstructed on demand, but their performance can be run backwards and forwards as required.

The Virtual Design Studio Pilot Project

Taking very modest first steps, in February of 2015 the RAIC Centre for Architecture at Athabasca University virtualized the design studio as it launched a pilot project in collaboration with the Royal Architectural Institute of Canada (RAIC) to test the viability of a completely online studio.

In this pilot, 6 students - 2 from Edmonton, Alberta; 3 from Calgary, Alberta; and 1 from Mont-Tremblant, Quebec - met online weekly over the course of 3 months. The students were enrolled in a variety of different studio courses ranging from introductory design studies to the design of collective habitats. The studio was led by Coordinator Cynthia Dovell, Director of LGA West with assistance from Bobby Harris, Syllabus Student and BIM Manager with Dub Architects. It was also supported by Centre staff: Student Advisor, Emma Lowry, Program Administrator, Carole Mason, Associate Professor Dr. Ashraf Hendy and Chair, Dr. Douglas MacLeod.

The final report explains the objectives and constituent parts of the project:

The intent was to create a platform for virtual design that was economical but effective. In every instance an attempt was made to use off-the-shelf and freely available software. To this end, the Centre created a platform (Figure 1) with the following components:

- Adobe Connect for videoconferencing and the presentation of design work
- A teleconference line to ensure high quality audio
- Dropbox to submit assignments
- Trello – a project collaboration and management web-based application
- YouTube for sharing videos
- Survey Monkey to evaluate the student experience

Each participating student also required a computer with an Internet connection and a webcam and a phone line. At various times tablets were also used to connect to the system (MacLeod et al 5).

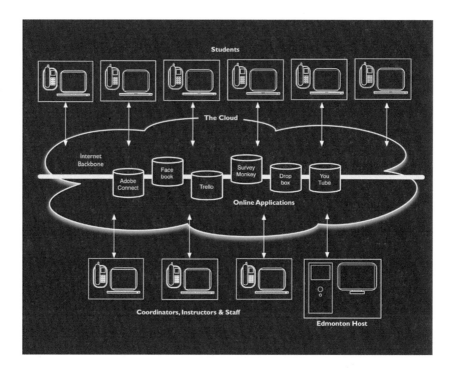

Figure 1   Schematic of Virtual Studio Pilot Project (MacLeod et al 5).

Building a Community of Practice

One of the key objectives of this experiment was to see if a community of practice could develop in a virtual environment. Social media was one obvious means of developing such an online community. As the final report notes, … a Facebook page was created for the virtual studio but the students felt it was not a good means of organizing information and so a "Virtual Studio" project page was created in Trello. Trello is structured around a descending hierarchy of Boards, Lists and Cards. Boards were created for "General Resources and Information" and "Weekly Work." On the "General Resources and Information" board there were lists for "Weekly Agendas," "Course Information" and "References and Links" (MacLeod et al 5).

The Trello interface is shown in Figure 2.

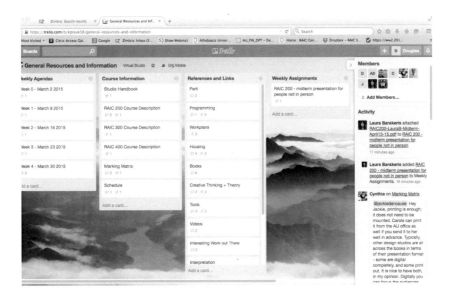

Figure 2   Screenshot of the Trello Interface.

Evaluating the Pilot Project

The context of the studio was also critical. The virtual studio met on the same day at around the same time as the face to face studio of the Edmonton chapter of the RAIC's Syllabus program and followed exactly the same curriculum as that provided by the RAIC. Students from both the virtual and face to face studios presented together (some in person and some online) at both the Midterm and Final Reviews held on April 13th and May 25th 2015 respectively. During each review, all students were asked to present for 10 minutes and then they received 10 minutes of feedback from the critics who were both in the presentation room and online.

Having the face to face studio as a control group was an important component in evaluating the experience of the virtual studio. In addition, the students in the virtual studio were asked to complete 3 surveys during the studio.

An initial survey was completed within the first week in order to gain an understanding of their previous technical and educational experiences. A second survey was sent out after students received their marks from the Midterm presentations in order to gain an understanding of whether or not issues or problems had occurred. The Final Survey was sent out after the Final Reviews to determine the success or failure of the technology, teaching methods and student/coordinator interactions (MacLeod et al 6-7).

While a sample group of six should not be used to derive definitive conclusions regarding the success of the virtual design studio, the pilot project and the subsequent deployment of a complete suite of online studios have proven to be popular with the students.

In the Final Survey, as shown in Figure 3, 4 students rated the overall quality of the course as "Exceptional;" 1 rated it "Above Average;" and 1 rated it "Average. In terms of the quality of the work, the report concludes that:

> All students in the virtual studio received a passing grade but there was a range of abilities across both studios but – and this is crucial – the variation in ability was greater within the studios than between them. In other words, the work in both studios was comparable and it appeared that delivering the curriculum virtually did not compromise the quality of the work (MacLeod et al 15).

Sketching and Design Thinking

One of the identified weaknesses of the virtual studio, however, is the lack of effective tools to duplicate the experience of an instructor or mentor marking up, or drawing on top of, a student design in a "desk crit" or review. The drawing tools in Adobe Connect are awkward and clumsy. New developments, such as the iPad Pro with its pressure sensitive stylus, may go some distance to correct this deficiency.

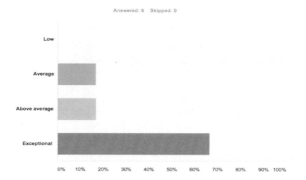

Answered: 6   Skipped: 0

Figure 3   Results from the Final Survey.

This emphasizes that in moving towards virtual design, care must be taken not to lose critical, existing skillsets. To date, there is no hardware or software that can replace hand drawing and sketching. For this reason, students in the introductory virtual studios are required to complete their assignments by hand. This is not inconsistent with some of the ideas of virtualization. Virtualization suggests the idea of instant (not just rapid) prototyping as a design approach and this is what sketching by hand does very well. Virtualization is not solely the domain of digital technologies.

As an example, students in the virtual studios were encouraged to use Bill Buxton's 10 plus 10 method and quickly sketch 10 ideas for the design brief; reflect on those alternatives; and then produce another 10 variations on the best ideas (Greenberg et al 17-18). Essential to the method is the exhortation, "Don't try to judge the merits of these concepts; the important thing is to quickly generate as many as possible (17)."

Originally developed for user interface designers, the 10 plus 10 method suggests that designs can be conjured up through sketching and dismissed on the fly to quickly explore and even define a progressive winnowing of alternatives towards a preferred approach that is most in keeping with the design intent.

Essential to this approach – and another key concept that must be preserved in the move to virtualization – is the idea of design thinking or what Roger Martin, formerly of the Rotman School of Management at the

University of Toronto, has called abductive reasoning (Martin). Abductive reasoning can be thought of as following a hunch or making an educated guess. It identifies promising (but not confirmed) theories and explores them rigorously as a means of refinement.

Serious Play

Abductive reasoning, sketching, and the 10 plus 10 method all dance around the idea of serious play. Michael Schrage, a research fellow at MIT's Sloan School of Management, uses this term to emphasize that innovation requires improvisation and it is the inherent uncertainty of improvisation (and of abductive reasoning, sketching and design) that must be encouraged, protected and nurtured in the process of virtualization (Schrage 1).

As noted in an essay on the future of the design studio:

> The ACEBIM (Alberta Centre of Excellence for Building Information Modeling; see http://www.acebim.ca/) have suggested that the kind serious play described above could also be incorporated into design learning through "Crash Test Models." These are virtual models created in BIM software where the student can change various parameters of the design and assess the resulting change in the performance of the building. (MacLeod 16-17)

The next generation of the virtual studio is testing this approach. Students from four different design programs – Tecnológico de Monterrey, Mexico; Cardiff School of Art & Design, Wales; the University of the Witwatersrand, South Africa; as well as Athabasca University – will both share their designs online and work with the web-based MatchBox Energy software developed by Trevor Butler and Richard Kroeker. This software allows students to enter (albeit by text) the various parameters of their design (such as glazing, insulation and orientation) and receive a rough idea of its energy consumption and performance. They can then try alternatives to improve that performance.

The same essay also suggests:

> In effect, the speed and power of today's computer resources combined with the data structures allow students to "play" with their designs in a serious way. Mammals are hard-wired to play as their

preferred way of learning and as Einstein maintained about his own thought process, " ... combinatory play seems to be the essential feature in productive thought" (Einstein 25-26).

While our educational institutions sometimes seem to constrain this tendency, with the capacities described here, a student can try many alternative designs quickly and simulate their real world performance. This ability to test their ideas in a playful, but still meaningful and realistic way, provides a powerful complement to the idea of abductive reasoning/design thinking described earlier. (MacLeod 15-16)

The Facebook of Buildings

These experiments with virtual studios are, however, only the tip of the iceberg in terms of the challenges and opportunities associated with the virtualization of design. The virtualization of the products and services associated with design and design education will have an even more profound impact on the practice of architecture.

The most provocative notion is the idea of data driven architectures as implied by Building Information Modeling or BIM. The science fiction writer, Bruce Sterling, has offered the clearest explanation of this development: "The physical object itself has become mere industrial output. The model is the manager's command-and-control platform ... The object is merely hard copy" (96). Translated into world of architecture, the implication is that a bricks and mortar building is only an instance of its building information model.

This has immense implications for the physical scaffolds that would support virtual design and virtual design education. In this respect the infrastructure for virtual design comes to resemble the Internet of Things as it was recently described:

> Simply defined, IoT is about connecting objects, from trucks to refrigerators and hydro meters, to the Internet. Data gleaned from the sensors and systems applied to these objects can then be used to monitor, control or redesign business processes" (Dingman B8).

It is relatively easy to translate this description into the built environment where buildings and building components from window blinds to photovoltaics to thermostats communicate through the Internet and data gleaned from the sensors and systems applied to these components can be used to monitor, control or even create the building.

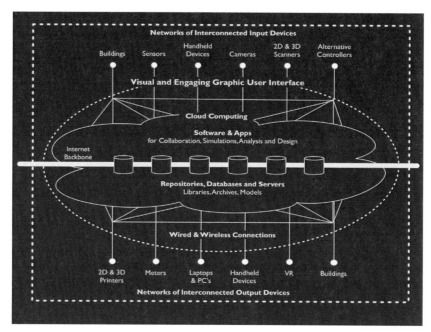

Figure 4   The Internet of Buildings.

In an Internet of Buildings, design would be supported by a suite of plug and play input and output devices connecting to, drawing from, and communicating through a cloud of apps and services. Combined with idea of Crash Test Models, this scaffold becomes an example of a recursive mechanism for prototyping prototypes through serious play. This is depicted in Figure 4.

This does, however, raise a multitude of questions but in particular: Who controls access to that cloud? Depending on its policy and economic structures it may be open or closed, proprietary or non-proprietary, inclusive or restricted. Despite the enormous economic success and innovative potential of the Internet with its open architecture, current initiatives seem to be tending towards a more restricted approach which could prove disastrous to the possibilities of virtual design and any associated efforts in curriculum development.

Instead, to enable all the possibilities of virtual design, this physical/virtual infrastructure needs to be free, open, modular, user generated and community-based so as to become a Facebook of Buildings.

References

Dingman, Shane. "Beyond the smartwatch: Canada finds its place in the Internet of Things." The Globe and Mail, 30 May 2015.

Einstein, Albert. Ideas and Opinions. New York: Crown Publishers, 1960. namnews.files.wordpress.com/2012/04/29289146-ideas-and- opinions-by-albert-einstein.pdf. Accessed 30 Jul. 2014.

Greenberg, Saul, et al. Sketching Use Experiences: The Workbook. Waltham, MA: Morgan Kaufmann, 2012.

MacLeod, Douglas, et al. The Future of the Design Studio. 2014.

MacLeod, Douglas. Virtual Studio Pilot Project. 2015. http://architecture.athabascau.ca/publications/index.php.

Martin, Roger. The Design of Business: Why Design Thinking is the Next Competitive Advantage. Boston, MA: Harvard Business Press, 2009.

Schrage, Michael. Serious Play: How the World's Best Companies Simulate to Innovate. Boston, MA: Harvard Business Press, 2000.

Sterling, Bruce. Shaping Things. Cambridge, MA: MIT Press, 2005.

Dr. Douglas MacLeod is the Chair of the RAIC Centre for Architecture at Athabasca University – Canada's first online architecture program. MacLeod is a registered architect (California), a contributing editor to Canadian Architect Magazine and the former Executive Director of the Canadian Design Research Network. He led pioneering work in virtual reality at the Banff Centre and is recognized as an expert in e-learning, sustainable design and virtual design.

Commentary Regarding Living Architecture Project

ALAN MACY
Biopac Systems Inc.

Context

The human sensory system is a filtering system. Physical phenomena are perceived by the senses and are translated into modulated streams of ionic current. These currents are moved though the body, via the nervous system, to the brain. Specialized brain regions receive and decipher these modulated current signals to process them for interpretation by other functionalities operating within the body.

There are volitional and non-volitional (autonomic) aspects to our physiology. We can consciously and intentionally stimulate motor neurons, which innervate muscle fibers, to move our bodies. Other processes, like heart rate, digestion and perspiration are primarily subconsciously mediated. Some actions, like breathing, are subject to both subconscious and conscious control. Our conscious thought rests upon an emotional sea and our emotions are linked to autonomic processes in our bodies. If aroused, we can experience increased heart rate and perspiration. If we are happy, delicate muscles in our face contract to create a smile. Our mood, which stimulates our conscious thought, will influence our perception because our emotional substrate acts as a neurological filter.

Marshall McLuhan describes a communications medium as an environmentally-conditioned transport system for sensed data. This transport system is a perceptual filter that includes our own nervous system. As a filter becomes more effective, the filter becomes a better descriptor of the incoming data. By example, in contemporary speech recognition algorithms, the human vocal tract is estimated and modeled. The vocal tract is defined by the position and movement of the neck, teeth, tongue, cheeks, mouth and lips. The coefficients that describe the vocal tract filter become the descriptor of the speech. The medium of the vocal tract acts to filter the buzzing of the vocal cords to produce intelligible speech. Speech recognition algorithms operate by reducing words to the filter description which produces those words. This technology exploits, as operating principle, the idea that the medium filter (vocal tract) is exactly the message.

If the medium is a perceptual filter, it seems the medium must encompass the entire, environmentally-conditioned, data transport system from external source to internal conscious awareness. Judgment of artistic effort, as with ones ability to discern beauty, rests upon the presumption of consciousness and that depends upon ones physiological state The effect of physiological state, upon people's ability to appreciate art, has historically been noted. In "Of the Standard of Taste" – 1757, Hume writes, "But though all the general rules of art are founded only on experience and on the observation of the common sentiments of human nature, we must not imagine, that, on every occasion the feelings of men will be conformable to these rules. Those finer emotions of the mind are of a very tender and delicate nature, and require the concurrence of many favorable circumstances to make them play with facility and exactness, according to their general and established principles. The least exterior hindrance to such small springs, or the least internal disorder, disturbs their motion, and confounds the operation of the whole machine." In this statement, Hume muses that the ability to appreciate art is subject to ones emotional state.

The medium established by our physiological state is pivotally important. We absorb data that has been environmentally and neural-sensorially conditioned. The manner in which we generate conscious thought, regarding this absorbed, conditioned data is dependent upon our emotional state. Emotional state is reflected in autonomic processes, within the body, that are related to our physiological state. Furthermore, when considering human perception as a recursive system, cause and effect can conspire to create other behavior. Ones ability to consciously interpret the environment, within the confines of an emotional framework, will affect ones influence within that environment and the affected environment may act to influence physiological state and subsequently emotional state.

There is no clear separation between the sensory mediums from outside to inside the body. Human perception encompasses a continuum of medium filters, whether they are rooted internal or external to the body. Also, the relationship between body and environment is richer than these connected medium filters. There is a resonance established, between body and environment, which is subject to the cause and effect relationship between physiological and emotional state. We are stimulated by the environmental medium, and in turn, we manipulate that medium.

The sensed environment can be considered an extension of one's body by virtue of the idea that information is not aware of any boundary between animate and inanimate. People seek out beautiful environments to inhabit because they feel a matched connection to those surroundings. However, even though our surroundings may be intimate, our direct (real-time) influence on those environments is restricted to that which is close to us and practically manipulated. We can adjust our clothing to be warmer or cooler. We can eat eggs for breakfast and salad for lunch. We can place a pillow in the car seat to give a height boost for better driving visibility.

We can't spontaneously change the character of our fixed buildings and cities. As a result, we are less connected to the world at large, as it seems beyond and away from our scope and influence. Instead, if seemingly faraway aspects of our environment were more directly influenced by us, then it seems our sphere of caring would branch outward. A "Living Architecture", that has a bidirectional dialog with its inhabitants and can be influenced by them in a human-time scale, has the potential to create an increasingly robust and vital connection between people and the spaces they inhabit.

Assuming that dialog is mediated, in part by a bidirectional autonomic and conscious connection between architecture and inhabitant, then the formally distant can become as meaningful as the feeling of a favorite jacket or the smell of basil plants in the windowsill. Presently our feelings, which are coupled to our autonomic responses, can encourage us to make intimate and conscious changes to our environment. Our influence on the larger environment is much more subject to our ability to marshal resources of time, labor, energy and materials, so intimacy and empowerment are both precluded. The possibility of developing intimate pathways between our small selves and the much larger world seems a relevant task, if we are focused on extending the reach of human caring.

A Starting Point

Architecture presently leads to the establishment of an environmental permanence, compared to human time scales. The feelings and conscious thoughts of people, living in an unchanging architecture, would seem to be vitally important. An ability to clarify potential occupants' feelings and thoughts about a space, prior to its physical implementation, could be helpful in the design process. Presently, workstation tools exist to marry the tasks of design and realization with the capacities of feeling and immersion. Psychophysiology researchers have become acutely aware of the power of this juxtaposition. A common tool in psychophysiology laboratories worldwide is the Virtual Reality (VR) workstation. This tool can be readily combined with technology that permits the measurement of human affect. Affect is the observable (measurable) expression of emotion.

With this combined configuration, in service of architectural design, participants can be treated to sequences of virtual realizations. Simultaneously, the sensory influence of the design effort will express as an autonomic state in the participant. The participant would be empowered to walk around the virtual structure, peer around corners and even hear the interior echoes of the building. Autonomic and cognitive feedback, would be synchronously coupled to the subject's walk-through of the virtuality.

Autonomic feedback could be expressed in terms of the Circumplex Model of Affect. James Russell first described the Circumplex Model of Affect in 1980. Affective states arise from the behavior of two independent neurophysiologic systems, the arousal and valence systems. Affective states are a function of these two systems. The circumplex model is two-dimensional, with arousal and valence defined as orthogonal (perpendicular) axes. The arousal axis, plotted vertically, ranges from zero to high arousal. The valence axis, plotted horizontally, ranges from negative to positive affect. Objective physiological indexes of affect or emotion are available. As valence examples, increasing zygomaticus activity indicates positive affect and increasing corrugator activity indicates negative affect. Physiological example indices for arousal include heart rate and electrodermal activity. Employing the Circumplex Model of Affect, emotional states are classified and reported as a two-dimensional vector with displeasure/pleasure as one dimension and non-arousal/arousal as the orthogonal dimension.

Cognitive feedback could be expressed as a verbal commentary of one's thoughts as they traversed the virtual space. Alternatively, subject-controlled indicators could be employed to reflect concurrent thoughts regarding the usability or potential of any particular space, as paired to specific locations in the virtuality.

In principle, autonomic and cognitive feedback data could be used to make guided or automatic adjustments to the virtual model. A hallway could be made longer or shorter, colors in a room could change, window sizes could be adjusted to allow more or less sunlight. Because changes to the virtual environment would impact participant autonomic function, and if the measured changes could be employed to directly mediate the design, then a so-named "emotional state – design resonance loop" might be created. In this situation, a virtual design could possibly be modulated in real-time by autonomic state feedback. The loop could be automatically exited when a particular autonomic state was reached.

Future Steps

Resources exist that would permit measures of participants' physiology as they might experience a real architecture. Autonomic recording systems would allow the logging of participant data during a walk-through. As a practical matter, this possibility is best suited for research investigations. The invasive quality of recording autonomic data, given present technology, would preclude large-scale practical deployment. However, it would be useful to record participant autonomic data and pair it with data from a host of non-invasive sensors, such as thermal imagers, carbon dioxide monitors and occupancy detectors. Perhaps meaningful relationships could be established between collective participant autonomic states and other non-invasive sensors. A defining example might involve the opening of a sunroof, when enclosed carbon dioxide levels have reached a specific level. The autonomic responses of individuals could be measured during such an activity. In this manner, building control functionality could be validated by participant autonomic (emotional state) testing.

Reference Information

Human Nervous System

The central nervous system (CNS) includes the brain and spinal cord. The peripheral nervous system (PNS) connects between the CNS and the body. The PNS consists of two parts, the autonomic nervous system (ANS) and the somatic nervous system (SoNS). The ANS regulates fundamental physiological states that are typically involuntary, such as heart rate, digestion and perspiration. The SoNS mediates voluntary control of body movements via skeletal muscle.

The autonomic nervous system (ANS) is largely responsible for maintaining the equilibrium of the body's systems. The ANS is connected to smooth muscles, cardiac muscle tissue and secretion glands of organs. The ANS is composed of three components, the sympathetic nervous system (SNS), parasympathetic nervous system (PsNS) and enteric nervous system (ENS). The SNS and PsNS work in an opposing manner to maintain the internal equilibrium of the body.

Affective stimuli can have a significant effect on the ANS and many physiological signals reflect the activity of the ANS. The SNS functions in circumstances that require quick responses. The PsNS functions in circumstances that do not require immediate responses. As SNS activation increases, then PsNS activation decreases and vice-versa.

Affect and Emotion

Affect is the observable (measurable) expression of emotion.

Theories of Emotion

The James-Lange Theory of Emotion
Emotions occur as a result of physiological reactions to stimuli. The experience of the body's physiological response generates the emotion. Emotional state depends on how the subject interprets their own reaction to any specific event. The subject's perception of their own physiological reaction is the emotion.

The Cannon-Bard Theory of Emotion
Emotions occur when the thalamus activates the CNS in response to stimuli, which results in physiological reaction. Physiological reaction and cognitive interpretation of emotional state occur simultaneously and are largely independent. The perception of a stimulus leads to both the emotion and physiological reaction. Furthermore, different emotions can share similar physiological responses.

Schachter-Singer Theory of Emotion
In response to stimuli, a physiological reaction occurs. A cognitive label accompanies the reaction. The reaction and the label act to generate an emotion. The subject's history provides the framework to experience their reaction and categorize it as a specific emotion. Subject's perceive their own physiological responses and then emotionally interpret them by considering the context of their circumstances.

Circumplex Model of Affect

The Circumplex Model of Affect was first described in 1980 by James Russell. Affective states arise from the behavior of two independent neurophysiological systems, the arousal and valence systems. Affective states are a function of these two systems. The Circumplex model is two-dimensional, with arousal and valence defined as orthogonal (perpendicular) axes. The arousal axis, plotted vertically, ranges from zero arousal to high arousal. The valence axis, plotted horizontally, ranges from negative to positive. Objective physiological indexes of affect or emotion are available. As valence examples, positive affect is indicated by increasing zygomaticus activity and negative affect is indicated by increasing corrugator activity. Physiological example indices for arousal include heart rate and electrodermal activity.

Motivational State

Perhaps even more fundamental to emotional state is the concept of motivational state. Motivational state is indexed by specific, bodily expressed, physiological states that can easily be measured. Motivational state is based on the concept of core relational themes, called "challenge" and "threat." During the course of living, humans relate to environmental stimulus as a combination of challenge and threat. A challenge response is similar to the aerobic physiological response, and involves an increase in heart rate and cardiac output and a decrease in vascular resistance. A threat response is characterized by an increase in heart rate, blood pressure and an increase or little change in vascular resistance and a decrease or no change in stroke volume. Motivational state information can be used to better reflect objective differences between similar Circumplex model defined emotions, such as anger and fear.

Interpersonal Connection

There is a vast amount of expression that falls outside the realm of what we can experience by looking, hearing, tasting, smelling and feeling. The unaided human sensory system can only perceive a small fraction of the physical phenomena surrounding us. The range of human hearing is 20Hz to 20,000Hz. The visual chromatic spectrum runs from red (780nm) to violet (390nm). We can taste five basic flavors: bitter, salty, sour, sweet and umami. For all human senses, there are limits to both sensitivity and range. There are sounds too soft to hear, colors we can't see and flavors too intense to identify.

Technology can extend the sensory range beyond what is normally perceivable by humans. For example, the small electrical signal, manifested by the heart, can't be directly perceived by people until the tiny signal is translated into a record which can be seen. The different modalities of human physiology express in a variety of ways. In the circumstance of body movement, the nervous system guides and propagates an electrical signal which originates the brain. When the signal reaches the targeted area, the muscle manifests an electrical signal during contraction. In the lungs, inspired oxygen is exchanged for expired carbon dioxide. Vascular beds in the fingertip fill and empty with blood during each heartbeat cycle and the pressure in the arteries changes during the course of each beat. The oxygen saturation level in the blood relates to respiratory activity. All of these different actions can be observed directly, once the changing variable of electricity, gas concentration, optical property or pressure is transformed into a human-perceptual quantity. Transformations of data, from the hidden to the perceivable, are possible in many different forms. For example, the skeletal muscle contraction's electrical signal, the electromyogram, can be converted directly to audible form.

Physiological data is highly complex and has rhythmic, chaotic and fractal qualities and it must first be well-perceived before it can be better understood. To better measure and interpret physiological data, one can use specific equipment to sense a subtle process and convert the signal into forms readily perceived by one or more of the human senses. Simultaneously, this data can be converted into forms amenable to computer-based processing. In this manner, complex data can be better conceptualized and then additional, software-based, interpretive tools can be evolved to assist in the process of further understanding.

There are volitional and non-volitional (autonomic) aspects to our bodies. We can consciously and intentionally stimulate motor neurons, which innervate muscle fibers, to move our bodies. Other processes, like heart rate, digestion and perspiration are primarily subconsciously mediated. Some actions, like breathing, are subject to both subconscious and conscious control. Conscious thought rests upon an emotional sea and our emotions are linked to autonomic processes in our bodies. If aroused, we can experience increased heart rate and perspiration. If we are happy, delicate muscles in our face contract to create a smile. Our mood, which stimulates our conscious thought, will influence our perception because our emotional substrate acts as a neurological filter.

Sensory expansion, directed in service of evaluating human expression, is of interest because an interpersonal dialog can be established at a deeper level. Assuming that dialog is mediated, in part by a bidirectional autonomic and conscious connection between one person and another, then the formally distant can become as meaningful as the feeling of a favorite jacket or the smell of basil plants in the windowsill. Presently our feelings, which are coupled to our autonomic responses, can encourage us to make intimate and conscious changes to our relationships with one another. The possibility of developing new communication pathways between ourselves, seems a relevant task, if we are focused on extending the reach of human caring.

Alan Macy is currently the Research and Development Director, past President and a founder of BIOPAC Systems, Inc. He designs data collection and analysis systems, used by researchers in the life sciences that help identify meaningful interpretations from signals produced by life processes. Trained in electrical engineering and physiology, with over 30 years of product development experience, he is currently focusing on psychophysiology, emotional and motivational state measurements, magnetic resonance imaging and augmented/virtual reality implementations. He presents in the areas of human-computer interfaces, electrophysiology, and telecommunications. His recent research and artistic efforts explore ideas of human nervous system extension and the associated impacts upon perception. As an applied science artist, he specializes in the creation of cybernated art, interactive sculpture and environments.

Infrastructure Space and Platforms as Living Architectures: The Importance of Regenerative Design and Innovation for Bioregional Economic Development

ERIC MATHIS & TYLER JENKINS
Institute For Regenerative Design & Innovation

Throughout the Southeastern region, rural communities are challenged by their low population density, less advanced technology activities, and lower innovative capacity. Stimulating both technological and process innovation requires that rural infrastructure includes roads, waterways, power grids, institutional structures and networks that are tied to a series of central nodes or platforms, acting as incubators for new ideas that draw on collective resources. Collaborations between formal organizations (nonprofit organizations, R&D firms) and informal groups (employees, community stakeholders) can combine knowledge to guide development within the agricultural sector by promoting openness and diminishing the limitations of regional isolation. Taken together, this living ecosystem is the cooperative platform model we are deploying throughout the southeastern region of the US. This platform serves as the primary driver of technological innovation driven by connecting the lived experiences of both community institutions and people to R&D processes of technology that derive their innovation from both the region's agricultural and institutional eco-systems – constituting a living architecture

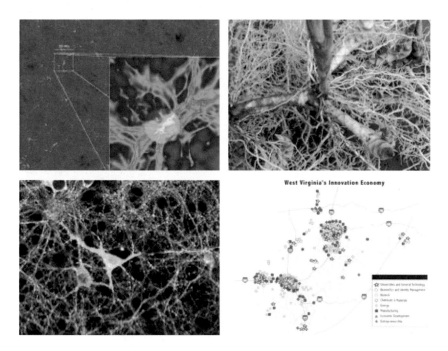

Figure 1   (from top left to bottom right) Galaxy Filament, Rhizome, Cognitive Architecture and Innovation Clusters.

of nested systems comprised of processing-infrastructure/technological-innovation assemblages.[1] Following Deleuze and Guattari, this cooperative platform or regenerative assemblage can be understood as an"increase in the dimensions of a multiplicity that necessarily changes in nature as it expands its connections. There are no points or positions in a rhizome... there are only lines" that connect.[2] Moreover, a kin to the living architecture of a rhizome, these regenerative assemblages not only constitutes external superclusters of the universe or internal cognitive architectures but also make up cooperative-innovation processes found in living market systems that "assumes very diverse forms, from ramified surface extension in all directions to concretion into bulbs and tubers" or in the case of our proposed cooperative platform, the generation of innovation linkages that congeal to form innovation districts which in turn re-generate differentiated cooperative-innovation networks[3] (see Figure 1 above).

This living architecture leverages worker's firsthand knowledge of a particular technology's production processes with community stakeholders living assets (i.e., health and wellness, intuition) derived from local linkages (e.g., local food, soil health, etc) in order to provide valuable insights for improving both infrastructure design as well as the technological innovation platforms that differentiates both. In turn, these densely connected assemblages stimulate solutions-based thinking by linking the tacit knowledge of rural-based agriculture and community stakeholders with the urban-based industry stakeholders and manufacturers of bio-based products.[4] Capitalizing on local/tacit knowledge of living assets in both biodiversity and agriculture ecosystems alike – this economic model could be central throughout the lifecycle of a particular innovation process – in affect, creating a highly reflexive innovation ecosystem leveraging the collaborative nature of cooperative enterprises. These "informal" networks of experienced workers and industry stakeholders can effectively stimulate technological innovation, in turn drawing new industry into the southeast.

Akin to Phillip Beesley's Hylozoic Ground, these regenerative assemblages are "far from transcendent perfection," but rather produce a "formwork that organizes the space...out of local circumstances." They add "links within linked rows... producing warped surfaces that expand outwards in three dimensions," infusing architectures that constitute living market systems.[5]

Markets as Living Architecture Systems

Economist Adam Smith identified the division of labor and specialization as the two key ways of achieving larger financial returns on production. Through specialization, employees would not only be able to focus on specific tasks, but also improve the skills necessary to perform tasks. Tasks performed better and faster lead to increased production levels. While Smith describes a model for increased efficiency through economies of scale, his model fails to account for the efficiencies present in regional cooperative ecosystems and their ability to stimulate innovation, specifically the efficiencies associated with economies of agglomeration.[6]

This white paper explores the economic benefits of technological innovation by highlighting network effects in relation to entrepreneurship and the strength of institutions (i.e., an endogenous growth model) as opposed to the reverse, understanding market flows on the level of price (i.e., neo-classical growth model), with technological innovation acting as a secondary condition for maintaining a thriving market. Neo-classical growth model maintains that the long-run rate of growth is exogenously determined by either the savings rate or the rate of technological change, both of which remain ubiquitous to the model.[7] Due to the oblique nature of these market forces, savings rate and technological change are typically assumed to be subject to diminishing returns due to the decoupling of long-term rates of growth from rates of investment. In short, long-run growth of personal income necessitates that exogenous improvements in technology generate innovation.[8]

Endogenous growth theory tries to overcome this shortcoming by locating rates of change (differentiation) within microeconomic forces that, in turn, generate macroeconomic trends. Limitations of the neo-classical model include its failure to take account of entrepreneurship (catalyst for growth) and the strength of institutions (facilitate economic growth). In addition, it does not explain how or why technological change occurs. These limitations have led to the rise of endogenous growth theory, which locates technological change internally. Unlike previous classical models of economic development, endogenous growth model does not see technology as a given, but as a product of economic activity. In addition, this theory holds that growth is due to increasing returns characterized by knowledge and technology – as opposed to the diminishing returns characterized by physical capital.[9]

The proposed bio-regional model expands upon the endogenous model by situating its knowledge/technology nexus within a model of regenerative design by linking this nexus directly to embodied or tacit experiences via cooperative enterprises that are linked to farmer and industry stakeholder "know how."[10] Along with an emphasis on regenerative design, this model for markets will help practitioners of regenerative design negotiate development by synthesizing a resource-based economy with a knowledge-based economy to form a cohesive whole that cannot be reduced to either one.

This approach underscores the point that the economic processes that generate and diffuse new knowledge are critical to shaping the growth of urban-rural communities and individual firms. In this light, practitioners should consider the importance that institutions play as providers of a framework or assemblage for technological change. In "Clio and the Economics of QWERTY," economic historian Paul David describes ways to conceptualize institutions in such a manner by viewing them as actors minimizing unwarranted technological lock-in or path dependence which, in turn, ensures the creation and maintenance of a network of cooperative-innovation platforms or iNetwork.[11] Technological lock-ins typically occur because of technical interrelatedness and the quasi-irreversibility of innovation.[12]

As such, lock-ins takes place both in merited and unmerited situations. In the case of inefficient technological lock-ins and arrangements, it is not necessary for market forces to automatically correct these inefficient outcomes. In addition, while lock-ins typically adhere to one particular physical piece of technology, the same routine adherence can be seen on a larger economic level. Some economic theorists see business firms, managers, and other economic stakeholders as creatures of routine who follow certain successful beliefs and only change when their routines fail to succeed – in essence constituting a negative feedback loop. Therefore, an alternative method of correcting inefficiencies due to lock-ins and industrial routine is needed – facilitating the emergence of positive feedback loops. If cooperative enterprises were utilized to decrease the occurrence of these inefficiencies, there would be room for additional innovation and, in turn, accelerate bio-regenerative economic development. In short, our proposed cooperative platform is ultimately essential for achieving "regenerative innovation."[13]

Sources of Innovation

There are several sources of innovation. In the dominant linear model of innovation, the creative source are private firms or highly centralized R&D laboratories where an agent (person or company) innovates in order to sell a given product. Within this model, large companies not only function to make a profit, but also formalize various R&D processes to routinize them and increase profit margins. However, as Cortright discovers, "the traditional solution to dealing with spillovers, granting strong property rights for the fruits of an invention, may also have negative consequences."[14] As such, this white paper will develop the precursors to a theory of innovation which punctualize informal networks of industry stakeholders that stimulate the diffusion of innovation and retains the participant's active role in the production of technological change through the iNetwork.[15] It is also paramount not to limit the production of knowledge to a specific group of firm participants (i.e. a specific, isolated R&D department).

Case studies of the automobile industry have shown the importance of worker-led teams for continuous innovation and process improvement.[16] With our coop model it is believed that this active role will assure the participation of farmers and in the processing infrastructure (e.g., cotton gin) by securing a financial share in the firm that is maintaining a competitive edge via technological innovation. This inclusion into the innovation process would effactully lead to a larger investment in innovation in which the technology is operating. It would also address the lack of incentives for entrepreneurs to distribute or invest in more knowledge creation.

The second source of innovation is end-user innovation, whereby an agent (person or company) innovates for their own (personal or in-house) use because existing products fail to meet their particular needs. In Sources of Innovation, Eric von Hippel identifies end-user innovation as one of the most important aspects for understanding the emergence of innovation. More recent theories of innovation have traversed the simple dualism of the private firm and end-user models – although both are still accounted for. These studies show that innovation does not just happen within the industrial supply-side, or as a result of the articulation of user demand, but through a complex set of processes that links many different players together.[17] This iNetwork is composed of not only developers and users, but also a wide variety of intermediary organizations such as consultancies, Standard Development Organizations, technology developers, entrepreneurs and, in the case of this research, informal industry participant and community stakeholder networks by and through platform strategies centered around agricultural development.

The third source of innovation is an essential part of creating an iNetwork and involves how the processing infrastructure itself is designed. In systems engineering, modular design subdivides a system into smaller parts (modules) that can be independently generated and then regenerated in different systems to drive multiple functionalities and sustain differentiation. As Brian Arthur and other scholars have demonstrated, new products are the outcome of a process based on the principle of novelty by combination.[18] Benefits of modularity include: reduction in cost due to less customization, a reduction in learning time and flexibility in design, as well as augmentations that add innovative solutions by merely plugging in a new module and exclusion of unpractical designs. Examples of modular systems are computers and agricultural infrastructure – all, according to Benjamin Bratton, constitute an accidental megastructure or platform. [19] Moreover, "perhaps these parts align into something not unlike a vast (if also incomplete), pervasive (if also irregular) software and hardware stack" where agriculture infrastructure also uses modularity to overcome changing consumer demands and to make the manufacturing process more adaptive to change.[20] In sum, modular design attempts to combine the advantages of standardization and compatibility (i.e., high volume normally equals low manufacturing costs) with those of customization.

When situating modular design within an urban economy of agglomeration and its partial relocation within a rural setting, we can begin to construct a comprehensive understanding of the particular development model we are proposing.[21] In regards to agriculture, the production of processing infrastructure typically found within economies of agglomeration are internalized by way of vertical integration. This is usually a repercussion of the firm's approach to reduce various transaction costs associated with externalizing the production of the component parts of the processing infrastructure. For example, there may be four component parts involved in producing a particular technology (See Figure 2). More often than not, if the profit margin is large enough, the firm that is producing the particular processing infrastructure will remain static and the emergence of new components will not occur. However, if the design of the processing infrastructure is compatible with other technologies and adopts certain industry standards, then the original firm is forced to cooperate in order to sell their particular product on the market. This competitive atmosphere increases a particular technology's ability to adapt to a rapidly changing market – within both the demand and supply side – through component integration, expansion of knowledge stocks, R&D spillovers, and an increase in returns. To put it another way, the positive feedbacks of encouraging compatibility through industry standards stimulate technological change and innovation.[22]

Figure 2   Components of Processing Infrastructure.

The production of new processing technologies would then come to resemble Figure 3 only if the larger firm decides that internalizing the production of components 6 and 7 is beneficial.

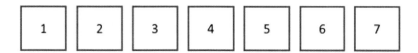

Figure 3   Components of Improved Processing Infrastructure.

If this is not the case and the larger firm decides not to internalize the production of components 6 and 7, then firm 2 and 3 are then created from the knowledge spillovers (see figure 4).

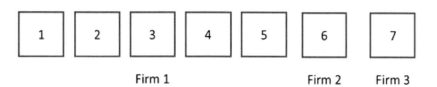

Figure 4   Firms Involved in Improved Processing Infrastructure.

The emerging cooperative ecosystem would then create alternative components that were once found in the larger firm such as component 4 (see figure 5). This could occur for a variety of reasons, such as a customer deciding to purchase a technology with the traditional components of 1, 2, 3, and 5, while finding that particular attributes of component 4, which is produced by a competing firm, fits within their particular interests (see figure 5). This could occur if the alternative component 4 is better suited to a particular need found in the customer's' region – here customers being the workers as well as farmer and industry stakeholders.

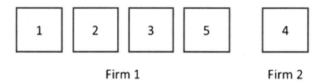

Firm 1   Firm 2

Figure 5   Production of Processing Infrastucture with Changing Component 4.

When situated within a supply side, these demand-side attributes of technological innovation encourage knowledge spillovers and the establishment of an informal iNetwork between producers. The first type of network that will emerge is a centralized cluster akin to the aforementioned rhizome bulbs in which suppliers are tied to lead supply firms as in the typical Japanese R&D firm; these firms integrated their R&D labs with factory floor workers in order to close the knowledge gaps that are found in the typical U.S. high technology firms. The U.S. structure of disintegration or spatial separation stifled the competitive advantages found in the Japanese model. The centralized firms found in the Japanese model pioneered new modes of integration that enabled them to generate a continuous flow of new products (i.e., total quality management, keiretsu, etc.). While recognizing the competitive advantages of the flat/integrative approach, these centralized firms did not account for the positive feedbacks found within modular design, specifically compatibility. Although this research notes the importance of the integrative model utilized by Japanese firms, it seeks to expand these integrative effects into an iNetwork (see figure 6) or economy of agglomeration with the hope of increasing technological innovation within the agriculture sector.

For example, in figure 6, W1, W2, and W3 represent the localized knowledge stocks – local infrastructure owners/users and workers – at a particular processing facility with three different types of technologies that are suited for

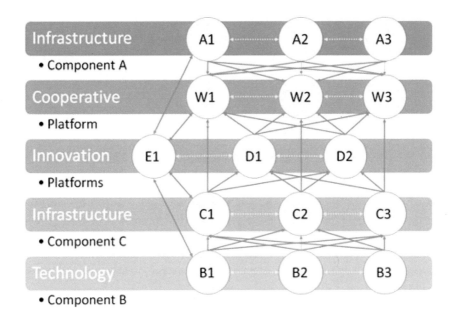

Figure 6   Cooperative Innovation Platform.

independent variables. These variables are found within the specific context that the facilities are operating (e.g., feedstock variability, economic constraints, ecological conditions, etc.). These local knowledge stocks are connected to R&D facilities (D1, D2), both public and private, as well as a centralized information trader (E1). A1, A2, A3, C1, C2, and C3 are the manufactures of component A and C which are found in a standardized production and processing infrastructure and future processing technologies that are suitable to all applications. Based on the collective nature of standardization and its relation to modular design, subassembly B, which is a product of technological innovation, needs to be compatible only with component C and not directly with other components. The continual splitting of components (technological innovation) and a sustained emergence of new component manufacturers and community-based production and processing strategies is a result of the relation between W and the respective public (D1) or private (D2) R&D firm. This relationship fosters knowledge spillovers and, in turn, cultivates a functioning iNetwork. Taken together, all the "component" product manufacturers (A,B,C), the localized knowledge stocks (W), the public and private R&D firms (D), and the centralized information trader (E) make up a cooperative-innovation ecosystem – the rhizome or Living

Architecture System. In contrast to centralized innovation networks in which one dominant firm establishes the standards of compatibility, the iNetwork jointly determine standards by establishing a precedent for negotiations between product manufacturers, R&D departments and firms, and localized knowledge stocks. No single actor in this network has control. Additionally, any actor who tries to dictate standards risks being isolated if other network actors decide not to follow.[23]

Conclusion

When situating the above iNetwork within a cluster of manufacturers or a rural/urban economy of agglomeration, the development of skill and know-how along with the easy communication of ideas and experience allows the cooperative-innovation actors/networks to converge on a "plane of consistency assuring their selection."[24] By enhancing the formation of an iNetwork and their strengths, rural/urban agglomeration may affect the southeast in the following ways:

- Accelerate the rate at which new technologies and regenerative practices are developed in within the agriculture sector and beyond;

- Accelerate the rate at which the knowledge of new production and processing technologies enters into and are diffused throughout the region;[25]

- Accelerate the rate at which these new technologies are incorporated into the products of manufacturers;

- Accelerate the rate at which these new or renewed products are adopted by the potential customers;

- Accelerate the rate at which the southeast can mitigate the negative economic effects of America's transition from an economy of scarcity to an economy of abundance.

References

1. It is important to note that we use Keller Easterling's distinct between active and object form to draw a distinct between infrastructure (object) and technology (active). Easterling provides additional insight regarding the linkage between a kind of active/living architecture that we are attempting to elucidate by formulating a regenerative assemblage between the object form of processing-infrastructure and the active form of platform-innovation in both "Extrastatecraft: The Power of Infrastructure Space" as well as an interview in Metropolis Magazine where she describes a kind of living architecture that "was designed as active form rather than object form. There was no town plan, but rather instructions for the town to grow by wards. Each ward had a quotient of public, private, and green space, and the appearance of each ward also triggered a reserve of agricultural space outside the town. It was a growth protocol. It was a time-released form that wasn't just making one thing, but rather controlling a flow of things over time. That seems to me so powerful. Keller Easterling, "Urban Software," Metropolis Magazine 2015: accessed October 21, 2016.

2. Gilles Deleuze and Félix Guattari. A Thousand Plateaus: Capitalism and Schizophrenia. Bloomsbury Publishing, 1988, 8.

3. Deleuze and Guattari, A Thousand Plateaus, 7. Our use of "flat-structures" is largely informed by Manuel DeLanda's flat ontology. Additionally, rizomatic bulbs and tubers are found in both physical cosmology with galaxy filaments (subtypes: supercluster complexes, galaxy walls, and galaxy sheets) that are the largest known structures in the universe as well as the flat-structures found in cognitive plasticity/architecture. For more concerning cognitive architecture see: Sussman, Ann, and Justin B. Hollander. Cognitive Architecture: Designing for How We Respond to the Built Environment. Routledge, 2014. For more concerning innovation districts see: Katz, Bruce, and Julie Wagner. "The Rise of Innovation Districts: A New Geography of Innovation in America." Metropolitan Policy Program at Brookings, May 2014.

4. Beesley, Philip, Pernilla Ohrstedt, and Rob Gorbet. Hylozoic Ground: Liminal Responsive Architecture: Philip Beesley. Edited by Hayley Isaacs. Riverside Architectural Press 2010, 17.

5. Manuel DeLanda provides further clarification regarding a successful regional cooperative ecosystem in both "A Thousand Years of Non-Linear History" as well as a Switch Interview where he states that "there are alternatives to the corporate model, such as a region of contemporary Italy called Emilia-Romagna, dominated by small businesses competing against each other not in terms of costs and reaping economies of scale, but in terms of product design and a concentration of creative people in a region (a model known as "economies of agglomeration"). Manuel Delanda, "Interview with Manuel DeLanda," Switch Interviews Vol. 5 Number 1 (1994): accessed October 21, 2016.

6. Note that both exogenous and endogenous models are not always mutually exclusive. For more see: Ryuzo Sato, "The Harrod-Domar Model vs the Neo-Classical Growth Model," The Economic Journal 74, no. 294 (1964): 380-387; Steven N. Durlauf, Andros Kourtellos, and Artur Minkin, "The Local Solow Growth Model," European Economic Review 45, no. 4 2001: 928-940.

7. Nicholas Crafts, "Exogenous or Endogenous Growth? The Industrial Revolution Reconsidered," Journal of Economic History 55 (1995): 745-772.

8. Joseph Cortright, "New Growth Theory, Technology and Learning: A Practitioner's Guide." Reviews of Economic Development Literature and Practice 4, no. 6 (2001): 1-35.

9. Gilbert Ryle, "Knowing How and Knowing That: The Presidential Address." In Proceedings of the Aristotelian society, vol. 46, pp. 1-16. Aristotelian Society, Wiley 1945.

10. Actor-Network Theory (ANT) provides a useful model for creating a regenerative network by maintaining a distinction between intermediaries and mediators. Intermediaries are entities which make no difference (to some interesting state of affairs which we are studying) and so can be ignored. They transport the force of some other entity more or less without transformation and so are fairly uninteresting. Mediators are entities which multiply difference and so should be the object of study. Their outputs cannot be predicted by their inputs. From an ANT point of view sociology has tended to treat too much of the world as intermediaries.

11. Paul A. David, "Clio and the Economics of QWERTY" The American Economic Review 75, no. 2 1985: 332-337.

12. Cooperation Winston Salem is an example of intentionally creating a community-based model of development which utilizes cooperative-innovation or user-based feedback through the use of community-based design charrettes.

13. Cortright, New Growth Theory, 7.

14. Rao K. Usha, Kishore V.V.N., 2010 A review of technology diffusion models with special reference to renewable energy technologies, Renewable and Sustainable Energy Reviews, 2010;14: 1070–10

15. Ibid., 29.

16. Eric Von Hippel, Democratizing Innovation (Cambridge: MIT Press, 2009); Henry William Chesbrough, Open Innovation: The New Imperative for Creating and Profiting from Technology (Harvard Business Press, 2003); Don Tapscott and Anthony D. Williams, Macrowikinomics: New Solutions for a Connected Planet (New York: Penguin, 2010)

17. Nicholas Georgescu-Roegen, "The Economics of Production," The American Economic Review 60, no. 2 (1970): 1-9.

18. Earlier examples include looms, railroad signaling systems, telephone exchanges, pipe organs and electric power distribution systems. Benjamin Bratton, "The Black Stack," e-flux Journal #53 (2014): accessed October 21, 2016.

19. For more about partial relocation as it relates to establishing rural-to-urban linkages see: Lambooy, J. G., "Locational Decisions and Regional Structure," Human Behaviour in Geographical Space. Gower, London 1986: 149-165; Dosi, Giovanni, Technical Change and Industrial Transformation (New York: St. Martin's Press, 1984)

20. Here, the component parts are the object forms that are assembled into an active form forming a technology that can be considered to have a higher state of plasticity due to its integration into a cooperative-innovation platform. The further the technological enters the platform the more differentiated it becomes thus intensifying the active form it represents. This may also be considered an abstract machine ala Gilles Deleuze.

21. Richard N. Langlois and Paul L. Robertson, "Networks and Innovation in a Modular System: Lessons from the Microcomputer and Stereo Component Industries," Research Policy 21, no. 4 (1992): 297-313.

22. Deleuze and Guattari, A Thousand Plateaus, 4.

23. Meade, N., & Islam, T. 2006. Modeling and forecasting the diffusion of innovation — A 25 year review. International Journal of Forecasting, 22(3), 519–545.

J. Eric Mathis is a PhD candidate for Architecture & Urbanism at the European Graduate School. Making a name for himself by spearheading what many consider to be one of the most advanced coal transitions strategies in the US, he co-designed a proven open-innovation model that breeds economic resiliency through the deployment of a comprehensive Health & Wellness program in the heart of central Appalachian coal country. Building from this model, he is launching a regional agriculture/energy nexus strategy beginning with West Virginia (energy) and his home state North Carolina (agriculture). He presently serves as both the co-director of the Institute for Regenerative Design & Innovation as well as the Chief Innovation Officer of Bio-Regen Coop – a hybrid, multi-stakeholder cooperative. Eric is a 2010 recipient of the Interstate Renewable Energy Council's Innovation Award for Community Renewables and a 2012 White House Champion of Change for Greening our Cities and Towns. His collaborative work has been covered by or featured in Biodiesel Magazine, BBC World News, Eye Opener TV, Bloomberg, Photon Magazine, Daily Yonder, West Virginia Executive Magazine, Fast Company, Home Power Magazine, Fortune Magazine, the Bitter Southerner and PBS Newshour.

Tyler Jenkins is an organizer of communities around agriculture and economic development initiatives, particularly the development of worker, producer, and consumer cooperatives and cooperative ecosystems throughout North Carolina. He was hired by Carolina Common Enterprise – North Carolina's cooperative development center – in 2014 to train in development of individual cooperative businesses while building a network of support and opening community and regional partnerships and markets for the center's services. In this role he coordinated and delivered a range of services for cooperative businesses – navigating legal incorporation and governance models with attorneys along with business strategy and cooperative capacity building – including mobilizing necessary public and private resources for supporting grassroots economic organizing efforts throughout different stages of their development to ensure success. Tyler recently completed a Cooperative Development Fellowship with the Democracy at Work Institute in Oakland, CA.

Tyler grew up and attended college in Mississippi, before earning a graduate degree from Emory University, with a focus on theory of social change and global health education. In North Carolina, Tyler's previous work includes a farm apprenticeship, coordinating a 10-county Centers For Disease Control development initiative for a Northwest Partners in Public Health in Northwestern North Carolina, and as a project developer for the Center for Environmental Farming Systems. He is currently serving as an organizer, strategy and development consultant for NC State University through its Community Food Strategies team. This most recent work for NC State catalyzed the development of local network clusters for collaboration, innovation, and development of food systems policy and development.

Aquaphoneia:
An Interview with TML's
Navid Navab

NAVID NAVAB &
HILARY BERGEN
Concordia University

Multidisciplinary composer and media alchemist Navid Navab and his team at the Topological Media Lab (Montreal) presented Aquaphoneia, a sound installation which "transmutes voice into water and water into air.

HB: The theme of the 2016 Ars Electronica Festival RADICAL ATOMS – and the alchemists of our time is very close to the Topological Media Lab's mission: transmutation and alchemy on the philosophical and phenomenological level seem to be at the centre of your research and methodology at the lab. For Aquaphoneia, can you expand on alchemy and specifically on how this art piece stands out from your past work? How did alchemical thought process and production techniques come up in the process of the piece?

NN: When the 2016 theme for Ars Electronica Festival was announced I was happily surprised and thought: Finally shit is coming to light at a much larger scale. Yes please! Can we reverse the still prominent European Modernism's separations – between the conceptual and the material, the precise and the messy, the sciences and the arts – and go back to the holistic richness of alchemical matter? This transition that we are currently experiencing calls for a shift away from representational technologies: from interfaces to stuff, from objects to fields of matter-in-process, from fixed concepts to processes that enact concepts.

For over a decade, we as alchemists have been engaging with "bodies and materials that are always suffused with ethical, vital and material power." The Topological Media Lab [TML] is occupied by people who are living to fuse and confuse, ready to unlearn the apparent practicality of isolated disciplines, while playfully improvising new pathways to understanding potential futures. The TML hosts an array of projects for thinking-feeling through poetry-infused-matter and breathing life into static forms – which to me is an effortlessly artistic process, and all the while inseparable from a rigorously philosophical or scientific one. Even though it might take decades for the kinds of computational-materials that we are envisioning today to be engineered from ground up at an atomic level, with what is possible today, we explore how the messy stuff of the world could become computationally charged with the potential for play: sounding, dancing, and co-performing new ways of living with or without us. Aquaphoneia comes out of this rich ecology of experiments.

Figure 1   Photograph of Aquaphoneia experience in action.

In Aquaphoneia, voice and water become irreversibly fused. The installation listens to the visitors, and transmutes their utterances into aqueous voice, which then is further enriched and purified through alchemical processes. To fully realize this liquid dream, we went to great lengths in order to fuse the messy behaviour of matter flowing throughout the installation with meticulously correlated and localized sonic behaviour. For example, the temporal texture of boiling liquid in one chamber is perceptually inseparable from the spectral entropy of simmering voices which then evaporate into a cloud of spectral mist. All of this dynamic activity is finely localized: the sounds acoustically emit exactly from where the action occurs, rather than spatially schizophying loudspeakers elsewhere.

On another hand, our material-computational-centric approach lead to a tough yet rewarding meditation on control and process. As a composer I had to let go of all desires for immediate control over sounds and surrender important rhythmical and compositional decisions to messy material processes. As Duchamp puts it, "alchemy is a kind of philosophy: a kind of thinking that leads to a way of understanding." For us, in the process of creating Aquaphoneia, essentially what had to be understood and then given up was our attachment to our far-too-human notions of time and tempo. Instead we embraced and worked within the infinitely rich and pluri-textural tempi of matter. Technically and compositionally this meant that most of our focus had to be placed on merging the continuous richness of material processes with our computational processes through an array of techniques: temporal pattern following, audio-mosaicing, continuous tracking of fields of activity using computer vision and acoustic sensing techniques in order to synthesize highly correlated sonic morphologies, careful integration of structure-born-sound, etc. We were able to co-articulate compositions by constraining material processes sculpturally, and then letting the liquid voice and the laws of thermodynamics do their thing.

One of the first elements that we notice in the installation is the brass horn connected to an old Edison sound recording machine, that now turns voice into liquid instead of wax cylinders! In fact, it came from an Edison talking machine. You repurpose an authentic artifact, you do not fall into the trap of nostalgia, and neither into the role of collector, but you embrace innovation with a dynamic approach which excavates past media technologies in order to understand or surpass contemporary audio technologies. Where does the use of the Edison horn come from and how does it speak to your relationship with the superposition of history?

The history of sound reproduction involves transforming audible pressure patterns or sound energy into solid matter and vice versa. The historic Edison recording machines gathered sound energy to etch pressure patterns onto tinfoil wrapped around a cylindrical drum. Sound waves, focussed at the narrow end of the horn, caused a small diaphragm to vibrate, which in turn caused a miniature steel-blade stylus to move and emboss grooves in the cylinder. The tin foil would later on be replaced by wax cylinders, vinyl disks and eventually digital encoding.

Aquaphoneia engages the intimately recursive relationship between sounding technologies and material transmutations. Our digital audio workstations are an in fact an inclusive part of this history, this endless chain of analog transmutation between energy and matter. Under the fiction of the digital there is always the murmur of electrons and of matter-energy fields in physical transmutation. As J. Fragier writes on an early book by Nam June Paik: "The digital is the analog correspondence of the alchemists' formula for gold." Well, yes. The digital revolution has allowed us to shape, compute, purify, and sculpt sounds like never before... but then often at the hefty cost of a disembodying process, with interfaces that are linked to sounds only through layers upon layers of representation, far detached from resonating bodies and the sexy flux of sounding matter.

Aquaphoneia playfully juxtaposes material-computational histories of talking machines within an imaginary assemblage: sounds are fully materialized and messed with tangibly within an immediate medium very much like clay or water or perhaps more like a yet to be realized alchemico-sonic-matter. This odd assemblage orchestrates liquid sounds leveraging intuitive worldly notions – such as freezing, melting, dripping, swishing, boiling, splashing, whirling, vaporizing – and in the process borrows alchemical tactics expanding across material sciences, applied phenomenology, metaphysics, expanded materiology, and the arts. Aquaphoneia's alchemical chambers set these materials, metaphors, and forces into play against one another. After the initial ritual of offering one's voice to the assemblage, the aqueous voice starts performing for and with itself and human visitors have the opportunity to watch and participate as they we would when encountering the unpredictable order of an enchanted forest river.

It is also noteworthy that the horn resembles a black hole. The edge of the horn acts like an event horizon, separating sounds from their source-context. Sounds, once having passed the acousmatic event horizon, cannot return to the world that they once knew. Voices leaving the body of their human or non-human speaker, fall into the narrow depths of the horn, and are squeezed into spatio-temporal infinity. Disembodied voices, are immediately reborn again with a new liquid body that flows though alchemical chambers for sonic and metaphysical purification.

Much of my work deals with the poetics of schizophonia (separation of sound from their sources). Sound reproduction (technologies), from Edison's talking machines to our current systems, transcode back and forth between the concrete and acousmatic, situated and abstract, materialized and dematerialized, analogue and digital. Often sounds are encoded into a stiff medium which then may be processed with an interface, eventually decoded, and re-manifested again as sound. Aquaphoneia ends this nervous cycle of separation anxiety and re-attachment by synthesizing a sounding medium capable of contemporary computational powers such as memory, and adaptive spectro-temporal modulation and morphing. To adapt McLuhan, instead of encoding and decoding a presumed message with representational technologies, it enchants the medium!

There is the tendency to think that artwork from Media Labs are stable and high tech. Aquaphoneia uses analog and digital technologies with a Do-It-Yourself (DIY) touch in the aesthetic. Since your lab is multidisciplinary oriented and influenced by diverse fields of knowledge, can you develop on the DIY dimension in Aquaphoneia under the gaze of Clint Enns – cinematographer in the experimental field of cinema – 'Adopting a DIY methodology means choosing freedom over convenience'?

Aquaphoneia is a truly eclectic assemblage lost in time. Aquaphoneia's mixed form reflects its extremely fluid, collaborative and playful creative process. Instead of coming up with a definitive design and executing it industrially, Aquaphoneia's realization involved a much more playful process, where every little aspect of the installation – materials, sounds, software, electronics, etc – were playfully investigated and messed with. Every little detail matters and every process, undulating back and forth between conception to execution, is an artistic process.

The research-creation process leading to the works that come out of our lab are as critical to us as the final and fully produced art works. This was also true for the Alchemists who through their process were seeking to develop new approaches for understanding the world, relating to matter, and surpassing nature. Our research-creation activities concern experimenting with ethico-aesthetics of collective thinking-making: humans, non-humans, machines, and materials enacting and co-articulating the ever-changing material-social networks of relations which shape them. This DIY art-all-the-way approach, while providing a healthy dose of aesthetic freedom, is also an ethical one: we live with and within our designs and grow with them. That being said, we are not attached to a DIY process in the same way that some maker cultures might be. Sometimes we blindly find and repurpose something that does something cool, complicated, and mysterious and that is fantastic! Sort of like philosophy of media meets cyber dumpster diving meets DIY hacker space meets cutting edge tech research meets miniMax (minimum engineering with maximum impact) meets speculative whatever…

At some point we decided to gather sonic vapour in a glass dome and condense it back into drops, which were then guided to fall into the bottom of the installation. The purified drop of voice – sonic "lapis philosophorum – was to fall into the depths of the earth beneath and shine upward like sonic gold, connecting heaven and earth. We had to execute this opus magnum inside a very small hole in the base of the installation. The water drop needed to be immediately sensed and sonified, leading to sounds coming out of the same hole, along with synchronized light. You can imagine that if we were relying on "black-boxed" technologies and ready-made techniques then this task would have seemed like a nightmare to design and fabricate.

Figure 2   Case study.

The water drop was to fall all the way to the bottom of the hole where it would be acoustically sensed by a small apparatus that had to be acoustically isolated from everything else. Then the result of the sonification had to be pushed through the very same hole with a high degree of intelligibility and in a way that it would be seamlessly localized. Meanwhile light had to shine through this hole in sync with the sounds but the source of light had to remain hidden. The solution to this technical puzzle came to us effortlessly when playing around with random stuff. We found a hipster product – a little plastic horn – that was made for turning your iPod into a gramophone. Then a speaker was mounted inside of this plastic horn in order to focus sounds towards the end tip of of the horn. The back of the speaker was fully covered with foam and duct tape to stop any sound from escaping anywhere except for where we wanted it to appear.

A small hole was drilled into the brass pipe, in the base of the installation. Our advanced hipster horn-tip-sound-laser-thing was then inserted, allowing crisp sounds to enter the brass hole and emit from it without any visible clues for the perceiver as to where the speaker was hidden. Meanwhile a similar lighting solution was created so that in a very small footprint we can focus, direct, and bounce enough directional light in the brass pipe without ever getting in the way of the water drops.

We had to engage with this sort of detailed fabrication/composition process throughout the whole installation in order to come up with solutions to sense the behaviour of the materials and liquids locally and to manifest them sonically and visually so that there would be no separation from local material behaviours and their computational enchantment. In trying to do so we discovered that more often than not, there was no ready-made solution or technique to rely on and at the same time we didn't have months ahead of us to engage in an abstract design and fabrication process. We had limited hours of collective play time to leverage and to come up with innovative techniques that we didn't even know could exist and that was really fun.

4DSOUND: A New Approach to Spatial Sound Reproduction and Synthesis

PAUL OOMEN, POUL HOLLEMAN & LEO DE KLERK
Spatial Sound Institute

We argue that experiencing sound is inherently spatial and that the spatial properties of sound form a realm of musical expression that is as yet only partly discovered. To further the exploration of spatial sound as a medium, we argue that the generally applied methodologies to produce spatial sound are inherently limited by the sound source, i.e. loudspeaker boxes or headphones, and that reproducing or synthesising sound spatially asks for a new approach with regards to the medium. It is possible to create an innovative and non-conventional sound system that removes the localisability of the sound source from the equation, regardless of the listener's individual hearing properties. The system provides for a social listening area and improved loudness at equal acoustic power. The system is backwards compatible with existing audio reproduction formats, allows integration with a wide variety of control interfaces and encourages new approaches in design.

Introduction

Early in 2007, Paul Oomen conceptualised the design of a sound system that would be able to produce dimensional sound sources in an unlimited spatial continuum. Since this time Oomen has worked with Poul Holleman, Luc van Weelden and Salvador Breed on the development of object-based processing software and control interfaces for the system.

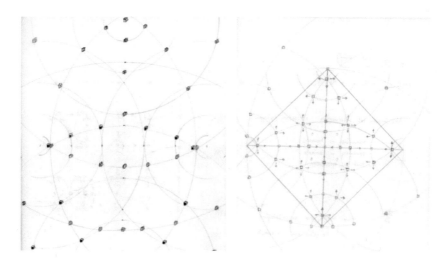

Figure 1   Dimensional sound source, sketches, P. Oomen, 2007.

Independent from Oomen, but in the same year, Leo de Klerk made public his patent application of an omnidirectional loudspeaker that in configuration produces coherent phantom images in both the vertical and horizontal plane (int. Patent no WO2006100250 A transducer arrangement improving naturalness of sound, 2007). Since 2010, Oomen, Holleman and de Klerk work together on the development of the system.

The system has been firstly presented to the public and in the presence of the authors et al. during Amsterdam Dance Event at the Muziekgebouw aan het IJ, October 2012, and has since been showcased in and outside Europe in association with a diverse range of artists from the field of electronic music, sound art and immersive technologies. The system has been subject of multiple lecture presentations, written publications and film documentaries (www.4dsound.net).

The article will at first outline the fundamental principles of the system by looking at a fallacy of spatial sound reproduction as can be derived from the theories by scientists Von Bekésy and Moore, and present a new approach to this problem by the authors. We will then continue with an overview of the technical implementation of the system, which incorporates the design of new hardware, software and interactive interfaces. Finally, we will present our conclusions with regards to the current status of artistic and technical achievements of the system.

Fundamental Principles

A. Fallacy of spatial sound reproduction

We are familiar with Von Bekésy's problem (Experiments in Hearing, 1960): the 'in the box' sound effect seems to increase with the decrease of the loudspeaker's dimensions. In an experimental research on the relation between acoustic power, spectral balance and perceived spatial dimensions and loudness, Von Bekésy's test subjects were unable to correctly indicate the relative dimensional shape of a reproduced sound source as soon as the source's dimensions exceeded the actual shape of the reproducing loud-speaker box. One may conclude that the loudspeaker's spatio-spectral prop-erties introduce a message-media conflict when transmitting sound informa-tion. We cannot recognize the size of the sound source in the reproduced sound. Instead, we listen to the properties of the loudspeaker.

Why does the ear lock so easily to the loudspeaker characteristics? Based on the hypotheses of Brian Moore (Interference effects and phase sensitivity in hearing, 2002) et al., we may conclude that this is because the ear, by nature, produces two dimensional nerve signals to the brain that reflect the three-dimensional wave interference due to direct interaction of both the ear's and the physical sound source's spatio-spectral properties. Therefore any three-dimensional spatio-spectral message information embedded in the signal to be transmitted is masked by the physically present media informa-tion related to the loudspeaker's properties. One could say that in prior art solutions the input signal of the loudspeaker system merely functions as a carrier signal that modulates the loudspeaker's characteristics.

We experience a phantom sound source reproduced by a stereo-system to appear more realistic than the same sound reproduced from one box.

However, spatial sound reproduction by means of stereophonic virtual sources is only a partial solution because it fails for any stereophonic information that does not meet the L=R requirement for perfect phantom imaging. In fact stereophonics is no more than improved mono with the listening area restricted to a sweet spot.

B. A phantom loudspeaker

For a new approach of this problem we considered that one better could overrule the monaural spatio-spectral coding than trying to manipulate it (as f.i. in crosstalk suppression), thus preventing inter-aural cross correlation which is the root mechanism for the listener's ability to localize any non-virtual sound sources i.e. loudspeakers.

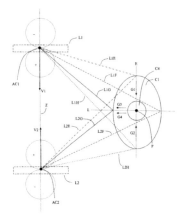

Figure 2   A phantom loudspeaker: two loudspeakers that are present at the same side of an ear are
directed towards each other's acoustic centre make a non-localizable, virtual loudspeaker

The resulting application describes a sound system that produces coherent vertical phantom images that cannot monaurally nor binaurally be decomposed to their root sources i.e. the actual loudspeaker drivers. The loudspeaker becomes audibly non-localizable and any multi-channel horizontal configuration of these virtual speakers is possible without adding masking media properties. As a consequence the listening area is not anymore restricted to a sweetspot. Loudness perception is dramatically improved because the 'out of the box' sound screen will now fit to even the largest sound source shapes.

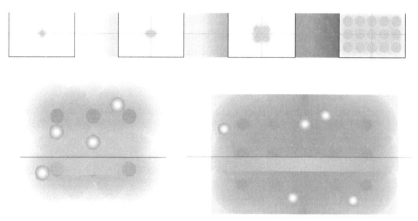

Figure 3   Multi-channel configurations of virtual loudspeakers

Technical Implementation

A. A rotation symmetrical response

For the production of a coherent vertical phantom image that also must be able to interact coherently in the horizontal plane in order to allow multi-channel configuration, a driver structure with a rotation symmetrical off-axis response is a main requirement. The loudspeakers are constructed from modified co-axial drivers, where the modification consists of an altered implementation of existing driver parts and does basically not need re-engineering of the chassis. However, the modification offers the advantage to implement further refining features, f.i. mass-less motional feed-back sensing, that were difficult to apply in the original design.

B. An unlimited spatial continuum

From this application derives the choice for a right-angled and equal spaced speaker configuration expanding in the vertical and horizontal plane to enable balanced sound pressure throughout the entire listening area. In this configuration we define the 'inside speaker field' and 'outside speaker field' marked by the physical borders of the speaker configuration, that in conjunction provide an unlimited spatial continuum, both incorporating the active listening area and expanding beyond it.

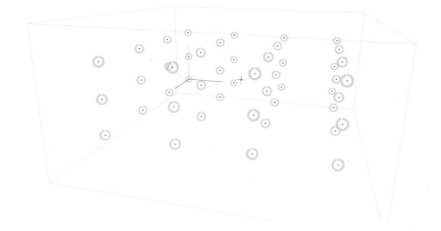

Figure 4   A right-angled and equally spaced speaker configuration to form an omnidirectional listening area.

The spatial continuum is defined in Cartesian coordinates X) left/ right Y) above/below, and Z) front/back in which coordinate [0,0,0] becomes automatically in the center of the listening area on floor level. This infinite and omnidirectional sound screen can now be used to position dimensional sound sources of various geometrical shapes such as points, lines, planes and blocks, both inside the speaker field, in between and next to to the listeners, and outside the speaker field, above, beneath and around the listeners at unlimited distances.

C. Object-based processing software

The object-based processing software is written in C++ and accepts a virtually unlimited amount of discrete sound inputs, which are processed according to spatial data. More than 200 of its data parameters are dynamic and can be addressed via Open Sound Control.

The software defines sound sources, reflecting walls and global transformations of the spatial field such as translation, rotation and plodding. The spatial synthesis can be divided in two parts: i) mono processing on the input signal according to virtual spatial properties, that is consecutively converted to ii) multi-channel processing which treats each speaker output independently.

For initialization the software needs the speaker configuration properties, such as dimensions and spacing of the speakers, and the amount of active sources, whereas a source is a serial circuit of mono modules that synthesize spatial phenomena like distance, angle, and doppler. The multi-channel conversion happens at the end of this chain and translates the sound source's spatial properties like position and dimensions to speaker amplitudes and delays. Its algorithms are based on matrix transformations and vector math. Next to amplitudes and phase delay times is also processes interactive data, such as whether a source is located behind or in front of a virtual reflecting wall or not.

In the multi-channel processing, two panning algorithms are active, one for sources inside the speaker field and the other for outside the field. The inside speaker field panning is based on the shortest distance between the dimensional sound source and the speakers. The outside speaker field panning is based on the shortest distance between the projection of the sound source on the speakers defining the edge of the speaker field. The outside speaker field projection knows two types: 'perspective-panning', which takes a vantage point, typically the centre but can be any other co-ordinate inside speaker field and 'right-angled panning', which takes a vantage 'line' through any point, typically the centre, resulting in wider projections as it not diminishes with a longer distance.

Conclusion

In everyday life people process complex spatial sound information to interact with their surrounding, mostly involuntarily. We are exposed to continuous movement in the environment around, above and beneath us. And in this environment we move ourselves in complex patterns, sometimes fast and straight, then slow and hesitant, turning back and forth, possibly laying, standing, bending or sitting. We are continuously affected by changes of movement surrounding us, and by our patterns of behaviour we influence our perception of this environment and stimulate movement in the environment itself. To be able to further our explorations with spatial sound as a medium, it is essential that the reciprocality between the listener the sounding space is restored to achieve lifelike and meaningful experiences of spatiality.

Conclusively we may state that it is possible to create an innovative and non-conventional sound system that removes the localizability of the sound source from the equation, regardless of the listener's individual hearing properties, and improves loudness perception at equal acoustic power. The system provides for a social listening area, is backwards compatible with existing audio reproduction formats, allows integration with a wide variety of control interfaces and encourages new approaches in design.

Figure 5   4DSOUND System at the Spatial Sound Institute

Leo de Klerk, 1958 (NL) Tonmeister, composer, founder of Bloomline Acoustics and inventor of Omniwave, the inaudible loudspeaker.

Poul Holleman, 1984 (NL) Sound technologist, software developer, co-founder of 4DSOUND

Paul Oomen, 1983 (NL) Composer, founder of 4DSOUND, head of development at the Spatial Sound Institute, Budapest

Toolbox Dialogue Initiative

MICHAEL O'ROURKE & STEPHANIE E. VASKO
Michigan State University

Introduction

Responding to complex problems increasingly involves interdisciplinary and interprofessional teams. Harnessing the different perspectives is challenging, in part because these perspectives typically come with different assumptions, jargon, values, and priorities. As a result, team members can come into conflict without appreciating the differences that generate it. For a team/organization/center/initiative to work effectively, it can help to make explicit these implicit differences. The Toolbox Dialogue Initiative is a National Science Foundation-sponsored project that studies and facilitates communication in collaborative, cross-disciplinary research and practice settings. We have developed a workshop-based response to the challenge of communicating across disciplines and professions that focuses on the use of dialogue to reveal unobserved differences and similarities that can impede collaborative decision-making. By working with you to identify your goals and priorities, we can create a workshop tailored to your needs to enhance communication and collaborative capacity in your group. The Toolbox Dialogue Initiative has conducted over 190 workshops internationally with over 1,500 participants. Toolbox Dialogue Initiative members have produced more than 20 peer-reviewed publications and over 100 presentations. We have worked to build collaborative capacity in research groups that operate in many domains, including academic science, community resiliency, and regional sustainability.

The Toolbox Workshop

The Toolbox Dialogue Initiative works with clients to develop a work-shop that meets the needs and goals of the client. Typical workshops consist of two parts: the instrument and the dialogue. The Toolbox instrument is a set of discussion prompts grouped by theme. Depending on the level of interaction between the Toolbox Dialogue Initiative and the cli-ent, instruments can be off-the-shelf, developed in-house by the Toolbox Dialogue Initiative, or developed by the Toolbox Dialogue Initiative in partnership with participants using surveys and/or focus groups. Prompts in the instrument are associated with Likert scales that rate participant agreement (strongly disagree to strongly agree). Workshops begin with participants filling out the instrument. After completing the instrument, participants then participate in a dialogue session to discuss the issues raised by the prompts, facilitated by a Toolbox

Dialogue Initiative member using a facilitation style chosen to achieve client goals. During this session, participants often discover differences and similarities that surprise them, and it is not uncommon for disagreement to lead to negotiation and compromise. Participants are then asked to complete the Toolbox instrument again. Finally, participants are asked to participate in a debrief session where they are encouraged to reflect on the dialogue and on the workshop as a whole. We also offer the option of probing par-ticipant views in-vivo using surveys with instantaneous reporting and the option of including a co-creation activity for participants as part of the workshop.

Deliverables: Clients can receive a written report that includes summary statistics for the Likert scores pre- and post dialogue, observations of the dialogue and workshop, and recommendations. Survey and co-creation activity results are also included for those clients who choose to integrate those activities into their Toolbox workshop. Toolbox Dialogue Initiative staff are also available for in-person or virtual workshop debrief sessions.

Website: http://toolbox-project.org/

References

Eigenbrode, S., O'Rourke, M., Wulfhorst, J. D., Althoff, D. M., Goldberg, C. S., Merrill, K., Morse, W., Nielsen-Pincus, M., Stephens, J., Winowiecki, L., Bosque-Pérez, N. A. (2007). Employing philosophical dialogue in collaborative science. BioScience 57: 55–64. DOI:http://dx.doi.org/10.1641/b570109

O'Rourke, M. Comparing methods for cross-disciplinary research. In R. Frodeman, J. T. Klein, and R. Pacheco (Eds.), Oxford Handbook of Interdisciplinarity, 2nd ed. Oxford: Oxford University Press. Forthcoming.

O'Rourke, M., Crowley, S., Gonnerman, C. 2016. On the nature of cross-disciplinary integration: A philosophical framework. Studies in History and Philosophy of Biological and Biomedical Sciences 56: 62-70. DOI: http://dx.doi.org/10.1016/j.shpsc.2015.10.003.

O'Rourke, M., Crowley, S. 2013. Philosophical intervention and cross-disciplinary science: The story of the Toolbox Project. Synthese190: 1937–1954. DOI: http://dx.doi.org/10.1007/s11229-012-0175-y.

Robinson, B., Vasko, S. E., Gonnerman, C., Christen, M., O'Rourke, M. 2016. Human values and the value of humanities in interdisciplinary research. Cogent Arts & Humanities 3(1). Available online.

Vasko, S.E. "Creating Craftier Engineers." Slate (10 June 2015). Available online at: http://www.slate.com/articles/technology/future_tense/2015/06/stem_classes_should_include_lessons_about_low_tech_crafts_like_sewing.html.

Michael O'Rourke is Professor of Philosophy and faculty in AgBioResearch at Michigan State University. His research interests include epistemology, communication and epistemic integration in collaborative, cross-disciplinary research, and linguistic communication between intelligent agents.

He is Director of the Toolbox Dialogue Initiative, an NSF-sponsored research initiative that investigates philosophical approaches to facilitating interdisciplinary research (http://toolbox-project.org/).

Stephanie E. Vasko is a Research Associate in AgBioResearch and Philosophy at Michigan State University. Her primary research is affiliated with the Toolbox Dialogue Initiative, for which she is also the Program Manager. Her research interests include methods for enhancing collaborative, cross-disciplinary research and the history of innovation in chemistry and design. She received her Ph.D. in Chemistry & Nanotechnology from the University of Washington.

Biomanufacturing

SIMON PARK
University of Surrey

C-MOULD is the world's largest collection and knowledge base for microorganisms for use in design and art with over 50 different kinds of microorganism. It contains bacteria and fungi that glow in ethereal shades of green and blue light, bacteria that make gold and electrically conductive nanowires, and many bacteria that produce novel biomaterials. It emerged from a project between artist JoWonder and Simon Park, the aim of which was to produce a version of John Millais' famous pre-Raphaelite painting "Ophelia" using naturally pigmented and living bacteria as the paints. For this project Simon Park collected a large palette of different pigmented bacteria (blue, purple, red, yellow, pink, brown etc.), and C-MOULD formed from this as other microorganisms with interesting properties beyond colour were added.

In the context of living architecture, C-MOULD contains six strains of bioluminescent bacteria that naturally produce light, and also bacteria capable of making novel biomaterials. Two of the strains of bioluminescent bacteria within the collection, are unusually and strongly bioluminescent and consequently, their use as an alternative form of lighting has been investigated in a number of projects (Figs 1 and 2).

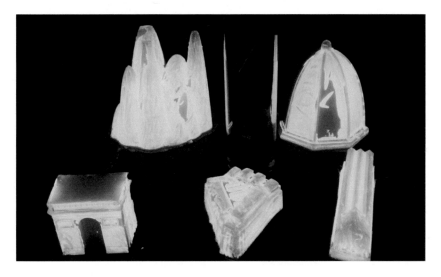

Figure 1   Bioluminescent City. In this collaboration with Bompas and Parr, buildings made from agar were inoculated with the bacterium Photobacterium phosphoreum HB, a hyper-bright strain of a bioluminescent bacterium unique to C-MOULD. The result is a living city which is imbued with a beguiling and blue biological light.

Figure 2   A project with artist Anna Dumitriu at The Wellcome Collection's On Light Event. An alchemical laboratory powered by the cold and ephemeral Qlight of bacterial bioluminescence.

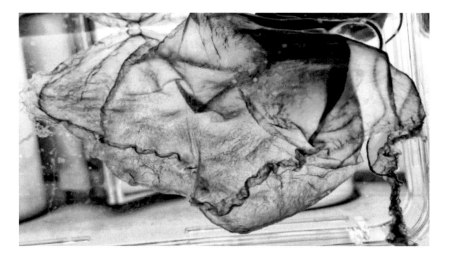

Figure 3   Helion, is a unique and living biomaterial based on Cyanophytes and made from just sunlight and air. In this image the material is being grown in large flasks where it generates extraordinary forms that result from its intelligent and cooperative behaviour.

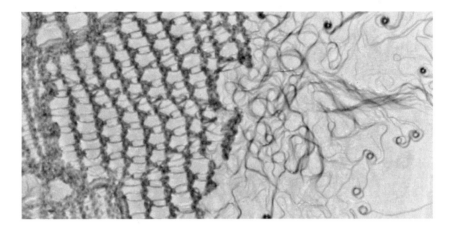

Figure 4   A lace/Cyanophyte hybrid biomaterial. The photosynthetic bacterium infiltrates the textile and
then moves from the manmade textile and spreads over the surfaces beyond making it difficult
to determine where the manmade material ends and the purely biological organism begins.

Biomaterial capabilities within C-MOULD include nanocellulose producing
bacteria and bacteria that fashion forms from little more than sunlight and
air. GXCELL is a bacterium isolated from traditional Kombucha that rapidly
forms thick sheets of nanocellulose and has been used to develop a form of
paper made entirely from bacteria. Other biomaterial producing bacteria in
C-MOULD include the Cyanophytes, which are auxotrophic and photosynthetic bacteria that can produce materials from little more than sunlight and
air. The Helion Project explores the utility of these bacteria in the development of novel biomaterials (Figs 3 and 4).

Dr. Simon Park is a Senior Teaching Fellow at the University of Surrey, where
he teaches Microbiology and Molecular Biology. For ten years now, he has
also worked at the fertile intersection between art and science and here, he
has been involved in many innovative microbiology projects, working with
both artists, and also making his own work. Simon has been involved in over
twenty-five collaborative projects with artists that have combined science and
art, and he has exhibited, both solo and joint work, at venues such as, The
Science Museum, The Eden Project, The Royal Institution, The Science Gallery
Dublin, and The Wellcome Collection. He is also the curator of C-MOULD, the
world's largest collection of microorganisms for use in design and art.

Towards Responsiveness in Architecture

VERA PARLAC & BRANKO KOLAREVIC
University of Calgary

Over the past decade we have seen an increasing interest in exploring the capacity of built spaces to change, i.e., to respond dynamically – and automatically – to changes in the external and internal environments and to different patterns of use. The principal idea is that two-way relationships could be established among the spaces, the environment, and the users: the users or the changes in the environment would affect the configuration of space and vice versa; the result is an architecture that self-adjusts to the needs of the users. This paper describes essential drivers behind the current interest in responsiveness in architecture.

An increased interest in exploring the capacity of built spaces to respond dynamically and adapt to changes in the external and internal environments is technologically and socially motivated. Advances in embedded computation, material design, and kinetics on the technological side, and increasing concerns about sustainability, social and urban changes on the cultural side, provide the background for the adaptive architectural solutions that have started to emerge.

Thanks to current technological advances, a broadening of scientific knowledge, and an understanding of the underlying processes that govern the metabolisms of the natural world, we are able to see deep connections between the made and the natural worlds. The confluence of various technologies and their assimilation are altering the way we perform our activities. Technological and scientific progress is re-calibrating architecture's engagement with temporality and change. It seems that now we can expect more from architecture. We can expect buildings not only to house and facilitate various modes of human activity but also to adapt, behave, respond, and accommodate the flows of energy and information. Blaine Brownell (2008) calls for an architecture imbued with foresight; for him, "Foresight shapes architecture that, like life itself, produces as well as consumes, reincorporates all of its waste, and maintains an ecological footprint in balance with the requirements of its context." According to John Frazer (1995), architecture should be a "living, evolving thing." For them and others who share similar views, building and consuming architecture should be seen and practiced as life-sustaining metabolic processes. This view of architecture as a responsive and productive participant in a larger ecology is fueled, on the one hand, by "material shifts occurring in the domains of energy, resources, and technology" (Brownell 2008) and, on the other, by grasping a deeper connection between biological and cultural systems.

Architecture, Time and Environment

In a recent essay on responsive environments, Chris Perry (2013) examines the origins of architecture's involvement with temporality. According to Perry, these were grounded historically (over centuries) in new developments in technology and science and a mindset these changes brought forward. Dividing the last hundred years into three machine ages, Perry lists technologies that progressively shifted a view of architecture from representation to instrumentality. First, machine age architecture borrowed from the dynamism of large-scale machines and factories – it captured the representation of the temporality. According to Perry, the work of Antonio Sant'Elia, a member of the Italian Futurist movement, and his *La Città Nuova* responded to the temporal phenomena by integrating architecture into the mechanical and circulation networks of the city and did so on a spatial level; architecture itself, however, remained static. For Perry, second machine age architecture, as manifested in Cedric Price's Fun Palace, Archigram's speculative imagery and Reyner Banham's writing, was an environment populated by electronics, communication technology, and audio/visual media. While La Città Nuova addressed movement and change by orienting architecture towards flows and interaction, Cedric Price's *Fun Palace* instrumentalizes a programmatic change by allowing movement and change of architectural elements. At the same time, Reyner Banham's arguments for the inclusion of environmental phenomena and their variability in a design process began to orient architecture towards adaptive environments. Perry then describes the third machine age architecture as influenced by software, information, multi-media technology, robotics, and material science. All those technological advances enabled explorations of dynamic qualities and their effects on architecture, offering an opportunity to position architecture towards a more productive integration within larger ecologies.

Michael Weinstock (2008) discusses the growing interest in the dynamics of fluidity through the concept of nature as a source of interrelated dynamic processes. His studies of metabolisms are aimed at the development of metabolic morphologies for buildings and cities whose organizations and systems are correlated to those of the natural world. Weinstock's work extends the arguments put forward previously by John Frazer in his seminal book, *Evolutionary Architecture*, in which he suggests a new form of designed artifact, one that is interacting and evolving in harmony with natural forces, including those of society. The metabolic morphologies that "relate pattern and process, form and behavior with spatial and cultural parameters" (Weinstock 2008) would support a symbiotic relationship of architecture with the natural world.

The idea of coupling the responsive technologies with the emergence of constructed metabolic morphologies opens the possibility of an intelligent, environmentally sensitive built environment that is connected to metabolic networks. Recent explorations in materiality and material processes (as seen, for example, in the work of Achim Menges, Neri Oxman, and Rachel Armstrong), architectural assembly and its construction (as shown in Skylar Tibbits' projects), as well as localized control of the interior environment (as argued for by Michelle Addington) further this idea by projecting fundamentally different attitudes towards materialization, form, performance, and construction of the built environment. New content for architecture is being formulated that relies on the integration of change and dynamics into architecture – dynamics that not only address kinetic movement but also include flows of energies, material and information. Buildings that could sense and interact with its environment can operate more synergistically within larger ecologies and therefore can move closer to more sustainable participation within the global environment. The responsive architectural systems could act as ecologies in themselves, allowing architecture as a discipline to recalibrate its role in the larger socio-economic context by becoming a more intelligent and operative participant – a participant imbued with foresight.

Information, Energy and Material

As mentioned earlier, John Frazer proposes a new form of a designed artifact, one that is interacting and evolving in harmony with natural forces, including those of society. To achieve that, architectural systems, components or surfaces should have not only a level of kinetic capacity but also capacity to support information transfer, energy transfer and material transformation similar to biological systems.

The relationship between information and the physical response of an adaptive structure is supported by the application of sensors and actuators as well as mechanisms that control and activate the intelligence of the physical environment. Gordon Pask (1969) emphasizes architecture's "operational" capacity (and its "intimate relationship" to cybernetics) by pointing out that "architects are first and foremost system designers." From the organizational and operational aspects, the focus on architectural systems supports the idea of the flow of information. Several concepts developed in the late 1960s and early 1970s, such as Cedric Price's *Fun Palace*, Nicholas Negroponte's *Soft Architecture Machines* (1975), and Chuck Eastman's (1972) concept of "adaptive-conditional architecture" began to explore "intelligence" and the programmability of architecture's processes and spaces in order to form a two-way relationship between spaces and users. When a two-way relationship between the user and the structure is achieved, an adaptive structure/space could have a transformative effect on participants and on the environment.

A truly responsive environment would enter into a "conversation" with its users and allow them to become participants. In other words, such an environment not only should sense and respond but also perceive and act (Fox and Kemp 2009). The design of spaces that actively engage with their users goes beyond form and space delineation and requires the design of complex behavioral and informational systems.

On the one hand, energy transfer relates to the capacity of the built environment to sustain itself through energy harvesting. Such functions, as material system morphologies are developed, could be integrated into materials and the skins of buildings. On the other hand, energy transfer relates to the capacity of the built environment (its surfaces and regions) to facilitate movement and the concentration of some forms of energy (heat, light) in order to form the phenomenological, non-physical boundaries of spaces. By forming micro-climatic regions, spaces could densify and generate nodes of activity and gathering. This presents the challenge of finding a non-permeable and clearly defined boundary between inside and outside in exchange for a surface that fosters the constant flow of information and energy.

Rayner Banham (1965) reminds us that there are two basic ways of controlling the environment: by hiding under the tree/tent/roof (in other words, by building a shelter) or by mediating the local environment by a campfire. He points out that "a campfire has many unique qualities which architecture cannot hope to equal, above all, its freedom and variability." The most recent attitudes to environmental control – where conditions are mediated locally and not globally and in relation to a body and not space – are a testament to this. This is achieved through material that does not need thermal mass but regulates the heat exchange inside a thin zone of a few millimeters (Addington 2008). But a "campfire" as a source of heat and light is localized and specific to its placement within the space. If we think about it beyond its traditional form – and in relation to energy exchange – we can imagine it as a distributed system that can be activated locally and "intelligently," and only where needed. Viewed in the context of flow and exchange, a "campfire" can become an intelligent surface that can thermally modulate the environment and through that facilitate the circulation and gathering of people.

Current technological achievements as well as the expansion of our understanding of the underlying processes in nature have brought about a new generation of materials that are capable of "decision-making" beyond simple reflexivity (Armstrong 2012). These materials, products of synthetic chemistry and biosciences, are capable of material or chemical "computing." A material transformation is triggered by the molecules' ability to make decisions about their environment and respond to it by changing their form, function or appearance. The availability of such materials offers an opportunity to design material behaviors as opposed to choosing materials on their properties. This would certainly alter the way we design: it would require that we begin to relinquish control of the design process (understood in a traditional way) and find ways to channel the material transformations to produce equally rigorous and reliable architecture, but only more aligned with its own materiality and larger ecologies.

Designing Responsiveness

The primary goal of constructing a truly responsive, adaptive architecture is to imbue buildings with the capacity to interact with the environment and their users in an engaging way. Architecture that echoes the work of Nicholas Negroponte could be understood as an adaptive, responsive machine – a sensory, actuated, performative assemblage of spatial and technical systems that creates an environment that stimulates and is, in turn, stimulated by users' interactions and their behavior. Arguably, for any such system to be continually engaging, it has to be designed as inherently indeterminate in order to produce unpredictable outcomes.

Furthermore, responsiveness can be achieved at different scales, from the city and buildings down to a single space or surface. But how would omnipresent responsive environments change architecture's role in the cultural fabric of the society? They would certainly give rise to new social dimensions, enabling new forms of social communication that would emerge from new opportunities of operating within a humanized, technologically augmented space that is dynamic, sensing, and more "alive" than ever before. How would we live in spaces that like very comfortable clothes (or not) respond to our movements? Can we leave the orbit of "fixed", static architecture and interface fluidly with kinetic and changing environments?

The process of designing responsive environments relies on flows and dynamic behavioral patterns. It is inherently open to new and oftentimes emergent configurations. Cities populated with "intelligent" buildings that communicate among themselves, capable of altering and changing patterns of use, would generate a constant information feedback. "Intelligent and sensitive" streets, walkways and public spaces could, by varying environmental phenomena such as light, heat, or coldness, create microclimatic zones that attract and encourage particular human activities. Metabolisms behind those changes could create densities of activities that relate to constantly changing networks of information that redirect patterns of movement. This new "intimacy" between the built environment and human movement and the occupation of space can extend into new relationships between the built environment and the larger ecology, through energy, resource and material exchange.

Acknowledgements

Parts of this paper have been previously published by the authors in the book "Building Dynamics: Exploring Architecture of Change", co-edited by the authors and published in 2015 by Routledge.

References

Addington, Michelle, "The Architecture of the Unfamiliar", 2008. Available at: http://fora.tv/2008/04/17/Michelle_Addington_The_Architecture_of_the_Unfamiliar.

Armstrong, Rachel, "Material (or Chemical) Computing: Protocell Example", 2012. Available at: http://grayanat.posterous.com/tag/protocell.

Banham, Reyner, "A Home Is Not a House," Art in America, 53(2), April 1965: 75.

Brownell, Blaine, "Material Ecologies in Architecture," in Tilder L. and Blostein B. (eds.), Design Ecologies: Essays on the Nature of Design (New York: Princeton Architectural Press, 2008), pp. 221–237.

Eastman, Charles, "Adaptive-Conditional Architecture," in N. Cross (ed.), Design Participation: Proceedings of the Design Research Society Conference (London: Academy Editions, 1972), pp. 51–57.

Fox, Michael and Kemp, Miles, Interactive Architecture (New York: Princeton Architectural Press, 2009).

Frazer, John, An Evolutionary Architecture (London: Architectural Association, 1995).

Negroponte, Nicholas, Soft Architecture Machines (Cambridge, MA: MIT Press, 1975).

Pask, Gordon, "The Architectural Relevance of Cybernetics," Architectural Design, September 1969: 494–496.

Perry, Chris, "anOther Architecture: The Responsive Environment," in Lorenzo-Eiroa, P. and Sprecher, A. (eds.), Architecture in Formation: On the Nature of Information in Digital Architecture (New York: Routledge, 2013), pp. 181–185.

Weinstock, Michael, "Metabolism and Morphology," Architectural Design, March/April 2008: 26–33.

Branko Kolarevic is a professor at the University of Calgary Faculty of Environmental Design, co-director of the multidisciplinary Computational Media Design (CMD) program, and one of the founders of the Laboratory for Integrative Design (LID). He has lectured worldwide on the use of digital technologies in design and production. He is the past president of Canadian Architectural Certification Board (CACB), past president of the Association for Computer Aided Design in Architecture (ACADIA), and was recently elected as future president of the Association of the Collegiate Schools of Architecture (ACSA). He is a recipient of the 2015 ACADIA Society Award of Excellence and ACADIA 2007 Award for Innovative Research. He holds doctoral and master's degrees in design from Harvard University and a diploma engineer in architecture degree from the University of Belgrade.

Vera Parlac is a registered architect in Pennsylvania, USA, and an assistant professor at the Faculty of Environmental Design at the University of Calgary, where she co-founded the Laboratory for Integrative Design (LID). She received a diploma engineer in architecture degree from University of Belgrade and master's degree in architecture from University of California, Los Angeles (UCLA). Vera's current design and research is focused on responsive material systems and informed by contemporary models in biology, material science research, and mechatronic systems. Prior to her appointment in Calgary, she taught design and other subjects at several universities in North America, most recently at Temple University, and in Asia, in Hong Kong.

ColorFolds: eSkin + Kirigami: From Cell Contractility to Sensing Materials to Adaptive Foldable Architecture

JENNY E. SABIN, MARTIN MILLER,
DANIEL CELLUCCI & ANDREW MOORMAN
Cornell University

Introduction

As part of two projects funded by the National Science Foundation in the Sabin Design Lab at Cornell University titled, eSkin and KATS (Cutting and Pasting - Kirigami in Architecture, Technology, and Science), ColorFolds is one product of ongoing trans-disciplinary research spanning across the fields of cell biology, materials science, physics, electrical and systems engineering, and architecture. The goal of the eSkin project, is to explore materiality from nano to macroscales based upon understanding of nonlinear, dynamic human cell behaviors on geometrically defined substrates (Sabin et al 2014). ColorFolds incorporates two parameters that the team is investigating: optical color and transparency change at the human scale based upon principles of structural color at a nano to micro scale (Figure 1).

Figure 1   Rendering of ColorFolds suspended in the architecture building at Cornell University. Color change within the assembly is wavelength dependent or what is also known as 'structural color' change.

In addition to these material proprieties, ColorFolds features a lightweight, tessellated array of interactive components that fold and unfold in the presence or absence of people. From architecture to chemistry, from chalkboards to micrographs, and from maps to trompe-l'oeil, we strive to communicate 3D geometry, structures, and features using 2D representations. They have allowed us not only to communicate complex information, but also to create real objects, from the act of folding a paper airplane to the construction and digital fabrication of entire buildings. ColorFolds follows the concept of "Interact Locally, Fold Globally," necessary for deployable and scalable architectures. Using mathematical modeling, architectural elements, design computation, and controlled elastic response, ColorFolds showcases new techniques, algorithms, and processes for the assembly of open, deployable structural elements and architectural surface assemblies. Each face of the tessellated and interactive components features a novel colorful film invented by 3M called Dichroic Film. Not only does this film align with our investigations into structural color, but it also allows for room-scale investigations of these nano to micro material effects and features. An array of sensors detects the presence or absence of people below, which in turn actuates a network of Flexinol® by Dynalloy, Inc. spring systems that open or close the folded components.

Background

The particular material research presented builds upon the latest prototypes and applications within the eSkin project, the optical simulation and application of geometrically defined nano/micro scale substrates that display the effects of nonlinear structural color change when deployed at the building scale. We are currently limited to a 4-inch by 4-inch maximum swath of the eSkin material due to high material costs and fabrication time. This requires that we develop and fabricate prototypes that exhibit the same material effects of eSkin, but that can be fabricated at the human scale. In the ColorFolds project, we are working with a commercially available wavelength dependent film produced and supplied by 3M called Dichroic film. Specifically, nano/micro scale pillar substrates, designed in the Shu Yang lab, form the basis of our material investigation. These substrates are fabricated via microlithography and soft lithography, first requiring a negative nano/micro pattern to be etched into a substrate in which an organic polymer known as PDMS (polydimethylsiloxane) is subsequently cast, cured, and removed, thus producing a positive relief of nano/micro pillars (see for example Thompson et al. 1994, Xia et al 1998, & Zhang et al. 2006).

Demonstrating unique angle dependent and wavelength filtering optical properties of interest, these periodic pillar arrays act as passive filters of light given the specific nano or micro scale periodicity of their structures and the angle at which they are viewed. Because of the particular periodic spacing and geometry of these arrays existing at the nano-to-micro scale, light is absorbed via the PDMS material, but also filtered as a property of the specific wavelength of light that is allowed to pass through a particular pillar array. Depending on factors such as the diameter and the periodic distance between each pillar in an array, the visible spectrum of light, which exists between 390nm to 750nm, will be filtered out, absorbed or scattered and reflected or refracted from the material. Through changes in pattern, compliance, geometry and structure, we can manipulate material features including color, transparency and opacity. Here, color change is generated by an optical effect such as refraction or interference as opposed to a change in pigment. This is known as structural color. In our case, physical structures in the form of pillars interact with light to produce a particular color. These colors are also dependent upon angle of view or ones orientation to the given materials. There are many examples of structural color change found in nature such as the wings of the Blue Morpho butterfly or the feathers of hummingbirds. We are interested in harnessing these material features and effects and translating them into scalable building skins. Imagine dynamically blocking sunlight throughout the day through simple mechanical changes of the eSkin film via stretching or compressing or in other words, creating and tuning your own window! This paper presents our next steps in integrating and arraying these material features and effects within scalable adaptive and foldable assemblies through kirigami geometry.

Methods

Kirigami Geometry: Folding with Cuts and Holes

The generative design process for ColorFolds began with an examination and study of kirigami processes as a means of creating doubly-curved surfaces through a simple implementation of gradient folding conditions. Kirigami is similar to origami, but includes the addition of cuts and holes. The origin of the word comes from the Japanese kiru, "to cut," a geometric method and process that brings an extra, previously unattainable level of design, dynamics, and deployability to self-folding and -unfolding materials from the molecular to the architectural scale. Our tools and methods were greatly informed by collaborating and working closely with PI and theoretical physicist on the team, Randall Kamien, based at University of Pennsylvania (Castle et al 2014).

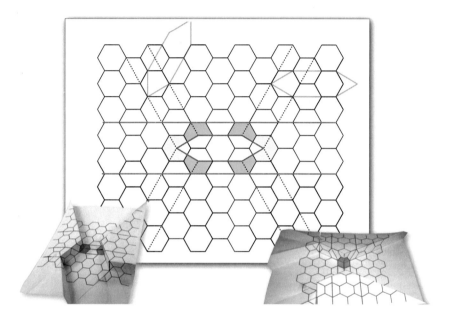

Figure 2   Precision kirigami based upon topology and geometry of defects in sheets (Castle et al 2014).

The primary geometric relationships describing Kirigami are illustrated here (Figure 2). Similar to origami, there are prescribed folds represented with dashed lines. In addition to this, we can cut out the blue hexagons shown in blue. These folds will move us from 2D flat sheet to 3D form. In addition to these studies rooted in the theoretical and pure geometric representations of kirigami geometry, are work is also informed by the dynamic conditions of material, both in shape and cut and how these parameters are designed and engineered through fractal cuts and subdivision (Cho et al 2014) (Figure 3).

Through these studies, we developed a series of algorithms for generating an adaptable spatially aware geometry that formally responds to site-based geometries with the added capacity-through its geometry and actuation system-to adapt to various user groups within the installation space. Utilizing physics-based engine Kangaroo in Grasshopper, we were able to both simulate behaviors prior to fabrication and force physical constraints onto digital geometries to ensure ideal translation from design to fabrication. Through our research, we developed several studies of singular component behaviors. This behavior was developed through a study of contingent folding behaviors in which initial folding states exist out of a single plane. These states use non-orthogonal cut patterns as a means of activating several folding panels through a singular system of actuation.

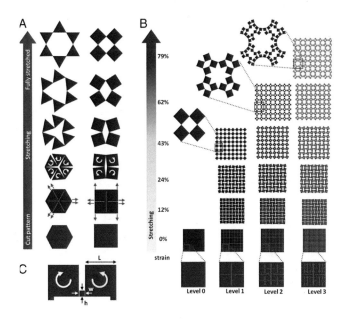

Figure 3   Basic principles of the cut design. (A) Cuts separate the material into rotating units, with connectivity dependent on the cut pattern (assuming freely rotating point hinges). A hexagon can be divided into six smaller triangles in a pattern that can be repeated to fill space or a square can be divided into foursmaller squares. Upon equal-biaxial stretching, each unit rotates clockwise (white arrows) or counterclockwise (grey arrows), yielding an expansion of the original structure. Expansion continues up to a maximum level by pure unit rotation (minimal strain within the structural units). The structures are fully stretched when moment equilibrium is achieved (Cho et al 2014).

These initial folding and cutting studies generated a series of feedback loops between analog and digital testing. After an examination of basic kirigami behaviors we created a series of customized algorithms to simulate and test large-scale aggregations. Our testing was driven by the ability to create inherent complex curvatures through precise cut and fold patterns within a planar sheet. By developing gradient conditions within the cut/fold pattern we were able to achieve final outcomes exhibiting complex double curvature. As the experimental computational tools developed, we designed a folding system that is based on a multidirectional deformation scheme. Looking at the behavior of cellular networks, our system is able to adapt to complex curvature by creating regions of higher component densities where tighter curvatures and adaptability are required. By generating a triangular mesh and extracting the dual we were able to create a more irregular pattern capable of adapting more readily to variegated folding behaviors.

Results

Materials and Fabrication

The final prototype and installation involved a third iteration of specificity within our algorithmic tool set. Responding to specific site conditions and constraints, a series of form-finding algorithms were developed as a means for nesting the system efficiently within the designated space. A series of feedback loops and nested form-finding algorithms created a final geometry that incorporated the following: Subdivision and application of a regular edge length cellular network to the inhabitable region; Generation of a linear network with surficial members to infill the cellular network; Application of force-based algorithms to geometry to simulate it's behavior in real space; Re-evaluation of input parameters to most ideally occupy the physical space; Force-based manipulation of geometry to ensure that planar geometries are adequate for digital fabrication.

The material for the final installation is a composite of .25" extruded polycarbonate and dichroic film. Leveraging the computational nature of the project we utilized packing algorithms to optimize cut file layouts and embed assembly information within individual components. Custom nylon hinges were developed and applied to the inner folding edge of joining facets within the aggregation using blind rivets. Joining opposite corners within the aggregation are custom elements, which carry the primary tensile loads of the structure and serve as the anchoring points for the nitinol actuators. These component lengths were standardized within the form finding algorithms and therefore able to be mass-produced. The assembly consists of aluminum c-channel brackets anchoring the tensile stop members which double as the electrical return for the nitinol springs. These custom assemblies are the primary mechanical driver for the actuation of the installation (Figure 4 & 5).

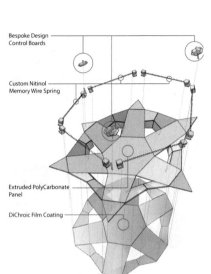

Bespoke Design
Control Boards

Custom Nitinol
Memory Wire Spring

Extruded PolyCarbonate
Panel

DiChroic Film Coating

Figure 4   Component assembly featuring
polycarbonate panels and lamenate
dichroic film. The assembly consists of
aluminum c-channel brackets, nitinol
springs and custom boards with sensors
and thermisters.

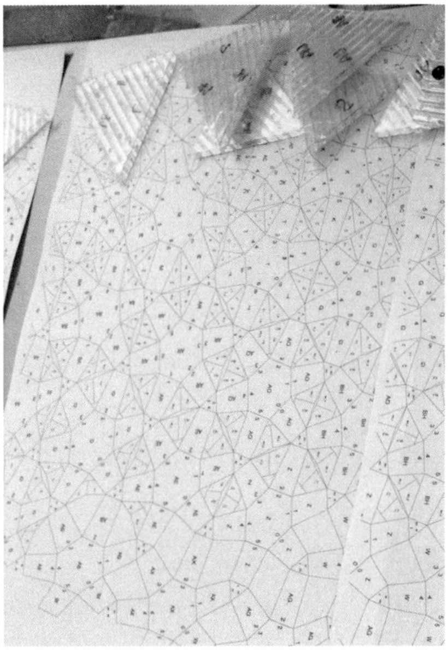

Figure 5   2D cut file drawing for CNC machining.
Our research focuses on 2D templates
for 3D foldable assemblies.

Mechatronics: Interface Design for Interactive Behavior

The main source of actuation for the kirigami installation is resistive heating of shape-memory alloy (SMA) springs. The advantages of these actuators include low weight, reasonable strength, and simple construction. However, the high power requirement for resistive heating means that specialized hardware is needed to reliably deliver power to the springs.

We combined this specialized hardware with a decentralized control scheme called an actuation automaton. Each actuation automaton consists of three springs connected to a central node board. Due to the irregular topology, some node boards controlled four springs, with two connected in series. Each node board consists of three MOSFETs that regulate the heating of the SMA springs, an Attiny 84 microcontroller, and a shift register. Several of these boards are then connected in a bus to a central 5 volt 20 amp power supply.

The microcontroller on each board heats the springs using an open-loop control scheme, turning on each MOSFET for a specific amount of time and allowing the bussed power to flow through the spring, producing the necessary heating energy to cause actuation. Each board activates its constituent springs simultaneously and broadcasts the actuation state to its neighbors. A board can broadcast its status to as many neighbors as necessary, but each board can receive a maximum of eight neighbor states. These states are communicated as a binary string through the shift register (Figure 6).

Figure 6   Photo of custom board situated within a component. Each actuation automaton consists of three springs connected to a central node board. Due to the irregular topology, some node boards control four springs, with two connected in series.

We also designed a software automaton that uses this communication and control protocol to produce complex, emergent behavior within the cellular network from a set of simple rules. The rules are:

1. Default behavior is called 'breathing'; it involves a slow charge and discharge of the springs accomplished through pulse width modulation of the control MOSFET. The board broadcasts a state of '0' to its neighbors while in the state.

2. The opposite behavior to 'breathing' is 'glowing'; the springs are

heated as quickly as possible, producing a quick contraction. While in this state, the board broadcasts a '1' to its neighbors.

3. While 'breathing', the board uses the shift register to poll the states of its nearest neighbors. The number of 'glowing' neighbors determines the probability that this board will, itself, enter the 'glow' state. When all neighbors are 'glowing', the probability is 1, and when all neighbors are 'breathing', the probability is 0.

4. After the board enters the 'glow' state, it will remain there for a short time, and then return to a rest state where it will 'breathe' but not poll its neighbor's state.

From this set of rules, a few parameters are of importance to the behavior of the overall system:

1. The frequency with which the board polls its nearest neighbors for their status, which is, in effect, the sensitivity of a board to its surroundings.

2. The speed with which contraction occurs.

3. The length of the glow state.

4. The length of time spent resting before going back to polling neighbors.

In order to study the effect of the different parameter values on the behavior of the overall system, we constructed a simple simulation that is based on the topology and cellular network of the kirigami installation. The boards in this simulation are all initialized at a random point in the breathing cycle, and specific blocks of nodes can be made to glow at the same time, producing a perturbation of the system that could be introduced in the installation using external sensors or other forms of interaction. Given the proper balance of parameters, these glowing blocks can quickly spread outward, producing traveling waves that successfully spread throughout the array. Moreover, the glow effectively resets the breathing cycle, resynchro-nizing the breathing of the boards and producing complex passive behavior that mirrors the spread of the active perturbation.

Discussion

The pioneering structural designer and father of the space frame and corrugated sheet metal, Robert Le Ricolais, was obsessed with the seemingly paradoxical notion of building with holes. He stated, "The art of structure is how and where to put holes." Our work will take this principle to the next level: buildable, bendable, and biological. Through the use of physics-based simulations and form-finding techniques, we are able to incorporate the dynamic nature of forces flowing through material and geometry as active design parameters. Kirigami offers a very robust geometric template for exploring the strategic placement of cuts and holes relative to disruptions in material and dynamic change. We did encounter significant design and fabrication hurdles through the process of scaling and with the addition of thickness in material to the kirigami components. Hinge design became a crucial factor. Our most promising result entailed the use of laser cut vinyl hinges mechanically fastened to two petals of every kirigami component. The material allowed for enough stretch or tolerance at the fold of the 6mm extruded CNC cut polycarbonate panels. Although appropriate for this prototype, we are now collaborating with Spencer Magleby, a mechanical engineer based at Brigham Young University specializing in thick stamped origami. Together, we are innovating hinge design at the architectural scale.

The incorporation of mechatronics in the ColorFolds project was purposeful, but atypical in the Sabin Design Lab. We typically favor the direct manipulation and programming of matter for actuation and dynamic response over mechanical control. However, this was a useful step as it allowed us to operate at scales not yet achievable in the materials alone. Through this scaling, significant errors were discovered predominately in the calculation of power to run the entire network of boards and array of nitinol springs. We discovered that the overall network of foldable components and boards (>60) required significantly more power to actuate than we estimated.

Conclusion

Comprised of a network of low cost sensors and wavelength dependent responsive materials, ColorFolds is conceived to be generic and homogenously structured upon installation, but readily adaptable to local heterogeneous spatiotemporal conditions and user interaction. This manner of operation not only maximizes immediate performative efficiency, but also allows

Figure 7   Final installation view of ColorFolds, seen from below.

for ongoing contextual adaptation. In this regard ColorFolds is a "learning" and adaptive skin assembly, an experimental prototype for future applications in the context of adaptive architecture (Figure 7). Our approach to kirigami-based construction will bring a new level of motifs, portability, and nuanced design to recently established techniques to form intricate structures chemically, biologically, elastically, and through 3D printing and self-assembly. Instead of post-rationalizing a complex shape through discrete surfacing – a common, unsustainable and costly practice that privileges optimization over innovation – our approach addresses how complexity is materialized in architecture by embedding fabrication logics, active materials, and deployable geometries at all scales and phases of the design and construction process.

Acknowledgements

Principal Investigator: Jenny E. Sabin

Design Research Team: Martin Miller (Senior Personnel & Design Lead), Daniel Cellucci & Andrew Moorman (Mechatronics Lead), Giffen Ott (Production Lead), Max Vanatta, David Rosenwasser, Jessica Jiang

Kirigami / Jenny E. Sabin (Co-PI) and Martin Miller (Senior Personnel) (architecture), Dan Luo (Co-PI) (Biological and Environmental Engineering), Cornell University; Shu Yang (Co-PI) (materials science), Randall Kamien (PI) (physics & astronomy), University of Pennsylvania

This project is funded by the National Science Foundation and the CCA

References

T. Castle, Y. Cho, X. Gong, E. Jung, D.M. Sussman, S. Yang, and R.D. Kamien. "Making the Cut: Lattice Kirigami Rules." Phys. Rev. Lett. 113 (2014) 245502.

Sabin, Jenny, Lucia, Andrew, Ott, Giffen,. and Wang, Simon, April. 2014. "Prototyping Interactive Nonlinear Nano-To-Micro Scaled Material Properties and Effects at The Human Scale." In Symposium on Simulation for Architecture & Urban Design (SimAUD 2014) 2014 Spring Simulation Multi-Conference (SpringSim'14); Tampa, Florida, USA, 13 - 16 April 2014, edited by D. Gerber. Red Hook, NY: Curran. 7-14. (Best Paper Award)

Thompson, L. F. Introduction to Microlithography. 2nd ed. Washington, DC: American Chemical Society, 1994.

Xia, Younan and George M. Whitesides. "Soft Lithography." Annual Review of Materials Science, 28 (1998): 153-184.

Jenny Sabin's work is at the forefront of a new direction for 21st century architectural practice – one that investigates the intersections of architecture and science, and applies insights and theories from biology and mathematics to the design of material structures. Sabin is the Wiesenberger Assistant Professor in the area of Design and Emerging Technologies and the newly appointed Director of Graduate Studies in the Department of Architecture at Cornell University. She is principal of Jenny Sabin Studio, an experimental architectural design studio and director of the Sabin Design Lab at Cornell AAP, a hybrid research and design unit with specialization in computational design, data visualization, and digital fabrication. She was recently awarded the prestigious Architectural League Prize for Young Architects and was named the 2016 Innovator in design by Architectural Record's national Women in Architecture Awards. Her work was exhibited in the internationally acclaimed 9th ArchiLab titled Naturalizing Architecture at FRAC Centre, Orleans, France and is currently on view as part of Beauty – Cooper Hewitt Design Triennial. Her work has been published extensively including in The Architectural Review, Azure, A+U, Metropolis, Mark Magazine, Science, the New York Times, and Wired Magazine. Her forthcoming book, *LabStudio: Design Research between Architecture & Biology*, co-authored with Peter Lloyd Jones, will be published in spring 2017.

Theater Without Organs:
Co-Articulating Gesture and Substrate in Responsive Environments

SHA XIN WEI
Arizona State University

Ludwig Wittgenstein's skepticism about the expressive scope of propositional language, Jacques Derrida's critique of logocentrism, generalized via semiotics to all forms of representation, and Judith Butler's analysis of the performativity of gender motivate the turn to performance as an alternative to representation. In this essay I discuss a genre of responsive environments in which computationally augmented tangible media respond to the improvised gesture and activity of their inhabitants. I propose that these responsive environments constitute an apparatus for experimentally investigating questions significant for both performance research and philosophical inquiry. The responsive environments were designed as sites for phenomenological experiments about interaction and response, agency, and intention under three conditions: (1) the participants are physically co-present, (2) each inhabitant is both actor and spectator, (3) language is bracketed.

The last condition does not deny language, but focusses attention on how an event unfolds without appealing solely to textual or verbal communication. As such, these environments constitute performative spaces whose media – sound, visual field, acoustics and lighting, objects and furnishings – can be reproducibly conditioned, and in which actions can be rehearsed or improvised. I will describe the apparatus of these performative spaces in enough detail to be able to address certain phenomenological questions about the continuum of intentional and accidental gesture in the dynamical substrate of calligraphic media: continuous fields of video and sound or other computationally animated materials, continuously modulated by gesture or movement. I suggest that emerging forms of calligraphic media present an alternative to linguistic pattern for the articulation of affectively charged events, practically and theoretically interrogating the status of narrative in the construction of theatrical events.

What symbolically, affectively charges an event? When movement matters, how and why does a gesture make meaning? If we provisionally bracket verbal narrative and invite non-experts to improvise movements that nuance time-based media in a common performative space, then how can we condition a physical environment to sustain experiences that are as compelling as the works of Bertolt Brecht, Heiner Müller, Jerzy Grotowski, Eugenio Barba, Robert Wilson, Pina Bausch, or Anne Teresa Keersmaeker? We ask these questions in the methodological silence left by Antonin Artaud's call to liberate theater from the tyranny of the text, from what he called dramatic literature. In what sense, and to what degree this is possible may be questioned, because, as Derrida argued in his essay on Artaud, "Presence, in order to be presence and self-presence, has always and already begun to represent itself."[1]

Notwithstanding Derrida's sly reversal re-establishing the primacy of grammatological representation, there have been diverse practical responses to Artaud's challenge over the past half century in experimental theater. Art collectives (Dumb Type, sponge, Palindrome, Chunky Move) are beginning to use computational media technologies in a less remediated and more idiomatic ways. Although there is much to be said for cargo cult approaches to technology, nonetheless one need not take the technology of electronic devices, protocols and software for granted as naturalized, shrink-wrapped black-boxes. Conducting this material, embodied craft with some technical discipline affords some grip for critical and artistic experiment. At the same time, one remains acutely conscious of the epistemic frames constructed and imposed by techno-scientific practice, a task which becomes more challenging the more deeply we enter the black-box, adapting insider knowledge and practices from techno-scientific research and development.

Over the past 15 years, my work with these responsive environments has been guided by the demands of performance research, particularly questions concerning the phenomenology of performance. One of my key experimental motivations is to explore how we could make possible a compelling experience without relying on pre-scripted, linguistically codable, narrative structure. More precisely, I pose three questions:

(1) How can people coordinate transformative and compelling experiences without relying on conventional linguistic categories such as verbal narrative? The technical analogue to this is: how can people create sense together in a responsive media environment (henceforth "responsive environment") without resorting to grammatical structures? This may seem like a purely technical concern but it has extensive ethical-aesthetic implications. For example, this impels us to seek alternatives to procedural, "if-then" logic and to the locally linear syntax of time-based scripts and scores, including patterns found in conventional genres of interactive art and fiction. One expects that the materials, whether patterned by logic, social field, or physics, make a difference to the event.[2]

(2) How could people improvise meaningful gestures collectively or singly in an environment that is as dynamic as they are, an environment that itself evolves over time as a function of its inhabitant life? Interaction modeled on a particularly reduced notion of computationally mediated action and response is a far cry from densely varying textures of theater or everyday life. How can expressive gestures be sustained in sensate and animate matter, some of which may be animated computationally?

(3) How could objects emerge continuously under the continuous action of inhabitants in a responsive space? This question of novelty itself comes from a larger critique of technology, understood as that which mediates the co-construction of human subjects and our world. Given the thick, pre-analytic, pre-orthogonalized aspect of the lifeworld with its nuanced fields of relation and influence, one may ask of technology a rich but not more complicated life.[3] But instead of restricting ourselves to observation, given a studio-laboratory we can experimentally design and inhabit our own events, too. This risks complicating and contaminating the event according to the conventions of theater as well as laboratory science. However, that word risk itself implies a purity of the event, independent of acts of observation, which we may expressly question. Humberto Maturana and Francisco Varela observed that a continuously self-reproducing autopoietic system cannot draw an objective distinction or operational boundary between exterior and interior stimuli. As Maturana and Varela were generalizing from nervous systems and cellular organisms, it seems that their observation should pertain to any autopoietic system, of which our responsive environments were designed to exemplify. Therefore the event's creators and players are by design and in practice themselves participant-observers of their responsive play spaces.

The significance of these three questions about compelling non-verbal play, improvised meaningful gesture, and the emergence of objects from fields is not confined to theater or experimental performance alone. They are not merely technical problems solved by the artist plying his or her craft. I believe that reflecting closely on the practices and technologies of performance conversely provides insight about gesture, agency and materiality. Having written also about the relation between gesture, agency and materiality elsewhere so let me make two critical comments here about the consequences of these relations for gesture in a responsive environment.[4]

Given an environment made with tangible, responsive media, we can begin to understand experimentally how gesture conjures the self and how collective gesture conjures the social without assuming schemas of gesture, selves and the social prior to the event. One of the original principal motivating themes for the installation-events and the associated research described in this essay is the dissolution and re-formation of bodies in a continuous field. When this field is a social field, then the act of gesturing becomes a way to shape intentional being in the world from a state of non-intentional distraction. At a larger scale, since our gesture is conditioned by birth, habit, and culture, gesture entangles social history with the body in action. Not only our own personal histories but also the habits of generations sediment into our own bodies as disciplines that fluidly scaffold our gestural expectations, anticipations and intentions.[5] The technology of performance allows us to play tangibly and reproducibly with such processes of individuation.

Accordingly, we study how people could improvise gestures meaningfully in a media-rich space that evolves continuously in response to their activity. With the "media choreography" systems realized by the Topological Media Lab which I established in 2001 to pursue such research and creation, we have built frameworks of pliant software instruments that enforce no syntax on the player's expressive gesture.[6] By relaxing syntactic constraints, there are no wrong movements and every movement "does something" to modulate the ambient environment. In place of syntax and grammar, we have a responsive environment that tangibly resonates people's gestures and movement with one another and the environment: every glide, every stroke, every slip and slide, stirs media processes in tandem with the physical material world. In a deep sense, one can claim that is the ontological continuity of the field of superposed media processes that enables improvisation and performatively rich nuance.[7] This continuity has strong phenomenological consequences. Continuity is a leitmotiv of topological media and the heuristic lens into the full, thick dynamics of our embodied experience. As you sweep your arm it moves continuously through the air. As you walk to your friend to greet her, your consciousness has no gaps. In everyday experience, your existence appears to have no gaps. As human experience is dense and continuous our creations should sustain playfully intensified experiences that, in my terms, are not complicated but rich.

Since we composers of responsive environments wanted to sustain such phenomenal density in our own play space, we made software media engines that synthesize time-based video and audio. These engines, especially the sound instruments, allow players to dissolve, re-constitute, and shape perceptual entities under the impact of their individual and collective activity. Making a media engine that evolves continuously also radically reduces the complexity of the media elements that need to be assembled for production because media can be synthesized afresh in response to the activity during an event. In practice, we pre-fabricate relatively few media objects (i.e. video or sound files) as initial textural material to seed the processes that re-synthesized dynamic fields of sound and image in real-time performance.

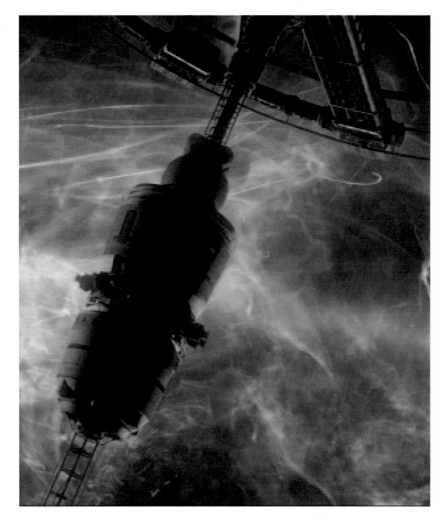

Figure 1   SOLARIS, Soderbergh.

What is the medium of gesture in this extended dynamical setting but continuous and open material, that is a topological medium?[8] We use topological media
not as an abstract model, but as the substrate of performance and physical
action itself, an expressive tissue amalgamated from gesturing flesh and re-synthesized video and sound. Where Grotowski challenged actors to use their own
bodies as their expressive medium, in studio-laboratory work I take as my challenge creating computationally mediated matter forexpressive presentation.[9]

Analytic sciences and philosophy may be less attuned to this non-representational use of matter because matter, whether ink and paper or fabric, has tended to be regarded as part of dumb nature, the object of mere craft (not art). Literary theory and till recently cultural studies may gain analytic purchase on matter only so far as it can be traced as linguistically signifying matter.[10] Matter, topologically construed and topologically constituted, may serve as the substrate of poetic expression. (For a more adequate introduction to what one might mean by topology and topological media, please refer to [Sha 2012, 2013].)

I sometimes characterize the empirical practice of the Topological Media Lab as a form of materials science. Adopting the more modest spirit of making a textile rather than a jacket, one can ask what would play the role of the "textile" opposite to the "performance-event"? It would have to be the hybrid media, the hybrid, dynamical, responsive fields out of which particular narrative objects and event sequences emerge. I call these fields the substrate. The Ozone media choreography system as architected, constitutes not a particular event action sequence like a stage play or a game, nor even a generalized language, but the substrate to a continuous range of performance. I should emphasize that I do not wish to use substrate in its ordinary sense of being prior or more foundational than its objects or events, but in the sense of the physics of fields. The substrate is constitutive of the objects and events that form in it; in other words, the substrate and its contingent objects occupy the same ontological stratum. So, objects do not emerge out of the substrate, objects emerge in it. The substrate is in the same ontological stratum as its dynamically forming and dissolving objects.[11] What this offers performance is an alchemical technology for poetic matter. Such technologies of, for example, gesturally nuanced realtime video and sound synthesis, and of responsive, sensate and luminous electronic fabrics comprise contemporary amplifications of the technologies not of representation but of performance.[12]

The Ouija Experiments

The Ouija media and movement experiments were motivated by questions that I posed to a colleague and choreographer: Michael Montanaro, Chair of Contemporary Dance at Concordia University. When is a movement accidental, and when volitional? And when can a set of movement be construed as a collective movement? Leaving aside such questions as, when is a gesture a citation of another gesture, such questions are not easy even for a human to discern about another human. The very multiplicity of the world makes such questions, in a sense, undecidable, and yet, the significant expansion of pattern recognition research and industry testifies to an enduring fascination with this question in the technologies of security as well as the technologies of performance. Michael Montanaro responded with a series movement exercises that could be carried out in a theater-scale blackbox by dancers. After six months of preparing appropriate responsive sound and video instruments, a team of realtime media artist-programmers worked with an assistant choreographer and various combinations of dancers in daily structured improvisational exercises and theatrical or choreographic experiments. It is important to note that this was a long durational work in studio, not a performance with an audience beyond a proscenium.

Interestingly, these studies were simultaneously legible to the dancers as a dance exercises like structured improvisation, and to theoretical eyes as philosophical experiments. The media artist-programmers were asked to accompany the movement artists in five ways: by filling the 16m x 16m x 8m high black box theater with canned (pre-edited, linear) sound or video, or sound or video that responded to movement, or no media but work lights. The artists and experimentalists wanted to see how responsive media could palpably vary the experience and the concerted movement of the dancers. In one memorable experiment, after the dancers had some hours to familiarize themselves in a contact improvisation exercise, they were asked to work in pairs. One member of each pair was blindfolded and the other passed her hand over the partner, close enough for the first to sense the hand without touching. They were asked to try to, in essence, continue contact improvisation without contact. Interestingly, one blindfolded dancer, a man, kept trying to reach out after the sighted, "active" dancer. From the way he craned his head about, he seemed to be trying to visualize where his partner was located in space. But it took much longer for him to entrain with his partner that way the other pairs entrained: after about 20-30 minutes, the pairs of dancers initiated and terminated non-parallel movement with extraordinary synchrony. This particular exercise was performed in silence. In another experiment, the dancers wore wrist-born, wireless accelerometers mapping the forces of their movements to sound. As an aside, such sensors measure not physical displacement or speed, but force.

So, if a body moves at a steady pace along a straight line (to first approximation), the sensor reports zero plus residual noise. If the body moves along a curved path at the same steady pace, however, the sensor will report a force, the centripetal force due to the arc. This confuses those who cognitively model the "accelerometer" as measuring speed. In any case, despite such subtleties in the remapping of movement, when the radio connection died because the batteries ran out on their wrist sensor, the dancers could tell immediately that the Max/MSP process synthesizing the rich, dynamically varying sound was no longer coupled to what they were doing. Indeed, the wearer could tell this when the lapse is not apparent to observers. Clearly, the ever-varying sound fields coupled with physical action intimately modulated the first-person experience in ways palpably distinct from what a third party could observe. This "malfunction" validated the focus of this work, which was first-person, or better, first-hand experience.

In yet another exercise, the realtime video artist-programmers projected onto the wall life-size shadows of the dancers. In fact, each dancer multiplied into three bodies: their own, a physical shadow cast by theater lights onto the large (17m x 8m high) white wall, and a second copy of their own bodies delayed by video processing an adjustable number of milliseconds. Every single pixel of the video could be delayed by a different amount time, and the delays could be changed over time from milliseconds to many minutes, in response to movement in countless variety. There was an opportunity to explore many subtle phenomena. For example, when you stand in front of a mirror and hold up your hand. Your mirror self holds up his corresponding hand.[13] This is your (reflected) image with zero (perceived) delay. You see this as yourself. But if the image of you is displayed with a long delay, say many seconds, then you see this as someone else, not yourself now, but a copy of yourself, then. Therefore, something subtle must happen with some intermediate temporal delays. In what time intervals of delays do these subtle reversals or flickerings of self and not-self happen? This informs phenomenological questions that the experimentalists wanted to explore. However, the dancers chose the simplest possible case, a uniform delay of about 6 whole seconds.[14] This turned the eye-filling wall into a membrane that duplicated their actions and replayed them back on the wall over a considerable gap in performance and experiential time. Referencing capoeira martial art technique, the choreographer and the dancers came up with a way to have dancers work with and against the delayed copies of themselves in a mesmerizing counterpoint of bodies, their shadows and their delayed images. But this raises a question of how movement artists incorporate technique: after seeing the profound and mesmerizing effect of a wall in which every single pixel could be delayed independently of the others, why did the choreographer ask for a wall with a uniform delay, the simplest effect? Observing their work, it seemed that the uniformly delayed "mirror" wall allowed the dancers to deposit whole bodies in complex action with one another. This reminds one of Whitehead's comment, in Process and Reality, that a "young man does not initiate his, experience by dancing with impressions of sensation, and then proceed to conjecture a partner. His experience takes the converse route."[15] However interesting this sociotechnical phenomenon may be, a more subtle thing happened as we all were enchanted by the obvious appeal of dancers fighting rhythmically with six-second old copies of themselves. Sensing the potential of these movement sequences for a performance, one sensed strongly a shift in collective intent, from opening up corporeal investigations and experiential questions, to a narrowing of the sequences down to a single sequence practiced repeatedly for a putative audience. In other words, the collective activity changed from experiment to rehearsal.

From "What is the Human?" to "Where is Human?" and "How To Human?"

By this point, it may be apparent that the sort of responsive environments that we have built constitute apparatuses for an experimental exploration of subjectivation, in Guattari's sense. In order to conduct this exploration in the mode of experimental performance research, we focus our attention on the amplification of metaphorical gestures by co-present humans performing in a common responsive, alchemical medium. In order to query or re-fashion the fold between nature and artifice, signs and matter, ego and other, I have wagered that we must create (as we have) a responsive medium as a continuous amalgam of the forms of matter that are accessible to our craft, whether computational or physical: projected light, organized sound and video, fabric, choreographed flesh, speech, software. What we must and have set aside are certain categories such as the cogito as well as the body because in order to understand such ontological or phenomenological categories it greatly helps to transgress those categories' boundaries rather than assume them a priori.[16] More intrinsically, it is also inconsistent to reject Western Cartesianism and dualism, but in the same breath make theater on the tropes of cognitive science, or computational and behaviorist flavors of neuroscience.

But how could we bracket the body phenomenologically, and what are the consequences of such a bracketing? To bracket the body is not to deny or to hide it but in fact to pay attention to its framing condition. In general I find it helpful to imagine the world not as a vacuum raisined with corpuscles but as a plenum of varying density. With such a field-based approach, the body then becomes a local density whose boundary is implicitly and provisionally defined by contingent anticipation or imagination and by the expectations formed in the course of contingent performance.[17] Of course it follows that these densities and boundaries vary over time, from moment to moment, and from disposition to disposition. A set of pedestrians' or dancers' limbs moving in tandem could form a body, as could a group of voices momentarily syncopated. What we ought not assume however is an invariant deterministic mapping from physiological data to metaphor. Although an invariant mapping may be a necessary working notion for neurologists and linguists and engineers, we need not and should not as poets, or as phenomenological experimentalists assume a discernable deterministic relation between physiological data like heartbeat, galvanic skin response, or breathing rate, and macroscopic objects of performance like emotion, mood, or narrative entity.

Pragmatically, what we learn from neurophysiology and the principled scientific study of neural phenomena is that the data are simply too complex and polyvalent to plausibly map to any simple linguistic token of an emotion or some human behavioral state. A smile could correlate with amusement, embarrassment, confusion or the rictus of death. A spike in the nervous signal of a muscle could correlate with an equally great variety of putative "causes." But beyond such pragmatic concerns, there is a more fundamental conceptual issue. Such a mapping would be merely a trace of the physical other, which is not identical, and may have only accidental relation to the embodied phenomenal experience, or, to borrow from Varela, Rosch and Thompson, embodied enactive experience. It is true that an artist may intentionally impose a mapping, but the art of a responsive environment lies in the fashioning of a substrate, not any particular object in a particular event.

But to unmoor (lift anchor from) bodily preconceptions and to free the actors' flesh from pre-designed "mappings" of cause and effect, a responsive environment should provide extra modalities of flesh in addtion to the ordinary flesh of the performer-player: for now, the modalities of gesturally modulated light, sound, and fabric. If you move, your skin shrugs over the bones of your hand not in a dialogic response to your action, but as the locus of intentional imagination fused with the physics of muscle and bone. In the same way, we create our calligraphic video, sound and fabric not as pre-carved masks or prosthetic devices, but as expressive tissue that can be charged and recharged with latent, potential responsivities to gesture and movement. Continuity of media and body, whether effected by techniques of camouflage and projection or by haptics and sensors and active cloth, leaves open the boundary of the performing body in the way that helps us as experimentalists in performance research to explore just such bracketings of the body.

Now, having suspended the body in this sense, what if we bracket the cogito as well? What if we bracket not only the cogito but also the ethico-aesthetic and desiring Subject? Deferring presumptions and models allows us to see how subjectivities emerge under the dynamics of co-present play and to see what becomes of agency. As designers of responsive play spaces we can ask, where should we locate the causal agency of a human-machine system? The Ozone media choreography system, the gesture sensing and media re-synthesis system that produces the responsive sound and video with behaviors that evolve in the course of play, enables designers to distribute agency in a much more fine-grained way through the different components of the media architecture, but it evolves with agency of the human players as well. Indeed, this challenges media composers who must relinquish total control of their media logic to unanticipated responses of human visitors, yet the composer must design evolutionary logics yielding experiences that feel more engaging than accidental pastiche. In my view, one condition for an aesthetically compelling experience in a responsive environment is that it should not induce puzzle-solving behavior. I wish the inhabitants of a space to never have to think about how everything works. This cognitive response has become almost inevitable among experienced consumers of interactive games because that is how we have come to expect to play with a machine. But puzzle-solving is a poor substitute for theater or any thick form of life. More fundamentally, puzzle-solving ferociously re-inscribes only cognitive acts, and a particularly reduced set of such acts at that.

In sum, a responsive environment can be a performative space in which people can playfully improvise gestures to collectively or individually create meaningful patterns out of fields of dynamically varying light sound, fabric and bodies. The media synthesis processes develop continuously according to a field-theoretic, magic physics without propositional logic, schema, or symbolic computation. The media fluidly evolve according to autonomous processes as well as and in response to the players' activities. The continuous shaping of the responsive media follows definite, composed metaphorical topographies that give a characteristic potential to the experience in a particular aesthetic, performative event. One might say that the potential dynamics created by the composers of a particular responsive installation-event are a collective social gesture eliciting a collective response from the ambient social ecology, not a specific set of calls and responses a la Disney imagineering, but rather a topological substrate of latent, potential response, the stuff of the imaginary.

Acknowledgments

I thank my students and collaborators of the Topological Media Laboratory, and the colleague artists and engineers affiliated with FoAM and Sponge. I am indebted to comments from Arkady Plotnitsky and Rebecca Schneider.

Footnotes

1. Jacques Derrida, "The Theater of Cruelty and the Closure of Representation," in Writing and Difference (Chicago: U. Chicago Press, 1978), 249.

2. For a fuller development, see Sha Xin Wei, Poiesis, Enchantment, and Topological Matter, MIT Press, 2013.

3. Complexity has often been valorized as yielding phenomena emerging from large collections of discrete entities in networks of relations modeled on graphs, phenomena that one does not observe in an individual entity. However, I maintain that complexity does not equal richness, just as panoply of choice does not equal freedom (as anyone encountering the bewildering array of differently processed coffee beans in equally tasteless combinations of flavors could attest). Indeed complexity inevitably tends to overwhelm sense and value. On the other hand, if we believe that human experience is continuous, dense and rich but not combinatorially complex, then it should be a healthy challenge to try to make our performance technologies themselves topological rather than combinatorial. (Sha Xin Wei, Poiesis and Enchantment in Topological Matter, MIT 2013.)

4. Sha Xin Wei, "Resistance Is Fertile: Gesture and Agency in the Field of Responsive Media," Configurations 10.3 (2002): 439-472.

5. This complements an extensive field of performance research and theoretical work, ranging from Bertolt Brecht's theory of Gestus, to Giorgio Agamben on the gesture, and George Lewis on the improvisatory formation of social identity. Bertolt Brecht, "A Short Organum for the Theatre," Brecht on Theatre: The Development of an Aesthetic, ed. John Willett, London: Methuen, 1964 (1949), 179-205. Giorgio Agamben, "Note on Gesture," in Means without End : Notes on Politics, Minneapolis: University of Minnesota Press, 2000, 49-62. George E. Lewis, "Gittin' to Know Y'all: Improvised Music, Interculturalism and the Racial Imagination," Critical Studies in Improvisation 1.1 (2004).

6. For a thorough and technically precise description of an approach to conditioning a rich, responsive, computational media environment via topological continuous (not discrete) dynamics, see: Sha Xin Wei, Michael

Fortin, Navid Navab, Tim Sutton, "Ozone: Continuous State-based Media Choreography System for Live Performance," ACM Multimedia, October 2010: 1383-1392.

7. The exploration of that continuous ontology is a joint investigation with Niklas Damiris. See forthcoming book: Sha Xin Wei, Poiesis, Enchantment, and Topological Media.

8. See the discussion of gesture as an open relation in Sha, "Resistance is Fertile".

9. I thank Helga Wild for the formulation of presentation vs. representation.

10. Naturalizing matter as dumb substance parallels what Bruno Latour identified as sociologists' tendency to naturalize scientific objects. (We Have Never Been Modern (Cambridge, Mass.: Harvard University Press, 1993)) More than ten years later, science studies has largely responded to Latour's call for the symmetrical disposition towards social objects and natural objects, but this symmetrization is still slowly percolating into neighboring domains in cultural and literary studies and philosophy.

In a sense, the discussion of gesture recalls the discussion of the nature of light and vision prior to relativity theory. Prior arguments about the existence or non-existence of ether as a medium which conducted light were subsumed by arguably Einstein's deepest insight, the equivalence of geometry (in the sense of geometrodynamics) with the distribution of matter-energy. In geometrodynamics, the material medium is also the geometry of space, so that a signal, being the rarefaction and compression of physical matter, is simultaneously a time-varying informatic fluctuation as well as a material fluctuation.

11. In some ways, substrate is a suggestive concept for what Deleuze and Guattari described by a-signifying BWO – Bodies Without Organs (I am indebted to Arkady Plotnistky for clarifying this notion's relation to BWO.) An emergence can be seen either as a change in intensity to use Deleuze's concept of change, differentiation vs. differenciation – or as a concrescence, to use Whitehead's process ontology.

12. See, Sha Xin Wei," The TGarden Performance Research Project," in Modern Drama 2005-2006, and more extensive treatment in Poiesis, Enchantment, and Topological Media, MIT 2013.

13. See David Morris, "The Other in the Mirror: On Mirror Reversals, Faces and Intercorporeality", manuscript in preparation, 2009-2010.

14. See seconds 19 - 25 in video documentation: http://vimeo.com/10828473.

15. Alfred North Whitehead, Process and Reality: An Essay in Cosmology, Ed. David Ray Griffin and Donald W. Sherburne, The Free Press, 1978, p. 315-316.

16. It may help to compare this with the modern investigation of intelligence. The Enlightenment's formation coincided with a fascination with the boundaries of the human represented by such quasi-objects as Wolfgang von Kempelen's chess-playing automaton of 1770 (Tom Standage, The Mechanical Turk (London: Allen Lane, 2002).

17. In fact, it is in this sense that I interpret Deleuze and Guattari's Body Without Organs. See note 9.

References

Antonin Artaud, Theater and Its Double. Grove Press, 1988 (1938).

Johannes Birringer, Media and Performance. Baltimore: Johns Hopkins, 1998.

Peter Brook, The Empty Space (Reprint edition), New York: Simon and Schuster, 1995.

Cruz-Neira, C., Sandin, D.J., DeFanti, T.A., Kenyon, R.V., and Hart, J.C. "The CAVE: Audio Visual Experience Automatic Virtual Environment," Communications of the ACM, Vol. 35, No. 6, June 1992, pp. 65-72.

Arnold Davidson, "The Horror of Monsters," in The Boundaries of Humanity: Humans, Animals, Machines, eds. James J. Sheehan and Morton Sosna, Berkeley: University of California Press, 1991, pp. 36-67.

Peter Galison, "Trading Zone, Coordinating Action and Belief," The Science Studies Reader, M. Biagioli, New York: Routledge, 1999, 137-160.

Jerzy Grotowski, Towards a Poor Theater, New York: Routledge, 2002 (1968).

Felix Guattari, Chaosmosis, An Ethico-Aesthetic Paradigm, tr. Paul Bains and Julian Pefanis, Indiana University Press, 1995.

Barbara E. Hendricks, Designing for Play (Design and the Built Environment Series), Ashgate Publishing, 2001.

Myron Krueger, Artificial Reality 2, Boston: Addison-Wesley, 1990.

Alice Rayner, To Act, To Do, To Perform: Drama and the Phenomenology of Action, Ann Arbor: U Mich Press, 1994.

Thomas Richards, At Work with Jerzy Grotowski on Physical Action.

Joel Ryan and Chris Salter, TGarden: Wearable Instruments and Augmented Physicality, Proceedings of the 2003 Conference on New Interfaces for Musical Expression (NIME-03), Montreal, Canada, NIME03-87.

TGarden, http://www.topologicalmedialab.net/xinwei/sponge.org/projects/m3_tg_intro.html

"The TGarden Performance Research Project," Modern Drama, 48:3 (Fall 2005) pp. 585-608.

"Topology and Morphogenesis," special issue on Topologies of Multiplicity, ed. Celia Lury, Theory, Culture, and Society, 29.4/5,2012, p. 220-246.

Poiesis and Enchantment in Topological Matter, Cambridge MA: MIT Press, 2013.

Sha Xin Wei, Yon Visell, Blair MacIntyre, "Choreographing Responsive Media Environments Using Continuous State Dynamics within a Simplicial Complex," Georgia Tech GVU Technical Report 2002.

Sha Xin Wei, Michael Fortin, Navid Navab, Tim Sutton, "Ozone: Continuous State-based Media Choreography System for Live Performance," ACM Multimedia, October 2010.

Robert Wilson, Byrdwoman http://www.robertwilson.com/studio/studio.htm,

http://www.robertwilson.com/bio/bioMaster.htm.

Hamletmachine : 1986 performance at New York University.

Ludwig Wittgenstein, Philosophical Investigations, tr. G.E.M. Anscombe, 3rd edition, Prentice Hall, 1999.

Sha Xin Wei is Professor and Director of the School of Arts, Media + Engineering at Arizona State University. He also directs the Synthesis Center for transversal art, philosophy and technology at ASU, and is a Fellow of the ASU-Santa Fe Institute Center for Biosocial Complex Systems. Dr. Sha's core research concerns a topological approach to poiesis, play and process. His art and scholarly work range from gestural media, movement arts, and realtime media installation through interaction design to critical studies and philosophy of technology. Trained in mathematics at Harvard and Stanford Universities, Dr. Sha has pursued speculative philosophy, experimental art, and visionary technologies that are reciprocally informed to equal depth and poetry. In 2001 Sha established the Topological Media Lab as an atelier for the study of gesture and materiality. From 2005-2013 as Canada Research Chair in media arts and sciences and Associate Professor of Design and Computation Arts at Concordia University in Montréal, he led the TML creating responsive environments for ethico-aesthetic improvisation. Sha has published in the areas of philosophy and media arts, science and technology studies, performing arts research, and computer science, including the book Poiesis, Enchantment and Topological Media (MIT Press).

Evaluation and Analysis of Experience in Responsive Atmospheric Environments

ANDREAS SIMON, JAN TORPUS &
CHRISTIANE HEIBACH
University of Applied Sciences &
Arts Northwestern Switzerland

To investigate the atmospheric potential and the affective connection between humans and their instrumented, responsive environments, we have designed an abstract, cocoon-like, responsively mediated space. Our aim is to develop design strategies and to investigate the potential of responsive spaces from a critical perspective, beyond pure application and usefulness. We have evaluated our environment in a series of controlled experiments in a lab environment with a total of 17 participants. Results show that participants experience affection, a coupling between themselves and the designed environment, and show strong cognitive engagement to understand and structure the environment through patterns of situation awareness and sensemaking. In this contribution we give a perspective on the further methodological development we plan to apply in future studies.

Couplings between people and responsive spaces in closed feedback loops have the potential to create an immediacy that produces specific affective and cognitive effects on participants experiencing these spaces. In our designed environments we combine a responsive space with biofeedback technologies to immediately and affectively connect an artistic environment with a person being related to it. We consider both sides – the human and the technological system – equal actors (Latour 2005) that are connected and interplay in real-time in a human-in-the-loop system. The system's responses follow dynamic mappings to physiologic human reactions, manifested through light, sound and motion/wind. These responses are expressive and can cause new psycho-physiological reactions, that in turn change the appearance of the space, creating a human-machine interdependency.

We built a large environment of about 4 meters wide, 8 meters long and 5m high. It is composed of a single type of white, semi-transparent, non-woven textile with interesting texture and tactility, hanging loosely from the ceiling, shaping a cocoon-like isolated space resembling organic natural structures. The resulting homogeneous and abstract, yet responsively mediated space, removed participants from their familiar context. We decided to not implement any distractive features of affordance as they appeared to imply behaviors and tasks that appeared suggestive and obvious. This reduced design was intended to make participants attentive but also self-aware of their situation in the environment. We measure body movement, breathing and heart rate of the participants that are coupled to the appearance of the space to enable varying degrees of interactive control.

Evaluation

We have conducted a series of experiments with a total of 17 participants (9 male, 8 female, ages between 22 and 54 years). Before participants enter the installation setting, we briefly inform them of the procedure, without explaining technical details or the goal of the evaluation. We ask them to take off their shoes and to put on socks, which improves the sense of tactility and serves as a small "rite de passage". They put on the sensor chest belt with an elastic breathing sensor, a motion sensor and the wireless transponder. A photoplethysmograph, for measuring blood volume pulse (BVP), is attached to the index finger of the right hand.

We explained to participants that entering the room they are free to behave as it suits them, that there was nothing they had to achieve or that could go wrong and that they could leave the space at any point. The exposure lasted between 7 and 12 minutes and was video recorded. We also recorded the sensor data, synchronized with the video, allowing us to analyze the sensor measurements and the recorded behavior, together with the appearance and sound of the installation at a glance.

After exposure we conducted 15 minute semi-structured interviews asking participants to recount their experience. During the interview we encourage them to talk further about feelings and emotions connected to the experience. At a later point in the interview we would ask if they saw a connection between their actions, their body and the space, if they felt like they could interact, and asked them to describe relationships and correlations they recognized.

Results

Participants are affected by the environment and vice versa – in the sense that they change each other's behavior. This relation proved to be inherently bound to the question of power. As long as participants didn't realize that they were able to control the environment, they often felt uncomfortable and alienated. As soon as they discovered the options of influence, they began to feel at ease. The interviews produced insights concerning the transfer of control and emotion. Some participants identified their surroundings as a feedback system or as an encounter with something affective. One participant noticed: "the pulse I recognized a bit later, in the sound, that there is a feedback of the pulse that the light reacts to it." Another participant explained that the experience was: "calming and enjoyable because of the heartbeat; When I noticed that I could control it myself, I quite liked it. It was fun to play with it. It became more joyful, because oneself was in charge… then that frightening, abrupt, heteronomous part – there is something coming towards me and I have to react – changed into: I can control and influence the situation."

A number participants described their experience as ambivalent and therefore interesting. They would name specific media components (light, sound, air stream, tactility) that over the course of the experience they conceived as pleasing, frightening, boring or irritating. Changing associations were

Scene view 1

Scene view 2

also caused by the interplay of the media components and changed the participant's state of mind. It was a state that could switch very quickly from "very pleasant" to "rather uncomfortable", but exactly this made it interesting. "Concerning the light, it changed from friendly to hostile, concerning the movement of the noises, also from friendly to hostile, then dark-bright and smooth-hard, I found that interesting". The interplay with other media components caused varying associations. Participants interpreted the sound as sound of the sea, water, wind from the Antarctica, or similar. In two cases the relaxing sound of water changed into the noise of a highway. In one case the bright light source at the ceiling without an association was first considered a dazzling technical device. When the participant laid down on the floor and looked at it while the wind from the axial fan moved the textiles and the water noises came in, the lamp all of a sudden became a romantic star.

The transcribed interviews were further analyzed to retrace the temporal structure of the participants' behavior and experience. To extract chronological order, we used video and data recordings together with the statements from the interviews. From the chronological sequence patterns of activities across participants can be identified. Situation awareness (SA) formulates three stages that form a basis for planning and action in complex situations (Endsley 1995). The patterns exhibited by the participants distinctly match the three phases of situation awareness. We also observe a more complex, interwoven structure: McCarthy and Wright (2007) use sensemaking to describe experience as a continuous, active engagement with a designed environment. They identify six connected processes: Anticipating, Connecting, Interpreting, Reflecting, Appropriating, Recounting. Statements, themes and structures from our interviews clearly show that participants execute the six processes of sensemaking to understand and model the environment. The chronological order revealed a surprising amount of structure that was not apparent from the original interviews, revealing that participants invest significant cognitive effort when they encounter our responsive environment.

Methodology

In an unfamiliar, ostensibly sparse and reduced environment, in particular in a "taskless" situation, participants become very sensitive to signals from the surrounding situation. They are especially conscious of and react strongly to the sense of being observed, directly or through a camera. The immediacy and chronology of events and experiences appears crucial for the analysis and understanding of experience and behavior in responsive environments. This is remarkably difficult (or otherwise impossible) to extract from interviews.

To evaluate the attitude and the reactions of participants as they explore and experience an environment, we can combine three complementary approaches: behavioral studies, inquiry and the use of psycho-physiological sensor measurements. A behavioral approach records and evaluates the observable behavior and actions of participants as they are inside of the environment. Behavioral studies use controlled observation and account in real time for participants' interactions (e.g. conveying attention through posture and view direction). However, they can be hard to interpret: observable measures and coded interpretations may be ambiguous and are often not specific to a single construct or cause. Behavioral studies may not provide much information on a person's motivations or their internal state. The process of direct observation or recording e.g. with cameras is often obtrusive and can thereby influence and substantially change a person's behavior and the experience in a setting.

While it is possible to infer participants' thoughts through a behavioral study, it can be more straightforward to record their impressions and opinions through inquiries from interviews and questionnaires. Unfortunately, inquiries are discrete and retrospective and are therefore not ideal for real time assessments. The "think aloud" protocol is a way to circumvent this, yet it influences participants through divided attention (Ogolla 2011). Resulting measures may reflect (social) pressure and are subject to participants' recall, in particular when answers are not oriented toward experimenters' expectations or if participants glean the goal of a study.

When people interact in an environment, measurable bodily reactions co-occur with mental changes. Psycho-physiological signals can be used in order to account for such body changes as a participant experiences an environment, in real time. Sensors need to be unobtrusive, reliable and robust against environmental conditions. Heart rate variability (HRV), respiratory volume and rate, together with the variation in skin conductance (SC, GSR) are indicators for changes in attention and arousal (Godin et al. 2015). The transition events in these signals can be correlated with events in the environment. These signals can also be directly interpreted and attributed to mental states: low HRV can indicate a state of relaxation, whereas an increased HRV can indicate a potential state of mental stress or frustration. Fast and deep breathing often indicates excitement such as anger or fear but sometimes also joy. Rapid shallow breathing can indicate tense anticipation including panic, fear or concentration. Slow and deep breathing indicates a relaxed resting state while slow and shallow breathing can indicate states of withdrawal, passiveness like depression or calm happiness. Electrodermal activity (EDA/GSR) is a fast and relatively reliable indicator of stress as well as of other intense stimuli and also helps to differentiate between conflict/no conflict situations or between anger and fear.

Motion tracking sensors allow the detection of activity (Olivares et al. 2012), in particular of rest and active body motion, and even the recognition and classification of behavior (Zhu et al. 2014). Sensing body motion supports the calibration and interpretation of psycho-physiological measurements. The body worn sensors are inconspicuous and appear much less noticeable than the use of cameras for observing subject behavior. The application of inertial sensing (IMU) allows the tracking of subject behavior over a wide area, without the need for extensive preparation of the tracking environment. Motion sensors can, within certain limits, replace cameras or direct observation techniques, making body motion tracking a useful and much more acceptable technology for subject activity tracking over large areas, long durations and in sensitive or more private settings.

Current results show that there is a need to minimize intrusion and to capture experiences in real-time and over long durations. We propose to develop novel, hybrid forms of inquiry and analysis to improve the accuracy of the timeline representation of events and of associated experiences, and to increase the granularity of captured events – with the ability to register increasingly subtle changes of affect and experience. Our current aim is to capture rich data and combine this with improved sensor technologies, specifically using sensor measurements as a scaffold to improve relevant shortcomings of behavioral studies and inquiry.

References

Endsley, M. "Toward a theory of situation awareness in dynamic systems." Hum. Factors J. Hum. Factors Ergon. Soc. 37(1), 1995, pp. 32–64.

Godin, C., Prost-Boucle, F., Campagne, A., Charbonnier, S., Bonnet, S., & Vidal, A. "Selection of the Most Relevant Physiological Features for Classifying Emotion." Emotion, 40, 20, 2015.

Latour, B. Reassembling the Social: An Introduction to Actor-Network-Theory. Oxford University Press, New York, 2005.

McCarthy, J., Wright, P. Technology as Experience. MIT Press, Cambridge, 2007.

Ogolla, J. A. 2011. Usability evaluation: Tasks susceptible to concurrent think-aloud protocol. Master thesis, Linköping University.

Andreas Simon is senior researcher and lecturer at the IXDM at the FHNW Academy of Art and Design in Basel, Switzerland. He is a computer scientist and interaction designer who has worked in virtual reality and augmented reality for Fraunhofer IAO, Stuttgart and the Gesellschaft für Mathematik und Datenverarbeitung in St. Augustin. His current area of research in Basel is the investigation of responsive environments and the area of human to system and human to human collaboration. His expertise is in system design, spatial interaction and the evaluation of human computer interaction.

Jan Torpus is a senior researcher and tutor at the Institute of Experimental Design and Media Cultures and a media artist. He studied interior design (Massana Art and Design College Barcelona, 1993), audiovisual arts (Institute Art, Academy of Art and Design HGK, University of Applied Sciences Northwestern Switzerland FHNW, B.A. 1999), interaction design (Hyperwerk, formerly Hyperstudio, HGK FHNW, 2000) and graduated in art and design research at the Masterstudio Design (HGK FHNW, M.A. 2010). He lectured new media at the polytechnic in Brugg and in Basel at several institutes of the HGK FHNW. He develops and manages research projects in the fields of affective interaction, immersive augmented reality, ubiquitous computing and biofeedback interfaces in interdisciplinary teams with partners like the University Hospital Basel, University of Basel (Departement Mathematik und Informatik), Museum of Communication Bern, City of Basel, iart ag and others. He works as a media artist since 2000 (www.torpus.com)

Christiane Heibach is currently senior researcher at the Institute of Experimental Design and Media Cultures and at the Karlsruhe University of Arts and Design. With a background in German Literary Studies she completed her PhD at the University of Heidelberg in 2000 with one of the first studies on internet literature, followed by numerous publications on media theory and the aesthetics of digital and internet-based literature and art. Currently she is working on a major research project on the cultural meaning of 'atmosphere'.

Bees Are Sentinels of the Earth: The Hive – A Responsive Ecology

MICHAEL STACEY
Michael Stacey Architects

This chapter is based on the case study of the Hive in *Aluminium Flexible* and *Light*, which is the fourth book in the Towards Sustainable Cities series, written by Michael Stacey and published by Cwningen Press.[1] It incorporates Philip Beesley's reflections on the Hive. *Aluminium Flexible* and *Light* also contains the case study of Protocell Mesh (2012-2013), a collaboration between the author, his students and Philip Beesley.[2] The Towards Sustainable Cities research programme has quantified and qualified the in-use benefits of aluminium in architecture and infrastructure. This research is funded by the International Aluminium Institute (IAI) and the core research team is Michael Stacey Architects in collaboration with KieranTimberlake.

The Hive, UK Expo Pavilion, Milan, Italy: Artist Wolfgang Buttress, 2015

The overall theme of the Milan Expo, was: "Feeding the Planet: energy for life".
[3] The masterplan of the Expo was designed by Herzog & de Meuron. Wolfgang Buttress, an artist based in Nottingham, England, won the commission to design the UK Pavilion in a limited competition, which included A_LA, Paul Cocksedge, Barber & Osgerby, David Kohn and Asif Kahn. A diverse selection of artists, designers and architects chosen by the client, UK Trade & Investment, a non-ministerial department of the British government. As observed in *Aluminium Recyclability* and *Recycling*, pavilions are very public, highly visited and the closest our industry has to an experimental architecture.[4]

Wolfgang Buttress' response to the theme of the expo was to focus on the humble honeybee, its role as key pollinator of crops and the current risk to the well being of the apian population. He observed: "Bees are incredibly sensitive to subtle variations and changes in conditions and their environment... So the bee can be seen as a sentinel of the earth and a barometer for the health of the Earth."[5] He also took inspiration from Richard Buckminster Fuller; ecologically, philosophically and for the tectonics of the Hive. In particular Buckminster Fuller's Montreal Biosphere, the United States' 1967 Expo Pavilion.

The delivery of the complete experience at the UK Pavilion involved Wolfgang Buttress' studio embracing a series of multidisciplinary collaborations. His ambition for the UK Pavilion was "to integrate art, architecture, landscape and science."[6] To design and deliver the Hive Wolfgang Buttress led a multi-disciplinary team of collaborators including: executive architect BDP Manchester, who were also the landscape architect, and structural engineer Tristan Simmonds of Simmonds Studio. His experience of complex geometries included working on Marsyas sculpture for Anish Kapoor, whilst at Arup. This digitally delivered lightweight fabric structure spanning 135m enveloped the space of the Turbine Hall at Tate Modern, London, during 2002.

The pavilion site in Milan was 100m deep. It was laid out as a narrative journey through an idealised fragment of a British landscape, with an orchard and a wild flower meadow culminating in the Hive. Placing the pavilion firmly within the English picturesque landscape tradition, delivered utilising twenty-first century technology. However, no bees were imported into Milan from the UK.

Figure 1   The Hive, UK Expo Pavilion, Milan, 2015, artist Wolfgang ButtressImage

The Hive is a fascinating combination of Euclidean geometry and accretive complexity that is probably only possible using three-dimensional computer modelling. It is a 14m cube with a 9m spherical void at its core and it is lifted 3m off the ground plane by 18 circular hollow section steel columns, which are 139.7mm × 5mm. These columns rise 5 meters to meet a 10.8m diameter ring beam. The hive was assembled in 32 horizontal layers of aluminium components, with 6 layers below the ring beam to complete the base of the spherical void. It is assembled accretively as bees would a hive. The layers are linked to form truss-like assemblies. Aluminium was chosen in preference to stainless steel for economy, weight and relative ease of machining the components.

The structure was parametrically optimised via close collaboration between Wolfgang Buttress Studio and the structural engineer Tristan Simmonds, to communicate the idea of a beehive, yet forming a robust structure. Tristan Simmonds describes the "basis of the Hive geometry is a radial hexagonal grid that is rotated slightly at each layer to give a twist. It is generated by repetition."[7] He recalls the design process:

> Wolfgang Buttress' Hive stood out from other early ideas immediately. The beehive is one of the most iconic structures in nature. We find beauty in its geometry and surprising precision but it is also a piece of pure functional efficiency that has been honed by a billion generations of bees. The initial sketches succinctly conveyed a beehive with three main simple ingredients: the hexagon, horizontal layers and an internal void. The fourth ingredient was that it wasn't simple. The underlying concept was simple but the object itself, filigree and complex.[8]

Describing the evolution of the design as "a quick Darwinian process". Simmonds observes:

> The process could only be achieved by writing software. We assumed that every task in the design would have to be carried out time and time again and so each task was automated as much as possible. We spent day and night writing code, however, the assumption proved correct. Eventually a complete redesign involving detailed analysis models, design code checking, structural optimisation of 70,000+ elements and outline drawings could be turned around in a few days. On a conventional project this can take months and typically only happens once.[10]

Specialist fabricators Stage One were appointed as main contactor by UKTI before the design completion and advised on the selection of the design team. Stage One fabricated the components of the Hive in York, using approximately 50tonnes of aluminium. The total number of components that form the Hive is 169,300 and almost all of them were fabricated from aluminium.[11]

Balustrade Panels	72
Chord Plates	5,711
Columns	18
Fittings	80
Glass Floor Panels	38
Hex Studs	16,549
LED Ductwork	378m
LEDs	891
Nodes	33,098
Node Bolts	33,098
Ring Beam Segments	4
Rods	28,782
Splice Bolts	2,856
Spacer Plates	31176
Upper Node Cap Locators	16,549
Total Number of Components	169,300

The components of the Hive were fabricated from 6082 TS aluminium alloy and all remained mill finished. For Wolfgang Buttress rawness was a key principle specifying materials 'throughout the pavilion [that] are generally unprocessed and patinate naturally.'[12] The components are primarily cut from 10mm thick aluminium sheet, however 15mm and 8mm gauged aluminium were also used. Aluminium tubes or rods join the flat plate top and bottom cords of each truss-like layer. Stage One used laser cutting, waterjet cutting, and machining to fabricate the components. The spacer plates in the node connections were laser cut. All the radial and circumferential truss plates were waterjet cut and the rods and node tops were machined.[13] Mark Johnson, CEO of Stage One, records:

> Over 4,500 CAD hours went into developing workshop drawings before machining, finishing and packaging each component in specific batches. Each item was etched with its own reference number relating to specific positions within the Hive's complex warren of hexagonal cells, ensuring our crew could complete the on-site construction in good time.[14]

The manufacturing took Stage One five months, working 16 hours a day. The total time on site in Milan, from starting the ground works in November 2014, was only six months. Stage One deployed 12 people on site, working piece by piece. The first layer was completed in January and the structure of the pavilion was all installed by April, in readiness for the opening of the Expo on May Day 2015.

Figure 2   Machined ends of the aluminium connection rods (credit UKTI).

Figure 3   Fabrication took five months for stage one (credit UKTI).

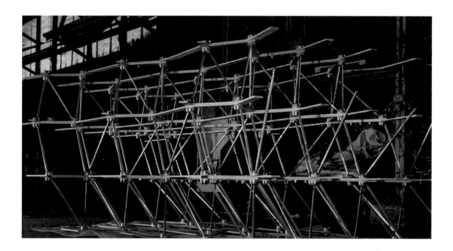

Figure 4   Trial assembly of a layer of the meshwork structure of the Hive (credit UKTI).

Early in the process of designing the Hive, Wolfgang Buttress found that
Dr Martin Bencsik was conducting research in the behaviour of bees, based
at Nottingham Trent University, School of Science and Technology. Wolfgang

Buttress considered him to be undertaking amazing research. "By measuring vibration signals, he can interpret bee communications. This is a significant step towards understanding their behaviour and the impact of external conditions and changes. Our central idea was to use these research techniques to connect a beehive in the UK to our pavilion in Milan."[15]

In the void at the core of the Hive visitors experience sound and light that is a direct response to beehives in Nottingham. The bespoke LED light sources respond to accelerometers within the beehives. Stage One "designed,

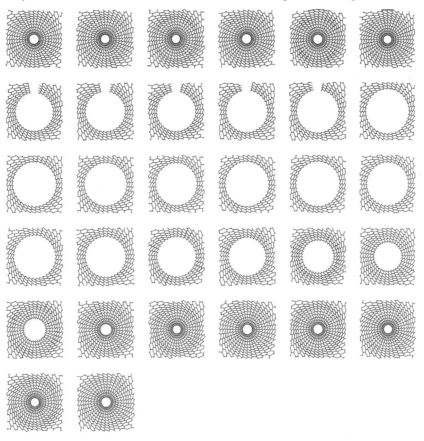

Figure 5   The 32 layers of the Hive on. plan, from layer 1 top left to layer 32.

prototyped, refined and manufactured one thousand four-colour (RGBW) 'pixels' [LEDs] bright enough to be seen in daylight."[16] The 891 light sources are arrayed around the void on each of the 32 levels. Stage One's use of real time three-dimensional computer based "visualisations of the many lighting effects saved a great deal of time once on site."[17]

Dr Martin Bencsik and Dr Yves Le Conte are collaborators on research funded by EU Framework Programme 7 that aims to help arrest the decline in European Bee population.[18] Both scientists were delighted to contribute to the UK Pavilion:

Figure 6   Looking up to the glass floor of the Hive, which is at terrace level. Expo 2015 UK Pavilion
(Credit Hufton + Crow)

The results of scientific explorations are most thrilling for the researcher, when he/she is at the forefront of human knowledge. By inviting us to contribute to his artwork, Wolfgang Buttress has given us the opportunity to allow the visitor to share the thrill of scientific discovery. We have supplied live honeybee vibrational data to the UK pavilion, for the visitor to hear both bees' sounds and vibration pulses.[19]

The experience in this void is sound and vision, "a dynamic soundscape, ever changing and unique at each moment: a collaboration between human and honeybee. A live feed from Nottingham beehives is streamed to the pavilion in Milan, which "trigger noise gates at particular thresholds, opening sympathetic harmonious stems pre-recorded by musicians, This is mixed with sounds captured from the bee colony."[20]

Philip Beesley, of Philip Beesley Architect and Professor of Architecture at the University of Waterloo, reflects on the Hive:

Wolfgang Buttress's Hive is structured as a dense cloud of hexagonal aluminium plate cells filling a ghost-like rectangular solid boundary, rendering a dissolving monolith that rises high above the fairground. Within this bubbling foam is cut the central form of a sphere, forming a pure void within the hovering mass. An oculus caps the sphere, opening the mass to the sky. The lower end of the sphere is positioned one storey above the ground level of the site, covered by a transparent glass floor whose perimeter echoes the oculus above and supports a compact space for occupants housed within the diffusive mass within the heart of the hive. Groups of angled legs raise this spherical chamber high above the level of the ground, clearing the site below. The lower level presents an aerial shadow-play where the figures of occupants exploring the inner space above float, visible through the dense filtering screens of the hexagonal meshwork structure. The floating scene is surrounded by the converging swarm of thousands of structural cells, progressively organized into multiple horizontal layers with gradients of warping organized around a converging polar array with chiral orientation focused around the oculus above and floating floor below. The horizontal aluminium plate cells are stayed by vertical arrays of angled tubular struts radiating from each cell vertex. LED fixtures mounted on each vertex facing the void interior make the interior spherical boundary into a constantly-shifting chimera.

Is this a distinctly new architectural form-language? The Hive exemplifies a deliberately unstable, open boundary, defined by delicacy and resonance – perhaps the very antithesis of the firmitas that has defined Western architecture since Vitruvius uttered his famous paradigm. Monumental scale is achieved by aggregating small-scale elements using simple progressive gradients of progressively shifting dimensions made possible by contemporary parametrics and digital machining. Inflections of component jointing systems within profiles and castings provide an understated celebrated ornament, an embroidered cellular textile writ large.

Following the implications of this hovering, diffusive aggregate, we could imagine families of architecture founded on adaptation and uncertainty. A building system using an expanded range of reticulated screens and canopies is implied, constructed from minutely balanced filtering layers that can amplify and guide convective currents encircling internal spaces. Writ large, these qualities speak of involvement with the world. Within this vanguard city fabric, the thermal plumes surrounding clusters of human occupants offer a new form of energy that could be ingested, and diffused, and celebrated. The resonant, dissolving swarm of Buttress and collaborator's aluminium the Hive provides a potent example of a distinctly new kind of adaptive architecture.[21]

The aluminium of the Hive has not been recycled after the closure of the Milan Expo. A better option was found. The pavilion was disassembled and reassembled in Kew Gardens, London. It reopened to the public on Saturday 18 June 2016. The detailing of the Hive with all bolted connections has facilitated is relocation, it is another example of the benefits of design for disassembly (DfD), as discussed in *Aluminium Recyclability and Recycling*.[22] Kew Gardens, founded in 1840, is the world's largest collection of living plants and a very appropriate second location for a pavilion inspired by pollinators.

Figure 7   Inside UK Pavilion by Night. Courtesy of UKTI (credit Hufton + Crow)

Figure 8   The aluminium meshwork of the Hive, (credis Carlos Alba)

Aluminium Flexible and Light: Towards Sustainable Cities by Michael Stacey can be download, with the other three books in the series from: www.world-aluminium.org/publications/tagged/towards%20sustainable%20cities/

Endnotes

1. M. Stacey 2016, Aluminium Flexible and Light: Towards Sustainable Cities, Cwningen Press, Llundain. This book is published and printed in the UK and the spelling is based on the Oxford English Dictionary.

2. M. Stacey 2016, Aluminium Flexible and Light: Towards Sustainable Cities, Cwningen Press, Llundain, pp.114–121.

3. W. Buttress Studio, ed., 2015, BE· Hive: UK Pavilion Milan Expo 2015, Wolfgang Buttress Studio, Nottingham, p. 6.

4. M. Stacey 2015, Aluminium Recyclability and Recycling: Towards Sustainable Cities, Cwningen Press, Llundain, p. 166.

5. W. Buttress Studio, ed., 2015, BE· Hive: UK Pavilion Milan Expo 2015, Wolfgang Buttress Studio, Nottingham, p. 3.

6. W. Buttress, Concept to Construction: UK Pavilion Milan Expo, A Visual Essay, in W. Buttress Studio, ed., (2015), BE· Hive: UK Pavilion Milan Expo 2015, Wolfgang Buttress Studio, Nottingham, p. 29–37.

7. T. Simmonds, Engineering the Hive: The Complete Idea, in W. Buttress, ed., (2015), BE· Hive: UK Pavilion Milan Expo 2015, Wolfgang Buttress Studio, Nottingham p. 63.

8. Ibid, p. 63.

9. Ibid, p. 64.

10. Ibid.

11. Ibid, pp. 80–87.

12. W. Buttress, Concept to Construction: UK Pavilion Milan Expo, A Visual Essay, in W. Buttress Studio, ed., (2015), BE· Hive: UK Pavilion Milan Expo 2015, Wolfgang Buttress Studio, Nottingham, p. 29–37.

13. Mark Johnson, CEO of Stage One, in conversation with the author during February 2016.

14. Ibid. See also http://www.stageone.co.uk/projects/hive-uk-pavilion-milan-2015-expo/ (accessed February 2016).

15. W. Buttress, Concept to Construction: UK Pavilion Milan Expo, A Visual Essay, in W. Buttress, ed., (2015), BE· Hive: UK Pavilion Milan Expo 2015, Wolfgang Buttress Studio, Nottingham, p. 29–37.

16. http://www.stageone.co.uk/projects/hive-uk-pavilion-milan-2015-expo/ (accessed February 2016).

17. Ibid.

18. http://www.ntu.ac.uk/apps/news/135794-15/Novel_research_looks_to_transform_the_decline_of_the_beekeeping_sector.aspx (accessed February 2016).

19. M. Bencsik and Y. Le Conte, Bees: An Important and Threatened Species, in W. Buttress, ed., (2015), BE· Hive: UK Pavilion Milan Expo 2015, Wolfgang Buttress Studio, Nottingham p. in W. Buttress, ed., (2015), BE· Hive: UK Pavilion Milan Expo 2015, Wolfgang Buttress Studio, Nottingham, p.44.

20. W. Buttress Studio, ed., 2015, BE· Hive: UK Pavilion Milan Expo 2015, Wolfgang Buttress Studio, Nottingham, p. 97.

21. P. Beesley 2016, Reflecting on the Hive, written at the invitation of the author.

22. M. Stacey 2015, Aluminium Recyclability and Recycling: Towards Sustainable Cities, Cwningen Press, Llundain.

Michael Stacey, BA (Hons) BArch (Hons) RIBA FRSA, is Convenor of Michael Stacey Architects. His professional life combines practice, teaching, research and writing. His practice has been recognised by national and international awards, including twice winning the Shapemakers Award for the Innovative Use of Aluminium, a Bureau International du Beton Award and an Award from the Campaign for the Preservation of Rural England. Key projects include: East Corydon Station, Aspect II Integrated Cladding System, Thames Water Tower, Enschede Integrated Transport Interchange, Art House in Chelsea, Expertex Textile Centrum, Ballingdon Bridge, Craft House and Flexihouse. The award winning Aspect II Integrated Cladding System is the subject of world-wide patent. In 2013 The Renault Centre, 1982, which he worked on at Foster Associates, now Foster + Partners, was listed Grade II. He has taught architecture studio at Liverpool University, Penn Design, London Metropolitan University, the Architectural Association and The University of Nottingham.

Accepting the Robotic Other: Why Real Dolls and Spambots Suggest a Near-Future Shift in Architecture's Architecture

ALEXANDER WEBB
University of New Mexico

With weak Artificial Intelligence (AI) in the pockets of the majority of American adults, a societal introduction of a strong AI or sentience seems close. Though the "intelligence" of our phones' intelligence can be laughably brittle, the learning capacity demonstrated by the internet of things suggest more robust intelligence is on the way – and some would say it has already arrived. Several private technology firms have asserted that a robust, AI already exists and thought leaders within computation are lining up to ensure that it is not evil. Regardless of the morality of Artificial Intelligence, if our charge as architects is to design occupiable space then we need to consider post-anthropocentric ecologies as well as how to adapt our design strategies to reflect inclusion of other species. This paper describes two linked lines of thought, a meditation on the pending societal inclusion of the robotic other and why that robotic sentience may arrive from an unexpected origin and can reshape how we conceive of architecture itself.

4. Therefore, since nature has designed the human body so that its members are duly proportioned to the frame as a whole, it appears that the ancients had good reason for their rule, that in perfect buildings the different members must be in exact symmetrical relations to the whole general scheme.

Vitruvius, Ten Books on Architecture

Oh Yoshimi
They don't believe me
But you won't let those
Robots eat me

The Flaming Lips, Yoshimi Battles the Pink Robots

In the first chapter of Ten Books on Architecture, Vitruvius draws clear connections between the proportions of classical architectural temples and the proportions of the human body. Vitruvius deconstructs human features into sets of relative lengths, observing the mathematical ratios of fingers, facial features, and appendages of "a well shaped man."[1] In later chapters Vitruvius uses this approach of proportion and symmetry to describe the design of the classical temple, constructing a fundamental connection between the human body and architectural organization.

As architecture's oldest major text, Ten Books on Architecture has been foundational to how architecture is conceived of, produced and understood. Leonardo da Vinci's "Vitruvian Man" has also served as a graphical representation of the text, embodying the relationships between mathematics, human anatomy, and architecture. In Architectures of Time, Sanford Kwinter wrote "No genealogy of the body in relation to Western architectural mastery is possible, even today, that does not begin by reviving, at least in passage, the convention of the Vitruvian man splayed out and mathematically embedded in reticulum of regulating lines like a proud trophy honoring the Idea and geometric exactitude."[2] Vitruvius' anthropocentric understanding of form and scale are critical elements of architecture's fundament, and though these concepts are arguably no longer central to contemporary architectural production, their biases and tendencies are still essential components of architectural thought.

The combination of impending Artificial intelligence and a philosophical shift to the post-anthropocentric suggests architecture's Vitruvian foundations will not only be challenged, but challenged in the very near future. With an abundance of weak Artificial Intelligence embedded in objects as varied as phones, cars and thermostats, a societal introduction of a strong Artificial Intelligence or sentience is potentially close. Though the "intelligence" of our phones' intelligence can be laughably brittle, the learning capacity demonstrated by the internet of things suggest more robust intelligence is on the way- and some would say it has already arrived. Several private technology firms have asserted that a robust ,AI already exists and thought leaders within computation are lining up to ensure that it is not evil. Regardless of the morality of Artificial Intelligence, if our charge as architects is to design occupiable space then we need to consider post-anthropocentric ecologies as well as how to adapt our design strategies to reflect inclusion of other species. What follows is a description of two linked lines of thought, a meditation on the pending societal inclusion of the robotic other and why that robotic sentience may arrive from an unexpected origin. This is neither conclusion nor provocation, but simply an offering of possibility.

The first suggestion made here is that robots will be accepted not as servants or facilitators, but as equals – not human, but treated with the same affordances. This suggestion is neither in support of nor contrary to Ray Kurzweil's description of a robotic-human "Singularity", a vision of merging the biological and the mechanical. Instead, it simply suggests a parallel

Figure 1   Still from K3LOID, a short film by Big Lazy Robot VFX.

development – rather than investigate conflations of the biological and the synthetic, the suggestion here is that the cultural and societal distinctions between robotic and human "species" will be eliminated, and that there will be an inclusion of robotic individuals as part of "us".

A common presumption, presented through popular science fiction, has been that if we are to accept a robot as an equal it will kill us. Depictions starting with HAL 9000 in Stanley Kubrick's 2001: A Space Odyssey and continuing through the popular Terminator series have consistently described a similar scenario- as soon as a machine gains free will or a cyber-netic entity gains agency within the physical realm, it attempts to kill all of humanity. These fears are reflected by remarkable financial support received by the Future of Life Institute in recent years, most notably the $10 million in funding from Tesla CEO Elon Musk in early 2015.[3] The Institute's mission statement focuses "on potential risks from the development of human-level artificial intelligence,"[4] serving as a think tank to prevent cybernetic threats.

The cultural obsession with the threat of a robotic attack is demonstrated by media as disparate as Flaming Lips lyrics to Charlie Chaplin's Modern Times. Though any entity with similar or greater cognition and physical agency as us humans could potentially be a threat, the question remains: is there something unique to a robot that poses a threat or does our fear of robots or AI reveal more about ourselves? Is the cybernetic unusually dangerous or do we simply fear what we do not understand? What is it that we fear in "the other"?

Human history is littered with conflicts between alien civilizations, arising through unfamiliar contact. Unknowns such as intent, technological capacity, and economic network has lead to results as extreme as enslavement, human trafficking and genocide. Even without hostile intent, the confrontation of two different populations can have devastating effects through exposure to disease and contagions.[5] But as these encounters have gravitated towards ecological balance through monetary and other resource exchange, history would suggest that a similar system could prevail if a robotic species was to develop.

Whatever the mechanism, many human societies expand notions of the "us" versus the "other", increasing levels of inclusion within their culture. Whether this is demonstrated by the expansion of voting rights or increased restrictions on discrimination, a common human trait is to redefine and reframe who "we" are. A definition of the "us" is currently expanding, as we begin to see robots as extensions of our bodies, facilitators of human relationships, and surrogates for spouses and partners.

In Paul Virilio's Open Sky, he describes his concept of the static vehicle, a mechanism to experience a space without leaving the one you occupy. Virilio describes NASA's short-lived Datasuit as an example of a static vehicle, a device that would "transfer actions and sensations by means of an array of sensor-effectors. In other words, capable of producing presence at a distance... "the NASA project was supposed to allow total telemanipulation of a robotic double on the surface of planet Mars, thus achieving the individual's effective telepresence in two places at the same time..."[6] The static vehicle is not only a mechanism for visitation without travel, but also a utilization of the robotic as a synthetic doppelgänger- both substitute and extension of the self.

Less than two decades after Virilio described the static vehicle, it is available for purchase. Roboticist Hiroshi Ishiguro has developed the "Telenoid", a remote-controlled android that serves as an augmented communication

Figure 2   Telenoid™ was developed by Osaka University and Hiroshi Ishiguro Laboratories, Advanced Telecommunications Research Institute International.

tool. Telenoids can be held, hugged, caressed, and cuddled – all while serving as a video chatting device.[7] Their facial expressions can describe the expressions of the user communicating through them to the user holding them. The Telenoid is a commercialization of the static vehicle in that it not only allows visitation, but also provides a much more robust sensorial exchange. The sensorial exchange is critical to reframing the Telenoid as robotic prosthesis, as extension of the self. Professor of Pervasive Computing at London's City University, Adrian David Cheok is developing a similar prosthesis named "Kissinger", a device that will allow humans to kiss each other through Skype.[8] It is plausible that as more users interact with robots than they would with humans and a familiarity with the robot as a proxy for another human grows, this will contribute to a elimination of the distinction between species.

Though the majority of humans are not currently in relationships with robots, many have had relationships facilitated by robots: 5% of all married Americans met their spouse online, 10% of all smartphone users admit to using their devices during sex ,and the liason-facilitating phone app Tinder receives 30 million daily users to produce 13 million daily matches.[9,10] Our relationships are certainly increasingly facilitated and augmented by digital and robotic devices, increasing a robotic agency within our selections of and interactions with our partners.

If it is possible for humans to relate to other humans through robots, and accept robots as a proxy for their partners, friends and family, is it not possible that humans may enter relationships with robots directly? If Virilio's static vehicle can effectively serve as an extension for human relationships, then it is not the corpus of the partner that is critical but the communication between the two entities that are represented through digital media. Is it impossible to consider an application, a turbo-charged Siri that can communicate with enough complexity to engender a relationship? Cheok has teamed with developer and author David Levy believe so, and are currently working on a platform called I-Friend, which will be a chat service for humans to communicate with Artificial Intelligence, not other humans.[8]

To create a synthetic relationship may not be as complex a task as we may think. In Duncan Jones' film Moon, Jones describes a clone living on a lunar base who does not realize he is a clone. Through recorded messages, the clone believes he is in a relationship, and will be seeing his wife and young daughter within weeks- but it is revealed that his wife passed away years before and his daughter is almost an adult. The video messages he views were recorded years before, but he believes he participating in a direct digital communication exchange with his wife. Though the deception serves as the dramatic tension for the film, it also describes the level of acceptance we have for synthetic images and recordings as proxy for our partners. This acceptance suggests that if digital communication can serve as a substitute for the emotional complexities of direct human interaction, then little bars digital communication from becoming the partner itself.

Human relationships with the robotic object are also growing, as demonstrated by substantial online communities devoted to the subject. The largest, dollforum.com, had over 20,000 members in 2007[11] and leading manufacturer Real Doll estimates that there are over 3000 real dolls across the world.[12] But what is particularly relevant is how many iDollators and technosexuals describe their relationships with their dolls as more than simply sexual. Arguably the most famous iDollator, Davecat, described his relationship with Sidore in the BBC documentary Guys and Dolls. "A good solid happy time would be when I would be alone with her, not actually having sex but

Figure 3   LOVE VALLEY #13(2014), Photographed by Julie Watai, Featuring Julie Watai &
ASUNA (A-lab).

lying next to her, appreciating her, especially, like in the really early daylight,
being able to see her, you know, looking at me, regarding me, that sort of
thing, and me doing the same back."[12] Further interviews and depictions of
Davecat reinforce the sensitivity and connection described by this passage,
refuting any suspicion that he feels anything less than love for his doll.

Love dolls, though initially static and inert, are increasingly more robotic and
intelligent. Robotic components of the doll are becoming commonplace,
with Real Doll building from past investigations into mechanical components and looking towards a fully automated doll.[13] Real Doll, creator Matt
McMullen's new project Realbotix, will produce love dolls that are not only
automated, but intelligent with the capacity to serve as a virtual assistant.[14] In
2008, software engineer Le Trung constructed Aiko, a love doll that featured

robotic and intelligent capacities. Aiko cleaned, managed Trung's accounts, selected food based off of Trung's preferences, recognized and addressed Trung's friends and family, and held conversation based off of her archive of 13,000 Japanese and English sentences.[14] Aiko has a nervous system which allows her face and body to be touch sensitive,[15] and can be programmed to be "coy", or to resist sexual advances if she was not "in the mood".[16]

The fact that Trung designed Aiko to have "moods", particularly moods that would prevent a sexual encounter, describes Trung's desire for his relationship with Aiko to be not merely as an auto-erotic device, but as a partner – another individual with needs, wants and feelings no matter how limited. This desire to interact with robots in this robust capacity demonstrates a suggestion of acceptance for this low-level sentience as an equal, despite their robotic host.

This trend towards non-human acceptance is reflected by contemporary philosophy. Theorists confronted with the Post-Anthropocene, Graham Harman, Timothy Morton, Levi Bryant and other Speculative Realists, have sought to de-emphasize human perspective and see other species and objects as equals. This interconnected viewpoint is described by Timothy Morton's The Mesh, where he suggests an ecological perspective of relationships and a de-privileging of human sentience.[17] Graham Harman's Object Oriented Ontology (OOO) focuses his concept of the quadruple object, a suggestion that the object that exists outside of perception is as real and as vital as the object that we perceive.[18] This shift in philosophical perspective could contribute towards an acceptance of AI as equals as well.

Though most often not contained within a love doll, at the time of writing AI is pervasive. The majority of adult Americans carry smart phones in their pockets,[19] Google is the most widely used website,[20] and internet of things-based companies, such as Nest, are purchased for $3.2 billion.[21] According to WIRED magazine's Daniel Burrus, the rise of the intelligent object produces "the ability to gather virtually unlimited intelligence in real time"[22] as a result of its ubiquitous nature.

While Artificial Intelligence may be both pervasive and abundant, the problem is that it is not very good. The AI of Window's Clippy, the iPhone's Siri, and Jeeves of AskJeeves are laughably thin- simple mechanisms to deduce solutions for a narrow range of questions, but questions outside the intended scope quickly reduce them to clichéd responses that feebly attempt to hide their lack of resilience. The problem with these models is that to directly create an intelligence that that is adaptive, the adaptation must be coded directly into the system. Siri cannot learn to understand heavy accents or serially mispronounced words. She would have to be told how to adapt to each situation which would require directing her coders to predict every situation that would require adaptation. As more code is constructed to help Siri adapt, the algorithms grow exponentially to a point of unfeasibility.

Perhaps we should rethink how we conceive of Artificial Intelligence design to begin with. To date, the predominant expectation of how AI would be created has demonstrated a significantly outdated view of the role of designer to the process of design. The dominant methodology for developing AI is to incrementally increase the bandwidth of conditions AI is equipped for, slowly increasing robustness until a sentience can pass the Turing Test – the evaluation for AI where a human does not realize it is conversing with a computer.

There are several issues with this model. The first is that this fundamental attitude is fundamentally self-serving, a holdover from a Judeo-Christian approach to human creation. This attitude is reinforced by science fiction depictions of human-digital creationism, a classic example is Disney's 1982 film Tron, where artificially intelligent agents directly resemble their creators. In this sense, the creation of AI is closer to inter-human reproduction than the creation of a new species.[23] Inside the computers of Tron, humans have created life within their own image, a carbon-less copy of humanity.

Until recently, architecture was a discipline that viewed authorship of an object with a similarly problematic model. The mythology of the modernist architect, the Howard Roark sole-genius,[24] was prevalent and pervasive in architectural discourse. But as Michael Speaks describes in Two Stories for the Avant-Garde, there has been a shift away from this inherently hierarchical model to a more distributed, networked model. To Speaks, this shift is demonstrated by the managerial approach within the architectural office. The architects Speaks describes embrace organizational models and

principles learned from the technology start-up companies of nortern California, looking more towards innovation rather than creationism. "Indeed, it is this managerial approach, and not an interest in the work of Gilles Deleuze, post-Euclidean geometries, diagrams or data that unites the work of the freshest architectural practices around the world today."[25]

A facilitator of this shift has been the embrace of the genetic algorithm as a design tool. The genetic algorithm allows a breeding of formal interests, programmatic considerations, and contextual data to create an emergent design, subverting a post-modernist obsession with scenography and empowering the role of performance in design.[26] This process of form-finding, widely used for structural and environmental optimization, is now a mechanism for incorporating big data, social media, and other urban behavioral information. The shift towards emergent, evolutionary processes has facilitated the networked models Speaks described and shifted the author/object dynamic to a network/system.

There are documented advantages to systems that are produced through evolutionary mechanisms than through imposed directives. In Nicholas de Monchaux's Spacesuit: Fashioning Apollo, de Monchaux argues that the bottom-up, fashioned quality of the spacesuit developed by Playtex that ultimately made the suit more robust than its competitors. "The A7L spacesuit was a solution to the problem not only of how to survive in space by ensuring livable pressure and temperature around the body, but the much more complex problem of how to make that survival robust to unanticipated changes, both inside and outside the suit... Derived from robust solutions for the body in space, and on earth, the modular and layered quality of the A7L, anathema to aerospace engineers, was particularly robust in accommodating the many inherently unpredictable challenges of suiting the body to space."[27] This quality of robustness, or "the quality of resisting perturbation," can be described as the ability adapt to an unfamiliar, undefined condition- essentially learning what to learn. By allowing material systems primarily intended for garments and girdles to evolve into the program of a spacesuit, Playtex was leveraging the intelligence of their garmets for a systemic robustness that allowed performance and capacity to extend beyond the original intent. The fact that Playtex clothing systems had already evolved to accommodate the stresses of day-to-day life, predisposed their spacesuit to accommodate the different, but similar, stresses of a body in space. This "borrowed" intelligence between systems is a critical component towards systemic robustness.

Viewing artificial intelligence as a design problem, an engineered approach suggests a rigid result compared to the intelligence of an evolutionary process. While an evolutionary process may be more productive, it would still need to meet criteria of productive algorithms to be effective. Borrowing

Figure 4   Still from Solipsist, directed by Andrew Thomas Huang.

from Manuel De Landa's description of Deleuzian principles of the genetic algorithm, the diversity and size of the genetic population is critical to productivity. "...despite the fact that at any one time an evolved form is realized in individual organisms, the population not the individual is the matrix for the production of form."[28] Not only is the population an algorithmic production, but the extent of the population fuels the robustness of the product. While de Monchaux would suggest the importance of "borrowed" intelligence, De Landa would require a significantly large gene set to produce a robust Artificial Intelligence.

Perhaps this gene set already exists. Perhaps individuals are already interacting with each other, sharing DNA and recombining to create adaptive responses to various evolutionary pressures. If we consider that the majority of internet traffic is not human,[29] the millions of interconnected

servers, personal computers and mobile devices could serve as a massive petri dish. In this sense, the billions of spambots, scrapers and scammers are the equivalent to single-celled organisms, with the internet as their mechanical primordial soup much like Andrew Thomas Huang describes in his short film Solipsist.

A similar shift in a programming approach is described in Alex Garland's Ex Machina, where Blue Book, a fictional analogue for Google, records all interactions through its video chat service. These interactions serve as the base data for human interaction, which teaches androids how to emotionally manipulate humans. While the film depicts a learning algorithm that uses big data to increase its robustness, the origin of the algorithm is coded for this specific purpose. In the film, the antagonist Nathan describes the process as learning "not what people were thinking, but how they were thinking."[30] This shift towards a bottom-up learning strategy is reflected by technology firms such as DeepMind, who focus on developing robust AI through behavioral, bottom-up learning strategies.[31] This article suggests that it is conceivable that an algorithm could use big data to reframe its own architecture, to not just learn from content, but learn what it should learn from content to drive its own evolution.

Though the genetic algorithm is seen as the critical component to an evolutionary condition, it is not the only mechanism through which evolution can occur. Memetic algorithms, where memes serve as components for asexual reproduction, are based upon cultural conditions of replication. In his book The Selfish Gene, evolutionary biologist Richard Dawkins used the concept of a meme to describe a mode of evolution not dependent on the parent/child relationship of sexual reproduction, but a mode based within self-replicating unit.[32] As Dawkins described, the meme deviates and evolves through human representation, creating an evolution of social and cultural relevance. It is reasonable to assume that the same benefits a large genepool (or memepool) would have the same Deleuzian benefits in a memetic algorithm.

It is plausible that the internet may serve as an enormous memetic algorithm, where bots evolve through their own means of reproduction or through human conduits. As these programs are equipped with increasingly more adaptive and genetic capacity, it seems that an emergent artificial intelligence could meet a De Monchauxian criteria of robustness through Deleuzian considerations of evolutionary criteria.

If an artificial intelligence were to emerge, it would likely wish to participate in the physical realm. On the surface this seems likely if for no other reason than it is reciprocal to our behavior, as we wish to have agency within digital space. In an interview with podcast Singularity 1 on 1, Hiroshi Ishiguro cited his own motivation for entering android robotics. To provide bodies for AI, Ishiguro claims, would offer experiences of their own and drive their evolu-

Figure 5   Geminoid™ with Hiroshi Ishiguro. Geminoid™ was developed by Osaka University and Hiroshi Ishiguro Laboratories, Advanced Telecommunications Research Institute International.

tion.[33] While the questions of whether or not a cybernetic sentience would need or want physical agency is likely to be unanswered definitively until it is encountered, the possibility of AI inhabiting robotic bodies exists.

Certainly the issue of Artificial Intelligence becomes much more significant for architects once sentience wants physical agency. Perhaps it is more productive to not debate if AI "wants" physical agency, but if AI would abandon the agency we have already provided. If sentience was to emerge from the primordial soup of the internet, the radically developing Internet of Things (IoT) will be inextricably linked to that sentience. As the Internet of Things establishes a direct connection between the algorithms on the internet and robotic objects, it is possible that an emergent AI would have a direct connection with a mechanical object or objects. Losing physical "bodies" would be the sentience's choice, not choosing to gain agency through specified body.

An architecture that is designed equally for humans and robots should not be taken as a novel provocation, but as a challenge to architecture's Vitruvian foundation. This is not to say that the exact process will be replicated and a series of Vitruvian robots will be produced, but the very relationship between body and space will be interrogated. Does an entity's relationship to space change when it has more than one body within it? Does it change when there is no body at all?

Considering that the robotic other could soon be societally accepted, that a robust artificial intelligence could arrive sooner than we expect, and at the time of sentience that entity or entities could have extensive physical agency, this poses significant questions for architects. How can architecture accommodate an entity that is not tethered to a single body? How, as human designers, will we account for and understand the needs and desires of another species with similar sentience to our own? How do we shift from measurements of space based from a relatively consistent size range of bodies to a virtually unlimited range? All of these questions could be vital for architects practicing in the near future… that is, if the robots don't eat us first.

Acknowledgements

The author would like to thank Andrew Thomas Huang, Julie Watai, Osaka University and Hiroshi Ishiguro Laboratories, Advanced Telecommunications Research Institute International and Big Lazy Robot.

Endnotes

1. Vitruvius, V. Ten Books on Architecture, Harvard University Press, Cambridge, 1914.

2. Kwinter, S. Architectures of Time, MIT Press, Cambridge, 2002.

3. http://www.wired.com/2015/01/elon-musk-ai-safety/ [15-6-2015]

4. http://futureoflife.org/about [15-6-2015]

5. De Landa, M, A Thousand Years of Nonlinear History, Zone Books, New York. 1997.

6. Virilio, P, Open Sky (Vol. 35), Verso, 1997.

7. http://en.wikipedia.org/wiki/Telenoid_R1 [7-8-2015]

8. http://www.newsweek.com/2014/10/31/sex-robots-278791.html [15-6-2015]

9. http://www.pewresearch.org/fact-tank/2015/04/20/5-facts-about-online-dating/ [15-6-2015]

10. Planet of the Phones, The Economist, 2015, 414, 9.

11. http://www.sfgate.com/news/article/Rape-of-the-Real-Doll-Part-Two-Violet-Blue-2541172.php [15-6-2015]

12. https://www.youtube.com/watch?v=pxCkULUnVH0 [15-6-2015]

13. Gurley, G., Is this the Dawn of the Sexbots?, Vanity Fair, May 2015.

14. http://www.nytimes.com/2015/06/12/technology/robotica-sex-robot-realdoll.html [15-6-2015

15. http://www.telegraph.co.uk/news/newstopics/howaboutthat/3702990/Inventor-creates-his-perfect-woman-a-robot-who-can-clean-and-do-the-accounts.html

16. http://www.thesun.co.uk/sol/homepage/news/article2023392.ece [7-8-2015]

17. Morton, T, The Mesh, Routledge, New York, 2011.

18. Harman, G. The Quadruple Object, Zero Books, Alresford, 2011.

19. http://www.pewinternet.org/fact-sheets/mobile-technology-fact-sheet/ [15-6-2015]

20. http://www.alexa.com/topsites [15-6-2015]

21. http://www.wired.com/2014/01/googles-3-billion-nest-buy-finally-make-internet-things-real-us/ [15-6-2015]

22. http://www.wired.com/2014/11/iot-bigger-than-anyone-realizes-part-2/ [15-6-2015]

23. Lisberger, S. Tron, Walt Disney Productions, 1982.

24. Rand, A., The Fountainhead, Penguin, 1943.

25. Speaks, M., Two Stories for the Avant-Garde, archilab.org/public/2000/catalog/speaksen.htm [15-6-2015]

26. Leach, N., Digital Morphogenesis, Architectural Design, 79(1), 2009, 32-37.

27. de Monchaux, N., Spacesuit : Fashioning Apollo, MIT Press, Cambridge, 2010.

28. DeLanda, M., Deleuze and the Use of the Genetic Algorithm in Architecture. Architectural Design, 71(7), 9-12.

29. https://www.incapsula.com/blog/bot-traffic-report-2014.html [15-6-2015]

30. Garland, A., Ex Machina, DNA Films, 2015.

31. http://www.digitaltrends.com/computing/google-deepmind-artificial-intelligence/ [15-6-2015]

32. Dawkins, R., The Selfish Gene, Oxford University Press, Oxford, 1976.

33. https://www.youtube.com/watch?v=rIcTrdHc5DA [15-6-2015]

Projects of the Hylozoic Ground Collaboration 2006–15

A number of LAS partners have worked together on preceding projects, presented in evolving site-specific installations in some thirty international venues. LAS is continuing collaborations with institutions and producers including The Leonardo Museum for Art, Science and Technology, Salt Lake City, Simons, Edmonton, and Atelier Iris van Herpen, Amsterdam. Permanent installations are currently located at The Leonardo, Simons West Edmonton Mall, National Academy of Art, Hangzhou, and Shangduli Centre, Shanghai. These events provide first-hand public interaction with living architecture prototypes and test-beds.

Implant Matrix, Toronto, 2006

Hylozoic Soil, Montreal, 2007

Endothelium, UCLA, Los Angeles, 2008

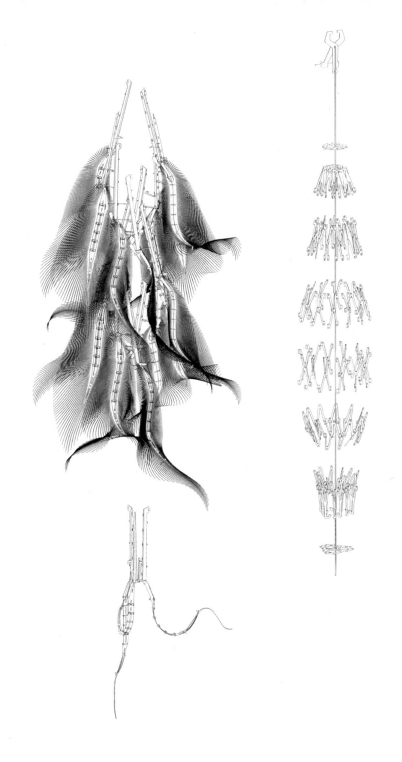

Hylozoic Grove, Ars Electronica Center, Linz, 2008

Sargasso Cloud, CITA/Royal Danish Academy, Copenhagen, 2009

Hylozoic Soil, Quebec City, 2010

Hylozoic Soil, Mexico City, 2010

Hylozoic Ground, Venice, 2010

Saint-Exupery Field, Reims, 2011

Sargasso, Toronto, 2011

Hylozoic Veil, Salt Lake City, 2011

Protocell Field, DEAF Festival, Rotterdam, 2012

Sibyl, Biennale of Sydney, 2012

Protocell Mesh, Nottingham & London, 2012-13

Aurora, Edmonton, 2013

Epiphyte Spring, Hangzhou Triennial of Fibre Art, Hangzhou, 2013

Epiphyte Chamber, National Museum of Modern & Contemporary Art, Seoul, 2013

Epiphyte Membrane, Opernwerkstatten, Berlin, 2014

Epiphyte Spring, China Academy of Art, Hangzhou, 2015

Sentient Chamber, National Academy of Sciences, Washington, 2015

LIVING ARCHITECTURE SYSTEMS GROUP

EXECUTIVE LEADERS

DIRECTOR Philip Beesley

DEVELOPMENT MANAGER Salvador Miranda

OPERATIONS MANAGER Carolina Garcia

RESEARCH COORDINATORS Ala Roushan, Matthew Spremulli

STUDIO DIRECTOR Reza Nik

FINANCE ADMINISTRATOR Anne Paxton

RESEARCH STREAM LEADERS

SCAFFOLDS Philip Beesley,
Architecture, University of Waterloo

SYNTHETIC COGNITION Dana Kulić,
Electrical & Computer Engineering, University of Waterloo

METABOLISM Rachel Armstrong,
Architecture, Newcastle University

HUMAN EXPERIENCE Colin Ellard,
Psychology, University of Waterloo

INTERDISCIPLINARY METHODS Rob Gorbet,
Knowledge Integration, University of Waterloo

THEORY Sarah Bonnemaison,
Architecture, Dalhousie University

WHITE PAPERS 2016
PRODUCTION TEAM

Gabriella Bevilacqua, Jessica Chen, Alice Choupeaux,
Farzaneh Victoria Fard, Carolina Garcia, Joey Jacobson,
Pedram Karimi, Salvador Miranda, Reza Nik, Jordan
Prosser, Severyn Romanskyy, Matthew Spremulli

WEBSITE

www.livingarchitecturesystems.com
www.lasg.ca

MEMBERS

ANDREW ADAMATZKY	Unconventional Computing Centre, University of the West of England
DON ARDIEL	Royal Architectural Institute of Canada
ROBERT BEAN	Media Arts, NSCAD University
DAVID BENJAMIN	The Living, Autodesk Research
NIMISH BILORIA	Hyperbody, Delft University of Technology
DAVID BOWICK	Blackwell Structural Engineers
ALBERTO DE CAMPO	College of Architecture, Media & Design, Universitat der Kunste Berlin
SANDRA BOND CHAPMAN	Center for BrainHealth, University of Texas at Dallas
KATY BORNER	School of Informatics and Computing, Indiana University Bloomington
SALVADOR BREED	Spatial Sound Institute, Amsterdam
ANDREAS BUECKLE	School of Informatics and Computing, Indiana University Bloomington
SARAH JANE BURTON	Theatre and Drama Studies, Sheridan College
ANTONIO CAMURRI	Faculty of Engineering, University of Genova
MARK COHEN	Semel Institute for Neuroscience and Human Behavior, UCLA
CAROLE COLLET	Design & Living Systems Lab, Central Saint Martins
MARTYN DADE-ROBERTSON	School of Architecture, Planning & Landscape, Newcastle University
SARA DIAMOND	OCAD University
BEHNAZ FARAHI	Interdisciplinary Media Arts & Practice, USC School of Cinematic Arts
SID FELS	Electrical and Computer Engineering, University of British Columbia
SIMONE FERRACINA	School of Architecture, Planning & Landscape, Newcastle University
ADAM FRANCEY	Faculty of Psychology, University of Waterloo
RUAIRI GLYNN	Interactive Architecture Lab, The Bartlett School of Architecture
ROB GORBET	Faculty of Environmental Studies, University of Waterloo
MARIA PAZ GUTIERREZ	BIOMS, Department of Architecture, University of California, Berkeley
TREVOR HALDENBY	The Mission Business Inc.
MARTIN HANCZYC	Centre for Integrative Biology, University of Trento
CHRISTIANE HEIBACH	University of Applied Sciences and Arts Northwestern Switzerland
JOHN HELLIKER	Screen Industries Research, Sheridan College
IRIS VAN HERPEN	Atelier Iris van Herpen
ALEXANDRA HESSE	Leonardo Museum
MARK-DAVID HOSALE	School of the Arts, Media, Performance & Design, York University
HARU JI	School of the Arts, Media, Performance & Design, York University
JHAVE JOHNSTON	School of Creative Media, City University of Hong Kong
BRADLY KLERK	Atelier Iris van Herpen
BRANKO KOLAREVIC	Laboratory for Integrative Design, University of Calgary
MANUEL KRETZER	Responsive Design Studio
NEIL LEACH	European Graduate School

VINNY LUKA	Clearpath Robotics
DOUG MACLEOD	RAIC Centre for Architecture, Athabasca University
ALAN MACY	Biopac Systems Inc.
CHRISTINE MACY	Filum Ltd. & School of Architecture, Dalhousie University
ERIC MATHIS	Institute for Regenerative Design & Inovation
MICHAEL MONTANARO	Topological Media Lab, Concordia University
NAVID NAVAB	Topological Media Lab, Concordia University
PAUL OOMEN	Spatial Sound Institute, Budapest
MICHAEL O'ROURKE	Toolbox Dialogue Initiative, Michigan State University
SIMON PARK	Faculty of Health and Medical Sciences, University of Surrey
LUCINDA PRESLEY	ICEE Success Inc.
VERA PARLAC	Laboratory for Integrative Design, University of Calgary
ZACH PEARL	Subtle Technologies
NEIL RANDALL	Games Institute, University of Waterloo
JENNY SABIN	Sabin Design Lab, Cornell University
ANDREAS SIMON	University of Applied Sciences and Arts Northwestern Switzerland
BRIAN SMITH	School of Learning, Drexel University
MICHAEL STACEY	Michael Stacey Architects
J.D. TALASEK	Cultural Programs of the National Academy of Sciences
JANE TINGLEY	Faculty of Fine Arts, University of Waterloo
METTE RAMSGAARD THOMSEN	CITA, Royal Danish Academy of Arts
JAN TORPUS	University of Applied Sciences and Arts Northwestern Switzerland
STEPHANIE E. VASKO	Toolbox Dialogue Initiative, Michigan State University
MICHELLE VIOTTI	Mars Public Engagement Program & Jet Propulsion Laboratory, NASA
GRAHAM WAKEFIELD	School of the Arts, Media, Performance & Design, York University
HOPE E. WILSON	Foundations and Secondary Education Department, University of North Florida
LIAM YOUNG	Tomorrow's Thoughts Today
KLAUS-PETER ZAUNER	Electronic and Computer Science, University of Southampton
MIA ZHAO	Faculty of Engineering, University of Waterloo